The Gestalt Shift in Conan Doyle's
Sherlock Holmes Stories

Michael J. Crowe

The Gestalt Shift in Conan Doyle's Sherlock Holmes Stories

To Margaret Humphrey

Possibly the most memorable student I have taught in my fifty years of teaching at Notre Dame

Michael J. Crowe

palgrave
macmillan

Michael J. Crowe
University of Notre Dame
Notre Dame, IN, USA

ISBN 978-3-319-98290-8   ISBN 978-3-319-98291-5   (eBook)
https://doi.org/10.1007/978-3-319-98291-5

Library of Congress Control Number: 2018952291

Cover illustration: © Samphire Arts, FJ
Cover design: Fatima Jamadar

This Palgrave Macmillan imprint is published by the registered company Springer Nature Switzerland AG
The registered company address is: Gewerbestrasse 11, 6330 Cham, Switzerland

This book is dedicated to two wonderful friends,
both Sherlockians:
Denis P. Burke
and
Frederick J. Crosson (1926–2009)

PREFACE

Numerous readers view Arthur Conan Doyle as the most skillful creator of detective fiction who ever put pen to paper. Doyle's four novels and fifty-six short stories featuring Sherlock Holmes are available in numerous languages, and his famous characters appear in dozens of plays and hundreds of films and television shows. Moreover, the studies of these stories number in the thousands. Hundreds of scholars and authors have sought the sources of Doyle's highly successful Sherlockian writings and investigated how Doyle achieved this extraordinary level of success. Such information makes one hesitant to propose a new analysis of Doyle's skills. Such, however, is the goal of this book, which draws on insights that emerged mainly in the latter half of the twentieth century in an area far from traditional literary studies. My book draws on a book published in 1962 by University of Chicago Press in an obscure series of volumes designed to be read mainly by philosophers and historians of science. In fact, the reaction to and interest in the book was extraordinary. As we shall later see in detail, one source of this book was ideas developed by Ludwig Wittgenstein, a German philosopher teaching in England, who himself dealt with ideas studied by perceptual psychologists. Another source was studies done by historians of science investigating the nature of scientific changes; for example, the adoption of the Copernican theory. The author of this relatively short volume was Thomas Kuhn, who titled it *The Structure of Scientific Revolutions*. Gradually Kuhn's book caught on. As of 2010, sales reached over 1.4 million copies. Many scholars believe it is the most influential book on the nature of scientific development published in the last half of the twentieth century. Moreover, scholars began applying Kuhn's approach to nearly every area of intellectual inquiry. One exception has been literature. My goal in this book is to suggest that Kuhn's ideas may significantly illuminate the study of Doyle's Sherlockian stories. My chief credential for attempting this is that for over four decades while teaching at the University of Notre Dame, I taught courses and published a number of books and essays on the development of astronomy, physics, and mathematics, many of which drew on Kuhn's writings.

Potential readers of this book may feel more confident that it is worth their time when I report on the reaction to it that came from a highly respected scholar who seemed to me to be the ideal judge of whether my thesis is plausible. This was not a personal friend; rather, what led me to contact him was that he is a highly respected scientist and historian of science as well as an active Sherlockian. This is Dr. Bradley Schaefer, Distinguished Professor at Louisiana State University and the author of a widely republished and now classic article on Sherlock Holmes and astronomy. A month after receiving my request and manuscript, he sent me a long email that began:

> I read your book fast, because it was a fun read. As a life-long Sherlockian, the whole discussion was dear to my heart. Your basic thesis is completely new, both within the Sherlockian literature, and within the literature about detective stories. (And coming up with anything new under the Sun within the Sherlockian literature is hard and rare.) I am convinced by your basic thesis. And I can see applications going past the Sherlockian stories.

Near the end of the letter, he added:

> I expect that your book will be comparable in sales to the best of the secondary Sherlockian literature. You are offering a completely new idea and of broad application, so I expect that every Sherlockian will want a copy. I don't know numbers, but this is not a small market.

My hope is that his endorsement will give readers confidence that my thesis merits their attention.

Various persons at the University of Notre Dame also contributed to the composition of this book. Notre Dame recognizes that emeritus faculty can still contribute to scholarship by supplying an office and some support for those who continue to wish to contribute. Moreover, various individuals at Notre Dame have been helpful in significant ways. Among these are Thomas Stapleford, Chair of the Program of Liberal Studies, my office mate Rev. Nicholas Ayo, C.S.C., and Denise Massa, Curator at Notre Dame's Visual Resource Center, who prepared most of the illustrations. Dr. Daniel Johnson, who is Notre Dame Digital Humanities Librarian and also teaches in the English Department, contributed significantly to locating publications relevant to my project. Elizabeth Sain very carefully indexed this volume.

For the last six years, I have co-taught a course on Sherlock Holmes at Forever Learning Institute, a local senior center, with Denis Burke, a retired attorney, who has been wonderfully supportive of my efforts to teach these materials. So has my wife, Dr. Marian Crowe, whose doctorate is in English and who has frequently supplied highly useful insights. Allie Troyanos and Rachel Jacobe of Palgrave Macmillan skillfully and graciously guided my efforts to put my manuscript into final form.

Notre Dame, IN   Michael J. Crowe

Contents

CHAPTER 1

Introduction

Goal of This Book

What makes the Sherlock Holmes stories so dramatic and engaging? This book offers an explanation of these effects in terms of the idea of a Gestalt shift or switch.[1] Gestalt is a German word meaning form or shape or configuration. A Gestalt shift happens when one first experiences an image or entity in one way and then in a quite different way. A famous example of such a shift is the duck/rabbit Gestalt shift.[2]

[1] In October 2014, I did a Google search for "Gestalt Shift" and "Gestalt Switch." The former name got 8640 hits, whereas "Gestalt Switch" produced 17,700 hits. In this book, I prefer the term shift.

[2] The duck-rabbit pair first appeared in a German humor magazine *Fliegende Blätter* (October 23, 1892), 117.

© The Author(s) 2018
M. J. Crowe, *The Gestalt Shift in Conan Doyle's Sherlock Holmes Stories*, https://doi.org/10.1007/978-3-319-98291-5_1

In looking at this image, one sometimes sees it as a rabbit, but then it turns into a duck. This remarkable ambiguity makes Gestalts and Gestalt shifts important in a number of ways, as we shall see. The word Gestalt is increasingly common in English. If one sees a silhouette composed of a human head with a deerstalker hat atop it and a pipe hanging from the mouth area, one readily recognizes it as a "Holmes Gestalt." Hundreds, perhaps thousands, of copies of this Gestalt adorn the Baker Street tube stop in London.

PART ONE: GESTALT FIGURES AND GESTALT SHIFTS

We shall begin by examining a few Gestalt figures and Gestalt shifts. The first diagram represents a Necker Cube.

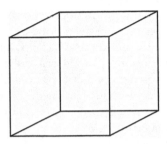

Is it a box pointing up and to the right or a box pointing down and to the left? Note that one cannot see both perspectives simultaneously. Or possibly you see twelve lines on a planar surface. Similarly, in the Rubin Vase, you can see either two faces or a chalice, but not both simultaneously).[3]

Typically, in Gestalts, the two or more sights are quite different; for example, a chalice is very different from two faces. Note that although it may take some time to see what is represented in a Gestalt diagram, one

---

[3] Sometimes dated as created in 1915, it actually appeared much earlier. See "Rubin Did Not Discover the Rubin Vase" on the internet at http://figuresambigues.free.fr/ArticlesImage/rubin1.html#axzz5CcbaTVFn. Viewed April 14, 2018.

typically sees it suddenly—and it may disappear suddenly. Discussions of the Rubin Vase frequently distinguish between the ground and the figure. In this case, the figure consists of the two faces, whereas the dark area is the ground. What is meant by a Gestalt shift is the shift between the two or more images seen on the page.

My thesis is that in a large number of Arthur Conan Doyle's sixty Sherlock Holmes stories one can detect one or more patterns that correspond to a Gestalt shift. Moreover, I will claim that the dramatic character of many of these stories results from the reader having an experience comparable to what one experiences in a Gestalt shift. I shall also claim that analyzing the stories in this manner provides a deeper understanding of their dramatic structure and effect. I do not claim that Doyle was aware of Gestalt figures or Gestalt shifts, at least in the ways that contemporary psychologists are aware of them.

Verbal Gestalt Shifts

The Gestalt experience or Gestalt shift can also occur in regard to verbal expressions, including jokes. Some examples: Think of the story of the panda that walked into a bar, ate his lunch, pulled out a gun, began shooting, and then left. When confronted by the police, the panda explained that he was just doing what the encyclopedia article on pandas directed. It said that a "Panda eats shoots and leaves."[4] Lowly commas are important, and can save lives: compare "Let's eat, grandma" with "Let's eat grandma." These sentences are very similar; their meanings are very different. Or consider these three headlines: "Teacher Strikes Idle Students," or "British Left Waffles on Falkland Islands," or "The President Wins on Budget, but More Lies Ahead." Or think of the story of the missionary who was very pleased by the natives wanting to have him for dinner, until he remembered they were cannibals. Note that as you go back and forth between the two readings, nouns may turn into verbs and vice versa.

Admittedly, these examples are all quite short. Visual Gestalts take up more space. Are larger verbal Gestalt shifts possible? A student once delighted me by presenting a paper similar to what follows. Hint: You do not need to know a word of Greek to read the following selection; you do, however, need to be familiar with the Greek alphabet and be acquainted with Sherlockian writings. Can you determine what the next paragraph says?

---

[4] This story is central to a best-selling book by Lynne Truss, *Eats, Shoots & Leaves: The Zero Tolerance Approach to Punctuation* (New York: Gotham Books, 2006).

Ιν τηε ψεαρ 1878 Ι τοοκ μψ δεγρεε οφ Δοχτορ οφ Μεδιχινε οφ τηε Υνιπερσιτψ οφ Λονδον, ανδ προχεεδεδ το Νετλεψ το γο τηρουγη τηε χουρσε πρεσχριβεδ φορ συργεονσ ιν τηε αρμψ. Ηαπινγ χομπλετεδ μψ στυδιεσ τηερε, Ι ωασ δυλψ ατταχηεδ το τηε Φιφτη Νορτηυμβερλανδ Φυσιλιερσ ασ Ασσισταντ Συργεον. Τηε ρεγιμεντ ωασ στατιονεδ ιν Ινδια ατ τηε τιμε, ανδ βεφορε Ι χουλδφοιν ιτ, τηε σεχονδ Αφγηαν ωαρ ηαδ βροκεν ουτ. Ον λανδινγ ατ Βομβαψ, Ι λεαρνεδ τηατ μψ χορπσ ηαδ αδπανχεδ τηρουγη τηε πασσεσ, ανδ ωασ αλρεαδψ δεεπ ιν τηε ενεμψ϶σ χουντρψ. Ι φολλοωεδ, ηοωεπερ, ωιτη μανψ οτηερ οφφιχερσ ωηο ωερε ιν τηε σαμε σιτυατιον ασ μψσελφ, ανδ συχχεεδεδ ιν ρεαχηινγ Χανδαηαρ ιν σαφετψ, ωηερε Ι φουνδ μψ ρεγιμεντ, ανδ ατ ονχε εντερεδ υπον μψ νεω δυτιεσ.

If you have succeeded in reading this paragraph, it seems probable that you puzzled over it for a period, possibly looked at a table matching up Greek and English letters, and then suddenly saw it as the opening lines of Doyle's *A Study in Scarlet*. Moreover, having managed this paragraph, you are able to supply the next paragraph, and hundreds more paragraphs if you wish. If still puzzled, see the information in the footnote that follows this sentence.[5]

More on Verbal Gestalt Shifts[6]

Cambridge University scholars have developed some new results on verbal Gestalts. Try reading the following passage:

7H15 M3554G3 53RV35 7O PR0V3 H0W 0UR M1ND5 C4N D0 4M4Z1NG 7H1NG5! 1MPR3551V3 7H1NG5! 1N 7H3 B3G1NN1NG17 WA5 H4RD BU7 N0W, 0N 7H15 LIN3 Y0UR M1ND1S R34D1NG 174U70M471C4LLY W17H0U7 3V3N 7H1NK1NG 4B0U7 17.[7]

This may explain your success or absence thereof in reading verbal Gestalts such as the one below.

---

[5] To produce this paragraph, I went to an electronic copy of the first Sherlock Holmes story, A Study in Scarlet copied it into my computer, pasted the whole thing into it, and converted the font to Symbol font. With this clue, you could within five minutes produce an entire book and if you learned to read Greek letters, even if you did not know a single Greek word, you could read the entire volume. Realizing that this is simply the opening paragraph of Arthur Conan Doyle's *A Study in Scarlet* would seem to qualify as a quite extended verbal Gestalt shift.

[6] I wish to thank Denis Burke for introducing me to this form of Gestalt shift.

[7] Googling this collection of letters will produce a number of discussions of such configurations.

it dseno't mtaetr in what oerdr the ltteres in a word are, the olny iproamtnt tihng is that the frsit and last ltteer be in the rghit pclae. The rset can be a taotl mses and you can still raed it whotuit a pboerlm. This is bcuseae the huamn mnid deos not raed ervey lteter by istlef, but the word as a wlohe. Azanmig huh? Yaeh and I awlyas tghuhot slpeling was ipmorantt!

Note the following:

- We do not always see what is really there.
- As in the preceding examples, the BRAIN corrects for errors.
- We want things to fit together in a recognized pattern.
- We see what we think we should see.[8]

Classes of Gestalt Shifts

Many kinds of Gestalt shifts exist. Considering some of these will both illustrate what constitutes a Gestalt shift and suggest how varied, even in form, Gestalt shifts can be.

Similarly, one can imagine a detective story that presents readers with an apparently chaotic array of clues but eventually the detective puts them in a comprehensible order. We can recognize a visual version of this pattern by considering the Dalmatian diagram (Fig. 1.1).

Fig. 1.1   Dalmatian Gestalt.

[8] For more information on this thought pattern, Google "7H15 M3554G3 53RV35 7O PR0V3 H0W 0UR M1ND5."

At first it appears as chaos, but then one detects the image of a Dalmatian.

Examples of the Bipolar Shift

Bipolar shifts are very common. In these cases, one moves from one image to another. A person cannot recognize two distinct images simultaneously. The Rubin Vase Gestalt shown earlier is of this type. We can see either a chalice or two people face to face. Note that we cannot simultaneously see both the chalice and the two faces. What we see are two wholes: One sees the chalice, but then two faces. One does not see a face on the left, and half a chalice on the right.

Another example of a bipolar Gestalt shift emerges from the next image, which has been named the Boring Figure[9] because it was analyzed in 1930 by the prominent psychologist Edwin G. Boring of Harvard (Fig. 1.2).

Fig. 1.2 Boring Figure.

[9] See Morton Hunt, *The Story of Psychology* (New York: Doubleday, 1993), 447. Edwin G. Boring, "A New Ambiguous Figure," *American Journal of Psychology*, 42 (1930), 444–445. Boring's figure can be traced back to 1915 when W. E. Hill published it in *Punch*.

Persons sometimes see a young woman looking away; then she exits and the person sees an older lady, chin downward, and looking parallel to the plane of the paper. A small circle serves as the left ear of the young woman, whereas it is the left eye of the other woman. What appears as a necklace for the younger woman is the mouth of the more senior woman. It is not vital that the reader succeed in seeing all these Gestalts as multi-faceted, but if one is to follow the claims later to be made, it is important to have struggled and sometimes succeeded at seeing these images as Gestalts.

The duck/rabbit shift, which dates back to the nineteenth century, has become well known not only to psychologists but also to philosophers. As will be shown later, it has had a long history and a surprisingly large influence. One can see either a duck looking to the left or a rabbit looking to the right.[14] Note that once you see the rabbit, you will probably notice the rabbit's mouth, which is nearly invisible when you are examining the duck.

Triple and Multiform Shifts

The Necker Cube (see p. 3) is an ideal image to show that it is possible to have three or more images emerge even from a relatively simple image. Note that in viewing this cube one can see it in any one of three (or more) distinct ways. One can see it either as a cube pointing up and to the top right or as a cube pointing down and to the left or as a set of twelve lines in a plane. Note also that one cannot simultaneously see it as more than one figure.

Multiple Gestalts are not impossible. A good example is a painting created in 1990 by the artist Octavio Ocampo. The name of the painting is *La Familia del General* (The General's Family), this name being appropriate because all his family members appear in the painting but hidden in the face of the General and elsewhere, as one can see from examining the portrait.[10] One might ask whether Ocampo created this technique. An examination of a painting by Johann Michael Voltz (1784–1858) of the Emperor Napoleon named *Triumph des Jahres* suggests that this is far from correct. Voltz's painting is an excellent candidate for being a source of Ocampo's artistry.[11] This suggests that the history of the idea of a Gestalt extends well into the past, although the term Gestalt shift is far more modern.

---

[10] To inspect the portrait, search Google images for Ocampo's "La Familia del General."

[11] To inspect Voltz's painting, search Google images for Johann Voltz's *Triumph des Jahres*.

Some Comments on Gestalt Shifts

If you like engaging with Gestalt shifts, you may want to visit one of my all-time favorite Gestalts, which is available on the internet.[12] If you wish to see more Gestalt shifts, insert the search term "Gestalt shift" or "Gestalt switch" into Google after clicking on the Images button on the Google web page. When I just tried this, Google reported that it could provide about 129,000 images in this category.

Do some novels contain Gestalt shifts? A very interesting candidate is Jane Austen's *Pride and Prejudice*. Think of the scene where Elizabeth Bennett goes through a transformation in her view of Fitzwilliam Darcy while visiting his estate called Pemberley.[13]

The Necessary and Sufficient Conditions Characteristic for a Gestalt Shift

Four characteristics must be present in a Gestalt shift. The Gestalts must be **distinct** and the change must be **rapid, unexpected**, and **global**. The Gestalt images must be distinct from each other. Associated with distinctiveness is the idea of contrast. Doyle as a writer was passionately interested in creating contrasts. His "Man with the Twisted Lip" story centers on the contrast between a deformed beggar, Hugh Boone, barely surviving on coins dropped into his cup by persons passing him on London streets and a successful businessman, Neville St. Clair, whom, it is believed, the beggar has murdered. The two characters are strikingly distinct from each other. The Gestalt shift in "Twisted Lip" occurs when Holmes applies some soap and water to the jailed beggar; then the beggar disappears and St. Clair appears. The associations of the beggar and businessman we would assume must be very different. But in fact a man suspected of being a capital murderer turns out to be a successful petty criminal, whose only crime is deceitful begging. The magnitude of a shift measures how impressive it is: a duck changing to rabbit is impressive; into a dinosaur is awesome.

---

[12] See http://www.liveleak.com/view?i=829_1360099797. This Gestalt is called the Speed Painter.

[13] Around 2002, when I was teaching Thomas Kuhn's *Structure of Scientific Revolutions* in an undergraduate class, a very gifted student, Kate Diaz, did a paper using Kuhnian ideas to analyze Jane Austen's *Pride and Prejudice*. I admired the paper and asked her to give me a copy. After this book was well along, I found her paper in my files and still believe she makes an interesting and plausible analysis. Kate is now a prominent physician, Kate Diaz Vickery.

Regarding **rapidity**, consider the "Boring Figure" Gestalt. We see the young woman disappear rapidly and the elderly woman appear quickly. It is true that it may take a long time to see the elderly woman, but finally she jumps onto the stage. The two images are quite distinct from each other. An ear becomes an eye. The women are looking in different directions. One does not expect that in the blink of an eye, a person in a picture will age by fifty years. And the associations of each woman are scarcely less different; one may be your wife; the other your mother-in-law. One does not expect a picture to shift in such a major fashion. One is surprised by the change. Magicians pull rabbits out of hats, whereas Gestalt psychologists within a few seconds turn a rabbit into a duck. We witness Holmes within a matter of seconds turn a deformed beggar suspected of murder into a successful businessman. The change must be of the form that the first image disappears and another view appears. It may take some work to get back to the first. Moreover, we have to be told to look for the young woman and to be told how to do this.

Just as we do not expect a rabbit to turn into duck, we believe it is **unexpected** that a beggar will turn into a businessman or that a murdered man will suddenly appear on the scene. It is also unexpected that an arch criminal will turn within seconds into a courageous guardian of the good, but Doyle delivers both these unexpected changes in his *The Valley of Fear*.

Global changes also occur within Holmes stories. Suddenly a pillar of the community turns into an arch criminal. Holmes reveals that a brilliant mathematics professor is the "organizer of half that is evil [in London] and all that is undetected."[14] The worlds of the beggar and businessman are very different. The former is a loner, living in a slum neighborhood; the latter is a married man with children living in an attractive house. The reformed beggar will disappear from the lives of those who drop coins into his cup. The businessman must now find employment in the business world and must dress for and act according to this role. Possibly the term global is too strong a word; I have chosen it to stress how extensive and pervasive the changes can be that result from a Gestalt shift. It is characteristic of a Gestalt shift that the reader experiences an "Aha!" feeling. The source of this feeling may be the major difference between the two images. Or perhaps it is the suddenness of the change or possibly the magnitude of the change.

One should not assume that the story is essentially over at the Gestalt shift point. Holmes typically must still find evidence that will satisfy authorities as to who has or will commit the crime or even that a crime can

---

[14] Arthur Conan Doyle, *The Complete Sherlock Holmes* (New York: Doubleday, 1953), II, 544.

or will occur. Holmes may also need to discover how to capture or convict the criminal. It is true that in *A Study in Scarlet* only moments separate the time when Holmes reveals the name of the criminal as well as his methods and motives, and the time at which Holmes captures the criminal, but this is an exception, a remarkable exception, which Doyle could not duplicate in *The Hound of the Baskervilles*.

The term global has the advantage that it suggests one very striking feature that very frequently occurs in stories that contain Gestalt shifts. Words and sentences may change their meaning when a new Gestalt comes into view. For example, the reader may come to see that a remark made by Holmes early in a story should be understood as said with ironic overtones. Numerous examples of this will be presented in the commentaries on the stories. One example: on a first reading of the "The Crooked Man" story, one identifies the crooked man as Henry Wood; a more careful reading leads one to see that the person meant is Barclay.

Must all four characteristics be present? Certainly not in the same degree. Suddenness is a major source of dramatic effect and is closely associated with surprise. We do not experience as a Gestalt shift the gradual emergence of a wall to which workers daily add bricks. The year-by-year growth of a person's net worth—this is not stuff for the dramatist. The chief point made by describing a change as a Gestalt shift is that it is no ordinary change; it is an extraordinary change.

Having found that it is not always easy to recall these four criteria for Gestalt shifts, I devised a method of recalling them; it is to recall the word DRUG, which provides the first letter of each criterion: DistinctRapidUnexpectedGlobal.

Measuring a Gestalt Shift: Category Mistakes

Not all Gestalt shifts are equally impressive. Nor are all tricks magicians perform. A magician who can turn a duck into a dog will get fewer bookings than a conjuror who can turn a dog into a dinosaur. One measure of a conjuror's competence is the magnitude of the change produced. Another measure is the difference between the object first presented and the object replacing it on stage. We are impressed when the author of a detective story has Joe—a character whom the reader rules out as killer of the heroine—turn out to be the culprit. An especially interesting example of this is what the philosopher Gilbert Ryle in his *Concepts of Mind* (1949) described as a "category mistake."[15] These are mistakes when one assumes that the answer to a question must be in a specific category, failing to see that there are perfectly good answers not in this category. An excellent example of this occurs in Doyle's "The Adventure of Silver Blaze," where it turns out that the culprit in the killing of the trainer was not a murderer; rather it was the horse, Silver Blaze, acting in self-defense. It does not seem possible to supply a metric to measure Gestalt shifts, but it is worth noting that such shifts are not all equally impressive.

The Gestalt Shift Point

In many Holmes stories, it is possible to locate what can be called a Gestalt shift point or Gestalt shift moment. We shall see cases where one can point to a sentence or a few lines after which the story dramatically changes. Holmes may announce: "I have solved this case." Of course, it may take some time for Watson and the rest of us to recognize that Holmes is right, but the change begins with these words. The Gestalt shift point for Holmes occurs rapidly in *The Hound of the Baskervilles*, but others need time to be convinced that Holmes's view is correct, On the other hand, in *A Study in Scarlet* developments rapidly follow Holmes's announcement which developments convince his associates of the correctness of his claims.

Did Conan Doyle Attain the Idea of a Gestalt Shift?

Also an Early Account of a Gestalt Shift Experience
Is there evidence that Doyle had the concept of a Gestalt shift? Did anyone in Doyle's day describe such an experience?

Historians of psychology typically trace the origins of Gestalt psychology to the year 1912, with the candidates as founders including Christian von Ehrenfels (1859–1932), Wolfgang Köhler (1887–1967), Max Wertheimer (1880–1943), and Kurt Koffka (1886–1941), by which time Doyle had written most of his Holmes stories. I can find no evidence that Doyle used the term Gestalt or that he read any of these authors. Moreover, although some figures now labeled Gestalt images were known even in the nineteenth century, they were not described as Gestalt figures. On the other hand, Doyle spent some time in Vienna and Paris in 1891–1892 studying ophthalmology, which indicates his strong interest in perception.

---

[15] See http://en.wikipedia.org/wiki/Category_mistake. Viewed January 25, 2015.

Everything considered, I have concluded that there is no direct evidence that Doyle attained the concept of a Gestalt shift.

In understanding the notion of a Gestalt shift it is important to examine carefully the process of a Gestalt shift occurring. The Gestalts discussed earlier in the book should provide readers some sense of this complex experience in which an image, at first invisible, becomes visible, typically only after some effort is made to perceive it. It will be productive to provide one detailed early account of such a Gestalt shift. This is particularly interesting because the author of the account was none other than Arthur Conan Doyle and the account appears in perhaps the most famous of his Holmes stories, *The Hound of the Baskervilles* (1901–1902). This account discusses a Gestalt shift experienced by both Holmes and Watson. Up to this point in the story, Doyle has portrayed Stapleton as a bookish butterfly fancier who roams the moors and is friendly to Henry Baskerville. During his visit to Baskerville Hall, Holmes, while meeting with Watson, Baskerville, and Lestrade, becomes absorbed in looking at portraits of the Baskerville ancestors. Although this hardly seems relevant to the case, it turns out that it transforms Holmes's view of the situation. My suggestion is that Holmes undergoes a Gestalt shift and discusses his experience with Watson. Holmes asks about various aspects of the portraits, but focuses especially on one (Fig. 1.3):

Fig. 1.3   "Good heavens!" I cried in amazement.

"And this Cavalier opposite to me—the one with the black velvet and the lace?"

"Ah, you have a right to know about him. That is the cause of all the mischief, the wicked Hugo, who started the Hound of the Baskervilles. We're not likely to forget him."

I gazed with interest and some surprise upon the portrait. "Dear me!" said Holmes, "he seems a quiet, meek-mannered man enough, but I dare say that there was a lurking devil in his eyes. I had pictured him as a more robust and ruffianly person."

"There's no doubt about the authenticity, for the name and the date, 1647, are on the back of the canvas."

Holmes said little more, but the picture of the old roysterer seemed to have a fascination for him, and his eyes were continually fixed upon it during supper. It was not until later, when Sir Henry had gone to his room, that I was able to follow the trend of his thoughts. He led me back into the banqueting-hall, his bedroom candle in his hand, and he held it up against the time-stained portrait on the wall.

"Do you see anything there?"

I looked at the broad plumed hat, the curling love-locks, the white lace collar, and the straight, severe face which was framed between them. It was not a brutal countenance, but it was prim, hard, and stern, with a firm-set, thin-lipped mouth, and a coldly intolerant eye.

"Is it like anyone you know?"

"There is something of Sir Henry about the jaw."

"Just a suggestion, perhaps. But wait an instant!" He stood upon a chair, and, holding up the light in his left hand, he curved his right arm over the broad hat and round the long ringlets.

"Good heavens!" I cried in amazement. The face of Stapleton had sprung out of the canvas.

"Ha, you see it now. My eyes have been trained to examine faces and not their trimmings. It is the first quality of a criminal investigator that he should see through a disguise."

"But this is marvellous. It might be his portrait."

"Yes, it is an interesting instance of a throwback, which appears to be both physical and spiritual. A study of family portraits is enough to convert a man to the doctrine of reincarnation. The fellow is a Baskerville—that is evident."

"With designs upon the succession."

"Exactly. This chance of the picture has supplied us with one of our most obvious missing links. We have him, Watson, we have him, and I dare swear that before tomorrow night he will be fluttering in our net as helpless as one of his own butterflies. A pin, a cork, and a card, and we add him to the Baker Street collection!"

He burst into one of his rare fits of laughter as he turned away from the picture. I have not heard him laugh often, and it has always boded ill to somebody.[16]

Doyle's description of the change that Holmes, and then Watson, underwent in viewing this portrait matches up very well with modern descriptions of experiencing a Gestalt shift. It seems surprising to me that neither William Baring-Gould nor Leslie Klinger mention this feature of the experience in their wonderful annotated versions of the Holmes stories.[17] In presenting Doyle's description of this Gestalt shift, I am not claiming that Doyle had the idea of a Gestalt shift. The term never appears in his writings. On the other hand, it does indicate that Doyle had experienced this process and in fact could describe it in impressive detail.

It is relevant to note that Arthur Conan Doyle was aware of the concept of a dénouement,[18] which concept dates back at least to Aristotle and his *Poetics*. One source defines dénouement as:

1. a. The final resolution or clarification of a dramatic or narrative plot.
  b. The events following the climax of a drama or novel in which such a resolution or clarification takes place.
2. The outcome of a sequence of events; the end result.[19]

Typically, the Gestalt shifts in a Holmes story are part of the dénouement of the story, but the two terms are not identical in meaning. A major difference is that a Gestalt shift must be swift, but a dénouement need not be.

Late in his life Doyle described how he wrote his Holmes stories. It is both an accurate description of what he typically did in his stories and shares some characteristics of a Gestalt shift.

People have often asked me whether I knew the end of a Holmes story before I started it. Of course I did. One could not possibly steer a course if one did not know one's destination. The first thing is to get your idea. We will suppose that this idea is that a woman ... is suspected of biting a wound

---

[16] Arthur Conan Doyle, *The Complete Sherlock Holmes* (New York: Doubleday, 1953), II, 879.
[17] Arthur Conan Doyle, *Annotated Sherlock Holmes: The Four Novels and the Fifty-Six Short Stories Complete*, annotated by William S. Baring-Gould, 2nd ed., 2 vols. (New York: C. N. Potter, 1975) and Arthur Conan Doyle, *New Annotated Sherlock Holmes*, annotated by Leslie Klinger, 3 volumes (New York: Norton, 2005).
[18] The term dénouement appears in *The Sign of the Four*, *The Valley of Fear*, and "A Case of Identity."
[19] See http://www.thefreedictionary.com/denouement. Viewed February 7, 2015.

in her child, when she was really sucking that wound for fear of poison injected by someone else. Having got that key idea, one's next task is to conceal it and lay emphasis upon everything which can make for a different explanation. Holmes, however, can see all the fallacies of the alternatives, and arrives more or less dramatically at the true solution by steps which he can describe and justify.[20]

One can easily imagine that an author recognizing that stories can benefit from containing a Gestalt shift would endorse the next to last sentence in this quotation.

---

[20] Arthur Conan Doyle, *Memories and Adventures and Western Wanderings* (Newcastle on Tyne: Cambridge Scholars Publishing, 2009), 75.

PART TWO: THE NATURE AND METHODS OF SCIENCE

Some Views on Arthur Conan Doyle's Relation to Science

To understand Arthur Conan Doyle's writings about Sherlock Holmes, it is important to understand Doyle's views on the nature of science. During most of the nineteenth century, it was widely believed that science has two fundamental methods: induction and deduction. An example of the use of induction is this. If we examine various swans, finding the first six white, we may conclude: all swans are white. Regarding deductive inference, an example would be examining various propositions and deducing a conclusion from them. From investigating triangles, we might draw the conclusion that the base angles of an isosceles triangle are equal. This is labeled deduction. It is sometimes suggested that these two forms of conceptual change, induction and deduction, provide us all that we know to be certain, that they give us conclusive information. Numerous references to induction and deduction occur in the Holmes stories. Doyle himself was trained in medicine at the University of Edinburgh and for a period practiced medicine. There are, however, three rather different descriptions of Doyle's relations to science.

One of the most respected biographers of Conan Doyle is Russell Miller, whose *The Adventures of Arthur Conan Doyle: A Biography* appeared in 2008. Miller suggests that the chief influence on Doyle in regard to science was Dr. Joseph Bell, who taught him at Edinburgh medical school and was famous for his ability to see a patient and almost immediately describe the medical issues that led the person to seek treatment. Miller describes Bell as "the talented and charismatic man on whom [Doyle] would model his most famous creation."[21] Moreover, Miller notes the physical similarities between Bell and Holmes; for example, both were tall and slim. It is interesting that three nineteenth-century scientists whose names never appear in Miller's book are Georges Cuvier, Charles Darwin, and Charles Lyell. Another well-known Doyle biographer, Daniel Stashower, quotes from a letter Doyle wrote to Bell: "It is most certainly to you that I owe Sherlock Holmes ... and though in the stories I have the advantage of being able to place him in all sorts of dramatic positions, I do

---

[21] Russell Miller. *Adventures of Arthur Conan Doyle: A Biography* (New York: Thomas Dunne Books: St. Martin's Press, 2008), 49.

not think that his analytical work is in the least an exaggeration of some of the effects that I have seen you produce in the outpatient ward."[22]

Another widely respected analysis is Lawrence Frank's *Victorian Detective Fiction and the Nature of Evidence*, which focuses on the detective fiction of Edgar Allen Poe, Charles Dickens, and Conan Doyle. Frank's study focuses on the impact that leading nineteenth-century scientists had on Doyle. The index of his book contains nearly a hundred references to Cuvier, Darwin, and Lyell, but no reference to Joseph Bell. One impressive example of Frank's analysis is that in Doyle's *Hound of the Baskervilles* Frank traces Holmes's prediction of the chief features of a potential client, Dr. Mortimer, from examining Mortimer's walking stick. Frank shows in detail that Doyle's model was probably Cuvier's famous ability, if given a fossil or two from some animal, to reconstruct intellectually the entire animal, even if the animal were extinct.[23] It is important to understand that the characterizations by Miller and Frank are not incompatible. Both give valuable insights into what Doyle was attempting.

If the question is asked: What author writing during the time when Doyle created Sherlock Holmes could have contributed most to Conan Doyle's providing a sophisticated presentation of scientific method, the best answer seems to be the American philosopher Charles Sanders Peirce (1839–1914), who proposed a method called abduction or abductive inference, later preferring the name retroduction. Most of an entire book explains and develops this claim about Holmes's methods: Umberto Eco and Thomas A. Sebeok (editors). *The Sign of Three: Dupin, Holmes, Peirce* (*Advances in Semiotics*) (Bloomington: Indiana University Press, c. 1983). The English philosopher and economist William Stanley Jevons put forth a method similar to Peirce's abduction in 1874 in his *Principles of Science*, naming his method inverse deduction.

The current name for this method is the hypothetico-deductive method (for short, the HD method). According to this method, the scientist creates a hypothesis, then deduces what follows from it, and if the phenomena it deductively predicts turn out as predicted, then this is a good indication that the original hypothesis is true. This cannot give complete certainty because it is possible that another hypothesis will also predict the

---

[22] Daniel Stashower. *Teller of Tales: The Life of Arthur Conan Doyle* (New York: Henry Holt, 1999), 77.

[23] Lawrence Frank. *Victorian Detective Fiction and the Nature of Evidence* (New York: Palgrave Macmillan, 2003), 156–161.

same phenomena. Example: If it rains, the grass will be wet. If we know that it has rained, we can know with certainty that the grass is wet. But the reverse does not necessarily follow; sprinklers can also produce wet grass. Applying this to the Holmes stories, one sees Doyle ascribing certainty to a number of results without realizing that the result cannot rest on inductive reasoning or on deductive reasoning. In fact, the argument conforms to the HD model, which in many cases can give only more or less probable results. A substantial number of Sherlockian scholars have adopted the position that the HD method is precisely the method that best describes many of the arguments used in the Holmes stories.[24] In some ways, this parallels what happens in a Gestalt shift. We are given an image and assume that only one concept corresponds to this image. We see, for example, a drawing of a rabbit. Persons experienced in perceiving Gestalt shifts are not totally surprised when the rabbit turns into a duck. This is comparable to seeing the grass is wet, concluding that it has rained, and then noticing that a sprinkler system is in operation.

Understanding the Nature and Development of Science

The nature of scientific method is an important issue; another important issue is: How does science develop? Over the last seventy or so years, a major development has occurred in views as to how scientific thought changes. Let us take one example: the Copernican revolution. In the first half of the twentieth century, the tendency was to believe that new empirical information led Copernicus to develop the heliocentric theory. The problem is that historical studies do not support this. Scientists invented the telescope more than sixty years *after* Copernicus's death. A sophisticated notion of inertia became available only decades later. Copernicus's chief arguments took the form that his system was more orderly and elegant than the geocentric system as developed by ancient astronomers,

---

[24] Umberto Eco and Thomas A. Sebeok (eds.). *The Sign of Three: Dupin, Holmes, Peirce (Advances in Semiotics)* (Bloomington: Indiana University Press, c. 1983). This volume contains essays by, among others, Thomas A. Sebeok, Marcello Truzzi, Carlo Ginzberg, Gian Paolo Carettini, and Jaakto Hintikka. The key essay in the volume seems to be Thomas Sebeok and Jean Umiker Sebeok, "You know My Method: A Juxtaposition of Charles S. Peirce and Sherlock Holmes," 11–54. Numerous Sherlockian scholars have accepted this analysis. See, for example, Douglas Kerr, *Conan Doyle: Writing, Profession, and Practice* (Oxford University Press, 2012), 128–129 and David Baggett, "Sherlock Holmes as Epistemologist" in Philip Tallon and David Baggett (eds.) *The Philosophy of Sherlock Holmes* (University Press of Kentucky, 2012), 7–21.

especially Claudius Ptolemy. What was crucial was that Copernicus had the insight that he could explain the motions of the Sun and planets in a radically different way from that adopted by his predecessors. Eventually, scholars came to see that the idea of a Gestalt shift could effectively be applied to numerous conceptual changes in science.

This leads us to investigate how the idea of a Gestalt shift arose and eventually entered the discussion of the nature of scientific change. As we shall see in what follows, the recognition of this pattern played a major role in the last sixty or so years in the formulation of theories of the proper and productive methods of science. One relevance of this development to the thesis of this book is that the thesis, if correct, shows that to some extent Doyle seemed well aware that the successful investigations carried out by Holmes were due in significant part to his skill in attaining new insights. Although at times Doyle stresses how much Holmes's knowledge of a vast number of tobacco ashes helped him solve a case, a careful reading of the stories shows that Holmes in a very large number of cases saw pretty much the same empirical information as the official detectives, but he also had the insight to see this shared information in a new and insightful way.

The claim made in this book is that the notion of a Gestalt shift can fruitfully be applied to the Holmes's stories needs further explanation, which can most effectively be provided by tracing in more detail how and when the idea of Gestalt shift arose and also by tracing the remarkable effects that it has had. But first a caveat. One might expect that the history of the study of Gestalt shifts was part of the history of Gestalt psychology. To a substantial degree, this does not seem to have been the case. From what I have been able to discern, the idea of a Gestalt shift arose primarily in the period around 1960 and for the most part independently of the history of Gestalt psychology.

The earliest clear-cut example of a Gestalt image may be Johann Voltz's painting *Triumph des Jahres* (mentioned earlier), which he created in 1813, long before the founding period assigned to Gestalt psychology (typically dated from 1912). After finding this, I happened upon the information that in 1832 the crystallographer L. A. Necker reported noticing the oddly shifting image of a rhomboid in a crystal, which led to Necker now being recognized as the first person to report on the characteristics of the figure now known as the Necker Cube.[25]

---

[25] Louis Albert Necker. "Observations on Some Remarkable Optical Phaenomena Seen in Switzerland; and on an Optical Phaenomenon Which Occurs on Viewing a Figure of a

Probably no Gestalt figure has received more attention or exerted greater influence than the duck-rabbit Gestalt, which first appeared in 1892 in a German humor magazine.[26] Placed above it was the question (written in German): "Which animals are most like each other?" with "Rabbit and Duck" written underneath. Although it is unknown who created the figure, various sources allow us to present information on its curious history. By 1893, it had migrated to *Harper's Weekly*,[27] where it attracted the attention of an American psychologist Joseph Jastrow, who discussed the figure in print in 1899 and 1900.[28] In his volume published in 1900, Jastrow devoted a section to showing how the mind plays a role in what we see. In order to stress this point, Jastrow discussed not only the duck/rabbit pair but also Necker's Cube, but without attributing it to Necker. In 1915, Edgar Rubin, a Danish psychologist, introduced his Rubin's Vase or Vase/Faces Gestalt,[29] and in 1930 Edwin Boring presented his "Boring's Figure" or Young Lady/Old Lady diagram. It is interesting that in his publication Boring notes that the picture "is not strictly new. It was drawn by the well-known cartoonist, W. E. Hill, and reproduced in the issue of *Puck* for the week ending November 6, 1915." And Boring adds: "This picture was originally published under the title 'My Wife and my Mother-in-law.'"[30] In fact, Boring was not quite right; the image has been dated back to an 1888 German postcard.[31] It is inter-

---

Crystal or Geometrical Solid," *London and Edinburgh Philosophical Magazine and Journal of Science, 1* (5) (1832), 329–337.

[26] *Fliegende Blätter* (October 22, 1892), 147, One of the best sources for the early history of the duck-rabbit figure is the Wikipedia article "The Duck-Rabbit Illusion." See http://en.wikipedia.org/wiki/Rabbit–duck_illusion. Viewed February 22, 2015. See also John F. Kihlstrom. "Joseph Jastrow and His Duck—Or Is It a Rabbit," http://ist-socrates.berkeley.edu/~Kihlstrm/JastrowDuck.htm (viewed March 3, 2015) and Peter Brugger and Susan Brugger, "The Easter Bunny in October: Is It Disguised as a Duck?" *Perceptual and Motor Skills, 76* (1993), 577–578 and Peter Brugger. "One Hundred Years of an Ambiguous Figure: Happy Birthday, Duck/Rabbit!" *Perceptual and Motor Skills, 89* (1999), 973–977.

[27] *Harper's Weekly* (November 19, 1892), 1114.

[28] Joseph Jastrow. "The Mind's Eye," *Popular Science Monthly, 54* (1899), 299–312 and Jastrow, *Fact and Fable in Psychology* (Boston: Houghton-Mifflin, 1900).

[29] For evidence that Rubin did not discover the Rubin vase, see "Rubin did not discover the Rubin Vase," http://figuresambigues.free.fr/ArticlesImage/rubin1.html#axzz41DIKsvFm.

[30] Boring, 445.

[31] See https://en.wikipedia.org/wiki/My_Wife_and_My_Mother-in-Law. Viewed September 17, 2015 for the postcard image and also the *Puck* image.

esting that none of the authors mentioned in this paragraph was a Gestalt psychologist, nor was the term Gestalt used in these publications.

It appears that the publication that launched the duck/rabbit pair and the Necker Cube on the main stage of western thought was a publication in 1953 by a scholar who was not a psychologist; this was the famous philosopher Ludwig Wittgenstein (1889–1951). In his well-known *Philosophical Investigations* (1953), he discussed both these figures as a way of distinguishing between "seeing" and "seeing as."[32] He listed Jastrow's 1900 volume as his source for the duck/rabbit pair. It is significant that Wittgenstein did not use either the term Gestalt or the term Gestalt shift.

In 1958, the philosopher of science Norwood Russell Hanson published his well-regarded *Patterns of Discovery: An Inquiry into the Foundations of Science*,[33] in which he drew heavily on Wittgenstein's discussion of the bird/rabbit drawing. Hanson substituted a bird/antelope pair for the duck/rabbit combo but like Wittgenstein included the Necker Cube and various other Gestalt figures, including Boring's young woman/older woman drawing.[34] On the one hand, Hanson discussed such diagrams in terms close to those used by Gestalt psychologists; on the other hand, his chief concern was to discuss whether, for example, the geocentrist astronomer Tycho Brahe and the heliocentrists Galileo and Kepler saw the Earth, planets, Sun, and moons in the same way. One of Hanson's main points was to claim that in science, "[t]here is a sense … in which seeing is a 'theory-laden' undertaking."[35] I do not believe the terms "Gestalt shift" or "Gestalt switch" appear in Hanson's book; in fact, I have been unsuccessful in tracing the first appearance of either of these terms.

In 1962, Thomas Kuhn (1922–1996) published his *The Structure of Scientific Revolutions*, the chief goal of which was to discuss how change occurs in scientific thought. Kuhn's volume has had a remarkable history, which strikingly illustrates the powerful impact that the idea of a Gestalt shift has had. For example, Kuhn's very academic book came to be seen as so important that by 2012 it had sold 1.4 million copies and became standard reading in a variety of academic departments in universities around

---

[32] Ludwig Wittgenstein, *Philosophical Investigations*, trans. by G. E. M. Anscombe, 2nd ed. (Oxford, U.K.: Blackwell), 193–197.

[33] (Cambridge University Press).

[34] Norwood Russell Hanson, *Patterns of Discovery: An Inquiry into the Foundations of Science* (Cambridge University Press, 1958), 8–30.

[35] Hanson, *Patterns of Discovery*, 19.

the world.[36] Also, Alexander Bird described Kuhn as "one of the most influential philosophers of science of the twentieth century, perhaps the most influential."[37] Kuhn's *Structure*, which is frequently described as having played the key role in ending the dominance of logical empiricism in philosophy, centers on the idea that scientists do not typically settle scientific revolutions solely by studying the available empirical information. Rather, revolutions can be seen as clashes between conflicting paradigms (a central term in Kuhn's philosophy, which term has now become common in many disciplines). Paradigms are holistic entities that encompass not only empirical information and theories but also convictions concerning methods, proper instrumentation, metaphysical and methodological claims, and groups of scientists. Kuhn called one of his key conceptual innovations a "paradigm switch," by which he meant to suggest that it was essentially a macro Gestalt shift.

Chapter X of Kuhn's book, "Revolutions as Changes of World View," is frequently seen as one of the most important chapters; in the present context, it is certainly the most relevant. The central claim in this chapter is that experiencing a scientific revolution—that is, moving from one paradigm to another—entails moving, in a sense, from one world to another. In a fundamental and literal sense, one **sees** the world differently within different paradigms. Even facts and observations can change when the paradigm changes. One cause of the incommensurability of competing paradigms is that no neutral set of facts and observations is accepted by the proponents of the two paradigms. In developing this point, Kuhn compares paradigm changes to Gestalt shifts. He does this partly by drawing on the writings, previously discussed, of Wittgenstein and Hanson. Kuhn states that in a scientific revolution:

> What were ducks in the scientific world before the revolution are rabbits afterwards. The man who first saw the exterior of the box from above later sees its interior from below.... Only after a number of such transformations

---

[36] John Naughton, "Thomas Kuhn: The Man Who Changed the Way the World Looked at Science," *Manchester Guardian*, August 19, 2012. Accessed on May 13, 2015 at http://www.rawstory.com/2012/08/thomas-kuhn-the-man-who-changed-the-way-the-world-looked-at-science/.

[37] Alexander Bird, "Thomas Kuhn," *The Stanford Encyclopedia of Philosophy* (Fall 2013 Edition), Edward N. Zalta (ed.), URL: http://plato.stanford.edu/archives/fall2013/entries/thomas-kuhn/. Viewed February 23, 2015.

of vision does the student become an inhabitant of the scientists' world, seeing what the scientist sees and responding as the scientist does.[38]

Kuhn devotes the rest of chapter X to insightful illustrations of this claim based on the examination of various developments in science; for example, Galileo's experiments with pendular motion, William Herschel's discovery of the planet Uranus, and the debate, crucial for the atomic theory, over whether chemical data support the law of definite proportions. One striking aspect of these portions of Kuhn's book is that although he mentions Gestalt psychology and draws on various Gestalt observations, such as the duck/rabbit diagram, he says almost nothing about the elaborate theoretical ideas of the Gestaltists.

Let us take one example. It is widely reported that on March 13, 1781 William Herschel discovered the planet Uranus, the first planet discovered in recorded history. The poet John Keats later celebrated this event when in a famous poem he compared his delight in reading a new translation of Homer to Herschel's discovery of Uranus: "Then felt I like some watcher of the skies when a new planet swims into his ken."[39] Kuhn carefully analyzes Herschel's discovery to show that what actually happened was radically different. It is true that Herschel soon reported his observation—in a paper entitled "Account of a Comet." Because no one had ever discovered a planet before and because comets look something like planets, Herschel literally saw the object as a comet. It took many months for Herschel to see his object as a planet. It was determined that that on 17 occasions before Herschel other astronomers had sighted this object, but failed to see it as a planet.[40] On a larger scale, Kuhn analyzed the Copernican revolution showing that the decision between the geocentrism and heliocentrism involved not only observations and mathematical theories but also more complex issues such as metaphysics, traditions, religion, the interpretation of observations, and much else.

---

[38] Thomas S. Kuhn, *The Structure of Scientific Revolutions*, 3rd ed. (Chicago: University of Chicago Press, 1996), 111.

[39] John Keats, "On First Looking into Chapman's Homer," available on the internet at http://en.wikipedia.org/wiki/On_First_Looking_into_Chapman%27s_Homer. Viewed May 18, 2015.

[40] Thomas Kuhn. "Historical Structure of Scientific Discovery," *Historical Conceptions of Psychology*, ed. Mary Henle, Julian Jaynes, and John J. Sullivan (New York: Springer, 1973), 7.

Paul Thagard in his book *Conceptual Revolutions* offers a relevant and helpful distinction. He describes major changes in scientific theories as taking the form of either "accretion theories or gestalt theories. On accretion views, a new conceptual system develops simply by adding new nodes and links."[41] Thagard adds: "Thinking of changes as gestalt switches has the advantage over the accretion theory of taking seriously the degree of conceptual reorganization that goes into important scientific developments."[42] In other words, the ideas and information in the old theory has become reorganized in a new way.

Practitioners in many areas of learning have attempted to determine how Kuhn's ideas can be applied to their specialty. Scientists, engineers, business management experts, financial analysts, as well as psychologists, philosophers, and theologians are among the experts who have taken up this task. Let us examine only one such development, but in the hope that seeing it will suggest the wide variety of changes brought on by the recognition of the importance of understanding the idea of a Gestalt shift. The incident I have selected has three features: (1) it presents an engaging instance that can be described as a form of Gestalt shift; (2) it illustrates how a Gestalt shift approach can be applied to much more than pictures and much more than natural science; and (3) it may give the reader a sense of the very extensive influence of the ideas of Thomas Kuhn. I have selected a single example (although two authors are involved). The person I have chosen is a philosopher concerned about ethical decisions. She is Peggy DesAutels, who has an interest in moral perception; in fact, in 1996, she published an essay titled "Gestalt Shifts in Moral Perception,"[43] which itself carried on a debate on this topic between Professors Carol Gilligan and Owen Flanagan. In order to illustrate how a Gestalt shift can be used to describe moral perceptions, she cited a passage from Stephen R. Covey, the author of a best-selling book titled *The Seven Habits of Highly Effective People*. Covey wrote:

[41] Paul Thagard, *Conceptual Revolutions* (Princeton, NJ: Princeton University Press, 1992), 48.

[42] Thagard, *Revolutions*, 49.

[43] Peggy DesAutels, "Gestalt Shifts in Moral Perception," in Larry May, Marilyn Friedman, and Andy Clark eds., *Mind and Morals* (Bradford/MIT Press, 1996), 129–143.

I remember a mini-Paradigm Shift I experienced one Sunday morning on a subway in New York. … It was a calm, peaceful scene. Then suddenly, a man and his children entered the subway car. The children were so loud and rambunctious that instantly the whole climate changed.

The man sat down next to me and closed his eyes, apparently oblivious to the situation. The children were yelling back and forth, throwing things, even grabbing people's papers. It was very disturbing. And yet, the man sitting next to me did nothing.

It was difficult not to feel irritated…. So finally, with what I felt was unusual patience and restraint, I turned to him and said, "Sir, your children are really disturbing a lot of people. I wonder if you couldn't control them a little more?"

The man lifted his gaze as if to come to a consciousness of the situation for the first time and said softly, "Oh, you're right. I guess I should do something about it. We just came from the hospital where their mother died about an hour ago. I don't know what to think, and I guess they don't know how to handle it either."

Can you imagine what I felt at that moment? My paradigm shifted. Suddenly I saw things differently, I felt differently, I behaved differently. My irritation vanished. I didn't have to worry about controlling my attitude or my behavior; my heart was filled with the man's pain. Feelings of sympathy and compassion flowed freely. "Your wife just died? Oh, I'm so sorry. Can you tell me about it? What can I do to help?" Everything changed in an instant.[44]

Professor DesAutels then discusses whether it makes more sense to view this as a Gestalt shift or a Paradigm shift, and commits to the Gestalt shift approach. My only comment is to agree with her that Gestalt shift language can be very appropriate for treating shifts such as this, which are rapid, unexpected, and global as well as incorporating Gestalts that are distinct from each other.

We can get an idea of the increase in popularity over the last fifty years of the ideas of a Gestalt shift and a paradigm shift by examining graphs produced using a technique called Google NGrams. Google has digitalized a very large number of books or portions thereof and placed them on the

---

[44] Stephen R. Covey. *The Seven Habits of Highly Effective People* (New York: Simon and Schuster, 1989), 30–31.

internet. This has given scholars a method of charting the level of usage specific terms have over a number of years. I have placed below NGrams for the terms "Gestalt shift" and "Paradigm shift" (Figs. 1.4 and 1.5).

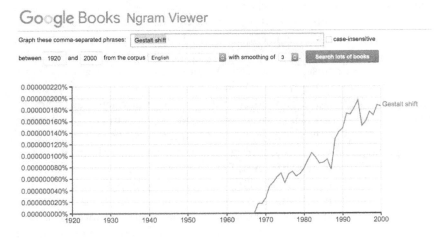

Fig. 1.4

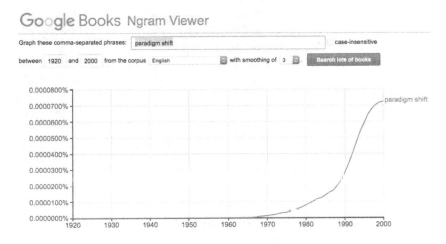

Fig. 1.5

In reflecting on the information discussed in this section, I am struck by the small role that the leading Gestalt psychologists seem to have played in these developments. Two of the most important Gestalt images appeared first not in journals of psychology but rather in humor magazines. A central one, the Necker Cube, came out of an investigation in crystallography. Rubin and Boring were psychologists, but not Gestalt psychologists. Wittgenstein, Hanson, and Kuhn were not psychologists, but rather scientifically interested philosophers. Overall, this information suggests two conclusions: The notion of a Gestalt shift has already had a major impact on modern thought, which suggests that there are grounds for centering this book on Gestalt shifts. It is of course true that many of these concepts took on a larger significance only after psychologists, including Gestalt psychologists, began to study them. It may also be true that specialists in Gestalt psychology will eventually be able to move this discussion to a higher, richer level. Put differently, the first graph seems to show that the idea of a Gestalt shift shows that traditional views about the nature of conceptual change need revision.

An interesting question that I have not yet succeeded in resolving is: When was the term Gestalt shift first used? Nonetheless, the graph above makes clear that it was only in the period after 1962 that it became an accepted, respected, and used term in publications. As the discussion of Hanson's book makes clear, the idea of a Gestalt shift was already in his mind even if the term wasn't yet in his vocabulary. It also true that various philosophers of science, most notably Michael Polanyi, were thinking and writing in the very early 1960s in relevant ways.[45]

Two more important points: First, it is my belief that this discussion will show that my claim that the idea of a Gestalt shift can be helpfully used in analyzing the Sherlock Holmes stories is a claim that many highly respected intellectuals would see as plausible. Moreover, my knowledge, built up over decades of employing the idea of a Gestalt shift in analyzing developments in science, gives me a significant background in applying this sort of analysis to a new area. Second, it is important to note that my claim is not that the whole structure of Thomas Kuhn's analysis of science can productively be applied to the Holmes stories; my claim is the more modest claim that one key part of Kuhn's analysis—the idea of a Gestalt shift—can productively be applied to the Holmes stories.

[45] See Michael Polanyi's *Personal Knowledge: Towards a Post-Critical Philosophy,* which was first published in 1958, with a revised edition in 1962. My edition is the 1964 New York: Harper and Row edition.

Final comment: It seems possible, given the large number of areas of learning in which scholars have drawn on Kuhn's writings, that literary scholars would attempt to apply Kuhn's Gestalt ideas to literature. Therefore, I began searching for just such attempts, using all the resources I could find. This included searching through books and journals and also employing electronic searches, where I received considerable help from some colleagues who possess greater skills than I. Of course I realized that detective fiction is only one area in literature, and possibly a somewhat distinct area. I entered this quest with mixed feelings: if I located an author who had applied Kuhnian Gestalt ideas to literature, it would have made my analyses less of a challenge, but also it might well have made them somewhat trivial. All my efforts failed, though I did receive a very interesting comment from a Notre Dame colleague, Laura Dassow Walls, who is a distinguished professor in Notre Dame's Department of English and also in its Graduate Program in History and Philosophy of Science. Her specialty is science and literature. She reported that she knew of no scholar who had attempted to apply Kuhn's ideas of literature in the way that I have adopted, but she added:

> Interestingly enough, I've never cited Kuhn directly in my own work, but I can't imagine how I would have proceeded in my career without having been introduced to Kuhn in graduate school. I took courses in history of science as well as science and literature, and was one of the earliest members of the Society for Literature and Science.… In my own research and writing I've concentrated on the nineteenth century, and Kuhn's concept of scientific revolution was very definitely in the background of my work on Alexander von Humboldt.[46]

Later she added:

> Kuhn allows for a historicist approach to scientific knowledge of a given era, something that's essential if a literary critic such as myself wants to understand how the world looked to the people we study. That is, Kuhn allows the historicist critic to approach a past world as engaged in an earlier paradigm, rather than as simply false. This is such a fundamental tool of historicist literary work that I think we take it for granted now!

---

[46] Letter of February 26, 2018 from Professor Laura Dassow Walls.

This suggests that overall Kuhn's writings had a significant role in developing the area literature and science, which I take to be an indication that my quite special use of his thought may be worthwhile.

The Genius of Sherlock Holmes: A New View

Numerous Sherlockians have attempted to describe the extraordinary genius of Sherlock Holmes. One of these was of course Arthur Conan Doyle, who enriched the Holmes stories by offering many accounts of Holmes's singular ability to solve criminal investigations. A few of Doyle's comments are:

> "It is a capital mistake to theorize before you have all the evidence. It biases the judgment."[47]

> "From a drop of water," said the writer, "a logician could infer the possibility of an Atlantic or a Niagara without having seen or heard of one or the other. So all life is a great chain, the nature of which is known whenever we are shown a single link of it. Like all other arts, the Science of Deduction and Analysis is one which can only be acquired by long and patient study nor is life long enough to allow any mortal to attain the highest possible perfection in it. Before turning to those moral and mental aspects of the matter which present the greatest difficulties, let the enquirer begin by mastering more elementary problems."[48]

There are certainly merits in these claims. Nonetheless, I believe it is possible in the context of this book to describe the genius of Holmes in a deeper and more satisfactory way and to do it a single sentence that differs from all previous characterizations of Holmes. My sentence: The essence of Holmes's detective genius was his extraordinary ability to colligate or to form an excellent Gestalt when presented with information. In other words, the genius of Holmes was his ability when encountering the information available in a case to put it together in a convincing manner. Thus Holmes demonstrates an extraordinary facility when presented with a duck to see a rabbit; when encountering the image of an elderly lady, to see a

---

[47] Doyle, *Holmes*, I, 18.
[48] Doyle, *Holmes*, I, 12.

younger lady; when presented with a twisted beggar accused of murdering St. Clair to see St. Clair himself. There are instances when Doyle comes close to recognizing something like this; for example, consider Holmes's statement in "The Reigate Puzzle": "It is of the highest importance in the art of detection to be able to recognize, out of a number of facts, which are incidental and which vital. Otherwise your energy and attention must be dissipated instead of being concentrated."[49] In short, Holmes ultimate genius was his ability to achieve Gestalt shifts, to see patterns beyond those recognized by the Scotland Yarders. His fantastic memory, clarity of thought, objectivity, stores of information, attention to detail, and similar attributes, were all part of this, but what above all defines his genius was his skill in recognizing and organizing patterns and relations that others could see only when he showed them what he had detected.[50]

Can Concepts Provide Explanatory Power? The Idea of a Tipping Point

The claim that effects are invariably proportional to causes is widespread and seems sound. A brilliant but largely unknown author in the year 2000 established his reputation by writing a book that in effect showed the flaw in this claim that causes and effects follow this pattern. The author was Malcolm Gladwell; his book, which sold over two million copies in the United States alone, was *The Tipping Point: How Little Things Can Make a Big Difference* (New York: Little Brown, 2000). Gladwell's starting point was that he noticed that epidemiologists view epidemics in an unusual way; they look for "tipping points," points at which the number of cases of a disease suddenly increases very rapidly. He came to see that an identical pattern might be seen in the crime rate in New York and the rate of sales of certain types of footwear. Suddenly, a major increase takes place. Gladwell showed that this pattern is widespread and can be measured, studied mathematically, and to a significant degree managed. He formulated laws that effectively applied to tipping point changes. The effect of his book was that persons all around the world saw that using the idea of

[49] Doyle, *Holmes*, I, 469.

[50] In recent years, a new verb has begun to appear in very diverse locations. The verb is to Gestalt or the activity can be described as "gestalting." One need only do a Google search on gestalting to estimate its frequency and to see the sometime quite diverse meanings that are being given to it. My search on January 15, 2016 produced 7220 hits.

a tipping point could provide them an understanding and methods of managing many forms of behavior that previously had seemed chaotic and ungoverned by laws.

This suggests that various ideas that may seem trivial or obvious can actually be very powerful in producing understanding. My suggestion is that the idea of a Gestalt shift is an instance of this. Moreover, I suggest that most Holmes stories contain a Gestalt shift point—that is, a time when suddenly Holmes sees that an array of evidence can be organized in a new way that points to the exact nature of the crime. Moreover, at the Gestalt shift point the detective typically sees who the criminal is and why the criminal behaved in a particular manner. The process is not a simple deduction or induction; it is more like seeing a picture in a new way that had been invisible before. From this point on, Holmes can convince others—for example, the Scotland Yarders or his client—to see the pattern that Holmes has detected.

The Structure of This Book

This book provides a separate discussion of each of the sixty Holmes stories, focusing on whether or not one or more Gestalt shifts are fundamental to the structure of the story. Initially, I planned to proceed through the stories in the chronological order of their publication. Eventually, I realized that a better method would be to lead off by discussing in chronological order the four book-length Holmes stories because they best illustrate my claim. This arrangement would early on clearly exhibit the mode of analysis that I have developed. I will then discuss individually each of the fifty-six short stories that appeared in five anthologies arranged in chronological order. An obvious benefit of this format is that a reader wanting to see whether one of the late stories has a Gestaltish structure can go directly to an analysis of that story. Each story analysis is meant to stand on its own, but my overall argument rests strongly on the level of agreement among the various analyses. In discussing most of the stories, I have sought to avoid summarizing the story in detail, which would very significantly extend the length of this book. Moreover, I frequently found that summaries of the stories were not a good source for revealing their structure.[51] Rather, I will present an analysis of whether the story is structured around one or more Gestalts and whether this enhances the story's dramatic effect. A summary chapter analyzes whether the approach taken in this book is successful. Appendix One extends the thesis of the book by examining a famous detective story told by Gilbert Keith Chesterton. Appendix Two, "Some Questions and Some Answers," asks whether the thesis of this book is applicable to the highly regarded television show *House, M.D.*, which some say is modeled on the Holmes stories. And Appendix Three provides a tabular synopsis of the analyses presented of the sixty Holmes stories.

---

[51] I have repeatedly consulted two sources for summaries. These helped me recall some of the main aspects of the stories, which I have read many times over a number of decades. Then I would reread the story, being repeatedly struck by the absolute necessity of carefully examining the story itself. I would also listen to each story as brilliantly read by David Timson. Typically, when I did this the Gestalts began to emerge far more effectively than they did from the summaries. The two chief sources of summaries that I have consulted are the summaries from "McMurdo's Camp," which are available at http://www.sherlockian.net/ and the summaries by a British barrister, James Hoy, which are available on the internet at http://www.diogenes-club.com/hoyadventures.htm.

BIBLIOGRAPHY

PRINTED SOURCES

Baggett, David. "Sherlock Holmes as Epistemologist," *The Philosophy of Sherlock Holmes*, ed. Philip Tallon and David Baggett (University Press of Kentucky, 2012).

Boring, Edwin G. "A New Ambiguous Figure," *American Journal of Psychology*, *42* (1930), 444–445.

Brugger, Peter and Susan Brugger. "The Easter Bunny in October: Is It Disguised as a Duck?" *Perceptual and Motor Skills, 76* (1993), 577–578.

Brugger, Peter. "One Hundred Years of an Ambiguous Figure: Happy Birthday, Duck/Rabbit!" *Perceptual and Motor Skills, 89* (1999), 973–977.

Covey, Stephen R. *The Seven Habits of Highly Effective People* (New York: Simon and Schuster, 1989).

DesAutels, Peggy. "Gestalt Shifts in Moral Perception," in Larry May, Marilyn Friedman, and Andy Clark eds., *Mind and Morals* (Bradford/MIT Press, 1996), 129–143.

Doyle, Arthur Conan. *Annotated Sherlock Holmes: The Four Novels and the Fifty-Six Short Stories Complete*, annotated by William S. Baring-Gould, 2nd ed., 2 vols. (New York: C. N. Potter, 1975).

Doyle, Arthur Conan. *Memories and Adventures and Western Wanderings* (Newcastle on Tyne: Cambridge Scholars Publishing, 2009).

Doyle, Arthur Conan. *The Complete Sherlock Holmes*, 2 vols. (New York: Doubleday, 1953).

Eco, Umberto and Thomas A. Sebeok (eds.). *The Sign of Three: Dupin, Holmes, Peirce (Advances in Semiotics)*, (Bloomington: Indiana University Press, c. 1983).

Frank, Lawrence. *Victorian Detective Fiction and the Nature of Evidence* (New York: Palgrave Macmillan, 2003).

Hanson, Norwood Russell. *Patterns of Discovery: An Inquiry into the Foundations of Science* (Cambridge University Press, 1958).

Hunt, Morton. *The Story of Psychology* (New York: Doubleday, 1993).

Jastrow, Joseph. "The Mind's Eye," *Popular Science Monthly, 54* (1899), 299–312.

Jastrow, Joseph. *Fact and Fable in Psychology* (Boston: Houghton-Mifflin, 1900).

Kerr, Douglas. *Conan Doyle: Writing, Profession, and Practice* (Oxford University Press, 2012).

Kuhn, Thomas. "Historical Structure of Scientific Discovery," *Historical Conceptions of Psychology*, ed. Mary Henle, Julian Jaynes, and John J. Sullivan (New York: Springer, 1973), 3–12.

Kuhn, Thomas. *The Structure of Scientific Revolutions*, 3rd ed. (Chicago: University of Chicago Press, 1996).

Miller, Russell. *Adventures of Arthur Conan Doyle: A Biography* (New York: Thomas Dunne Books: St. Martin's Press, 2008).

Necker, Louis Albert. "Observations on Some Remarkable Optical Phaenomena Seen in Switzerland; and on an Optical Phaenomenon Which Occurs on Viewing a Figure of a Crystal or Geometrical Solid," *London and Edinburgh Philosophical Magazine and Journal of Science, 1* (5) (1832), 329–337.

Polanyi, Michael. *Personal Knowledge: Towards a Post-Critical Philosophy* (New York: Harper and Row, 1964).

Stashower, Daniel. *Teller of Tales: The Life of Arthur Conan Doyle* (New york: Henry Holt, 1999).

Thagard, Paul. *Conceptual Revolutions* (Princeton, NJ: Princeton University Press, 1992).

Truss, Lynne. *Eats, Shoots & Leaves: The Zero Tolerance Approach to Punctuation* (New York: Gotham Books, 2006).

Wittgenstein, Ludwig. *Philosophical Investigations*, trans. by G. E. M. Anscombe, 2nd ed. (Oxford, U.K.: Blackwell).

INTERNET REFERENCES

"7H15 M3554G3 53RV35 7O PR0V3 H0W 0UR M1ND5".

"Duck-Rabbit Illusion." See http://en.wikipedia.org/wiki/Rabbit–duck_illusion. Viewed 22 February 2015.

"Rubin did not discover the Rubin Vase," http://figuresambigues.free.fr/ArticlesImage/rubin1.html#axzz41DIKsvFm.

"Rubin Did Not Discover the Rubin Vase," on the internet at http://figuresambigues.free.fr/ArticlesImage/rubin1.html#axzz5CcbaTVFn. Viewed 14 April 2018.

Bird, Alexander. "Thomas Kuhn," *The Stanford Encyclopedia of Philosophy* (Fall 2013 Edition), Edward N. Zalta (ed.), URL: http://plato.stanford.edu/archives/fall2013/entries/thomas-kuhn/. Viewed 23 February 2015.

Fliegende Blätter (October 23, 1892), 147. Viewed 14 April 2018.

http://en.wikipedia.org/wiki/Category_mistake. Viewed 25 January 2015.

http://www.thefreedictionary.com/denouement. Viewed 7 Ferbruary 2015.

https://en.wikipedia.org/wiki/My_Wife_and_My_Mother-in-Law. Viewed 17 September 2015.

Keats, John. "On First Looking into Chapman's Homer," https://en.wikipedia.org/wiki/On_First_Looking_into_Chapman%27s_Homer. Viewed 18 May 2015.

Kihlstrom, John F. "Jospeh Jastrow and His Duck—Or Is It a Rabbit," http://ist-socrates.berkeley.edu/~Kihlstrm/JastrowDuck.htm. Viewed 3 March 2015.

Naughton, John. "Thomas Kuhn: The Man Who Changed the Way the World Looked at Science," *Manchester Guardian*, August 19, 2012. Accessed on May 13, 2015 at http://www.rawstory.com/2012/08/thomas-kuhn-the-man-who-changed-the-way-the-world-looked-at-science/.

CHAPTER 2

The Four Holmes Novels

PART ONE: *A STUDY IN SCARLET* (NOVEL, 1887)

A Study in Scarlet is important in numerous ways, many linked to its being Arthur Conan Doyle's first Sherlock Holmes story. It is also noteworthy that, like Doyle's *The Valley of Fear*, it consists of two linked stories of comparable length, with the second story filling in background for the first story. In both cases, Sherlock Holmes has no direct role in the second story, which is set much earlier and in the United States.

We shall begin by considering the first story. My claim regarding this story is not only that it is structured in a form that highlights a Gestalt shift, but that it also contains a clearly defined Gestalt shift point. In outline, the story reports on the murder in London of an American, followed slightly later by the murder of the American's companion. On one level, the Gestalt shift takes the form of a major change in how Watson and also Inspectors Lestrade and Gregson of Scotland Yard view Holmes, who up to this point seems to be a person of some intelligence but desultory interests, with a propensity for making preposterous inferences far beyond what the evidence indicates. Watson and the inspectors do at times see a certain genius in Holmes, but for the most part they remain skeptical, as no doubt the reader does as well. A minor Gestalt shift occurs in Chap. 6: "Tobias Gregson Shows What He Can Do." This title leads the reader to expect that the chapter will report the accomplishments of Gregson. The chapter records Gregson's seemingly impressive results, but at its very end, Lestrade arrives with results that totally contradict Gregson's claim that he has apprehended the murderer. In particular, Lestrade reports that Stangerson had been murdered this morning, precisely at a time when Gregson's culprit was in jail. The chapter title remains true: We have seen what Gregson can do, but it turns out to be to botch the investigation!

Skepticism about Holmes, however, persists until late in the story. It resolves only after both Gregson and Lestrade admit that they have failed to solve the mystery. This leads to Watson, Lestrade, and Gregson challenging Holmes to put up or shut up. Give us the murderer's name so that we can catch him! Holmes gives them the murderer's name, Jefferson Hope, but provides no evidence, and of course this leaves open the issue of how to apprehend this supposed murderer and establish his guilt. Then unexpectedly a cabman arrives and Holmes directs his efforts to talking to this new person who has arrived to pick up some luggage (Fig. 2.1).

Fig. 2.1 Holmes cuffing Jefferson Hope.

Seconds later, Holmes skillfully puts the cabman in handcuffs and announces that the cabman is the double murderer, which the cabman confirms by a violent struggle! As a result of what happens in these few moments, the Gestalt shift point, a global transformation has occurred, not only for the cabman but also in the view held by the official detectives and by Watson of the airhead consulting detective. The reader has beheld the first major appearance of the brilliant Sherlock Holmes, now known throughout the world. Conan Doyle, moreover, far better than earlier writers of detective fiction, ties up nearly all the loose ends in the story.

One of these is that Hope had not strictly speaking murdered the first victim. He had offered him a choice between two identical pills, one of which contained poison, promising that after the fellow had made his choice, Hope would consume the other pill. The one loose end that remains is the question of the background of the skillful if determined culprit, Jefferson Hope. This information is the focus of the second story.

In the second story, titled "The Country of the Saints," Doyle transports the reader across the ocean and presents the piety and practices of the then polygamous Mormons. By the end of the story, we have another view of Jefferson Hope, though this transformation is more gradual. We meet John Ferrier and his adopted daughter, Lucy, whom Ferrier had rescued. We also meet Jefferson Hope, who falls in love with Lucy, only to have two ruthless Mormons claim her hand. These are Enoch Drebber and Joseph Stangerson, who subsequently murdered John Ferrier, sought to murder Hope, and ruined the life of Lucy Ferrier by forcing her to marry Drebber. And we learn that Drebber and Stangerson are the two men who had died in London after being confronted by Jefferson Hope, who goes from being seen as a ruthless if efficient murderer to being a possibly justified and highly effective executioner. We have also seen a transformative shift in our image of the murdered Americans, Drebber and Stangerson, from being members of a religious movement to being carnal and ruthless brigands intent on murdering Hope as they had earlier ruined the life of Lucy Ferrier, who was Hope's great love.

The gradual success of Doyle's *A Study in Scarlet* played a major role in transforming an unsuccessful ophthalmologist into a strikingly successful author and also transformed the format of the traditional detective story. Part of the cause of this transformation was probably Doyle's skill in instilling a level of drama into these stories by such scenes as that set in Holmes's rooms where occurred the remarkable shift that Watson, Lestrade, Gregson, and readers experienced in their image of Sherlock Holmes.

PART TWO: *THE SIGN OF THE FOUR* (NOVEL, 1890)

A major Gestalt shift (in fact, two such) occurs in *The Sign of the Four*, but they are less evident than the shifts in the other novels. The two shifts culminate on the same point, but one of them seems less evident than those encountered so far. This second shift becomes more evident if one recognizes the curious fact that sometimes a detective story may have a plot curiously similar to a romance. These two types of stories in many instances share the feature that a person comes to see someone else in a radically new way. In romance, a chance encounter of a character may become the love of one's life, with that recognition (whether happening slowly or suddenly) representing a very great change. Similarly, in many detective stories the detective finds that someone who at first appears irrelevant to the crime is in fact the culprit. This parallel is illustrated in *Sign*, if the reader sees the story as an account of a romance and also as an account of the detection of a criminal. In the opening scene, Holmes and Watson encounter Mary Morstan, whom they see very differently: Holmes views her as an effective client; Watson begins by seeing her as an attractive woman, and eventually proposes marriage. Thus it appears that Doyle has written *The Sign of the Four* on two levels, which, as we shall see, culminate at the same instant. Readers inclined to seek detective stories in detective story books may overlook this aspect of *The Sign of the Four* even though Doyle provides many clues. These commence with Watson's rather extraordinary comment about the client whom he had just met: "In an experience of women which extends over many nations and three separate continents, I have never looked upon a face which gave a clearer promise of a refined and sensitive nature."[1] After her departure, Watson immediately remarks: "What a very attractive woman!" Holmes response: "Is she? ... I did not observe." So smitten was the good doctor that he accuses Holmes of being "an automaton—a calculating machine."[2]

Three pages later, Watson records that as the plot thickened:

Miss Morstan's demeanour was as resolute and collected as ever. I endeavored to cheer and amuse her by reminiscences of my adventures in Afghanistan; but, to tell the truth, I was myself so excited at our situation and so curious as to our destination that my stories were slightly involved. To this day she declares that I told her one moving anecdote as to how a musket looked into my tent at the dead of night, and how I fired a double-barrelled tiger cub at it.[3]

[1] Doyle, *Holmes*, I, 97.
[2] Doyle, *Holmes*, I, 100.
[3] Doyle, *Holmes*, I, 103.

Soon after this, they learn the magnitude of what appears to be at stake in this case: a treasure worth "not less than a half million sterling."[4] Alas for Watson, who realizes that if Holmes could secure Morstan's rights to the treasure it would change her "from a needy governess to the richest heiress in England. Surely it was the place of a loyal friend to rejoice at such news; yet I am ashamed to say that selfishness took me by the soul, and that my heart turned as heavy as lead within me. I stammered out some few halting words of congratulation, and then sat downcast."[5] The ever observant Holmes, one suspects, missed much of what was going on between the two, though Watson recorded that Holmes had observed that Watson had provided problematic medical advice regarding insomnia to Thaddeus Sholto: "Holmes declares that he overheard me caution him against the great danger of taking more than two drops of castor oil, while I recommended strychnine in large doses as a sedative."[6] Soon Watson, Holmes, and Thaddeus arrive at Bartholomew Sholto's home, where they sense problems. Watson recounts his response:

> Miss Morstan and I stood together, and her hand was in mine. A wondrous subtle thing is love, for here were we two who had never seen each other before that day, between whom no word or even look of affection had ever passed, and yet now in an hour of trouble our hands instinctively sought for each other. I have marvelled at it since, but at the time it seemed the most natural thing that I should go out to her so, and, as she has often told me, there was in her also the instinct to turn to me for comfort and protection. So we stood hand in hand, like two children, and there was peace in our hearts for all the dark things that surrounded us.[7]

Let us turn now to the detective part of the story. The focus is on finding the treasure, which Doyle traces from the time that one British soldier (Jonathan Small) along with three Indian soldiers (the Four of the title) stole the treasure, committing murders in the process. We learn of Small, his wooden leg, his Andaman Island co-conspirator Tonga, and of Small's pact with two British officers, Major Sholto and Captain Morstan, who in effect steal the treasure from Small and bring it to England. We are told that Small then killed Morstan and scared Sholto to death, but failed to secure the treasure, which fell into the hands of Sholto's two sons, one of

[4] Doyle, *Holmes*, I, 111.
[5] Doyle, *Holmes*, I, 111.
[6] Doyle, *Holmes*, I, 113.
[7] Doyle, *Holmes*, I, 113.

whom Tonga had dispatched with a poison dart, which made it possible for Small to acquire the treasure from Bartholomew Sholto's attic. To recover the box of precious jewels Holmes must locate the resourceful Small, which he does with an assist from the trained nose of the dog Toby. Finally, Holmes, Watson, Inspector Athelney Jones, and other police pursue Small down the Thames, their police boat finally overtaking the launch rented by Small. They thereby recover the locked box of precious jewels, which had occasioned a number of murders and a chase half way around the world. But this is not the culmination, the shift point in the story. This occurs when Watson and a policeman take the treasure to Miss Morstan, while Holmes and Jones take Small to 221B Baker Street to hear Small's story. Watson recounts greeting Mary Morstan by explaining he had brought her "a fortune." He adds that it will bring her "an annuity of ten thousand pounds. There will be few richer young ladies in England. Is it not glorious?"[8] Watson, after recounting the chase down the Thames, the shooting of Tonga, and the capture of Small, proceeds to force open the locked treasure box, which reveals a remarkable surprise: it is empty. They later learn that Small, who had come to hate the treasure, had emptied the box into the Thames just before he was apprehended. Watson recounts how he and Mary Morstan reacted to the empty treasure box:

"The treasure is lost," said Miss Morstan, calmly.

As I listened to the words and realized what they meant, a great shadow seemed to pass from my soul. I did not know how this Agra treasure had weighed me down, until now that it was finally removed. It was selfish, no doubt, disloyal, wrong, but I could realize nothing save that the golden barrier was gone from between us. "Thank God!" I ejaculated from my very heart.

She looked at me with a quick, questioning smile. "Why do you say that?" she asked.

"Because you are within my reach again," I said, taking her hand. She did not withdraw it. "Because I love you, Mary, as truly as ever a man loved a woman. Because this treasure, these riches, sealed my lips. Now that they are gone I can tell you how I love you. That is why I said, 'Thank God.'"

"Then I say, 'Thank God,' too," she whispered, as I drew her to my side. Whoever had lost a treasure, I knew that night that I had gained one.[9]

[8] Doyle, *Holmes*, I, 154.
[9] Doyle, *Holmes*, I, 154–155.

In short, the recovery and opening of the treasure box is the shift point for each of the intertwined story lines, one being Holmes's search to secure the treasure and the other being Watson's desire to link up with quite another treasure. Whereas Conan Doyle presented *A Study in Scarlet* and *The Valley of Fear* as each consisting of two separate but linked stories, he devised *The Sign of the Four* as two stories woven together and converging on the same point but from different directions.

PART THREE: *THE HOUND OF THE BASKERVILLES* (NOVEL, 1901–1902)

This famous novel contains at least two very different Gestalt shifts. The first shift is an excellent illustration of the thesis of this book. We need not examine it in detail because it was featured in the first chapter. The long quotation there recounts how Holmes, still seeking to find who murdered the former head of Baskerville Hall, begins staring at the portrait of the nefarious Sir Hugo Baskerville and soon sees in his visage the features exhibited by Stapleton, the supposedly pleasant, bookish, butterfly fancier who becomes a friend of Sir Charles Baskerville, Holmes's client. It is important to note what actually happens in the extended passage quoted in the first chapter. On the one hand, it records in considerable detail an excellent account of a perceptual Gestalt shift. First Holmes and then Watson see in the portrait of the visage of the wicked seventeenth-century Baskerville the face of Stapleton, who up to this point has seemed almost insignificant in the story: he is just a good-natured neighbor. Then Holmes, and eventually Watson, recognize a pattern much more significant: they come to see that nearly all of the difficulties they have been having can be resolved by "seeing" Stapleton as a part of the Baskerville family, indeed as a person who is seeking to secure the estate for himself. This is not just a visual Gestalt shift; it is a brilliantly formulated image of what is central to Holmes's case. It is the Gestalt shift point in the story, as the text clearly indicates:

> "Yes, it is an interesting instance of a throwback, which appears to be both physical and spiritual. A study of family portraits is enough to convert a man to the doctrine of reincarnation. The fellow is a Baskerville—that is evident."
>
> "With designs upon the succession."
>
> "Exactly. This chance of the picture has supplied us with one of our most obvious missing links. We have him, Watson, we have him, and I dare swear that before tomorrow night he will be fluttering in our net as helpless as one of his own butterflies. A pin, a cork, and a card, and we add him to the Baker Street collection!"
>
> He burst into one of his rare fits of laughter as he turned away from the picture. I have not heard him laugh often, and it has always boded ill to somebody.[10]

[10] Arthur Conan Doyle, *The Complete Sherlock Holmes* (New York: Doubleday, 1953), II, 879.

This experience provides Holmes with far more than a "missing link," as Holmes realizes and expresses with his "we have him" and by his comment "I dare swear that before tomorrow night he will be fluttering in our net."[11] The remaining parts of the story confirm Holmes's prediction.

This experience transforms the case, making it natural to assume that Stapleton, rather than being a pleasant neighbor, was probably in line to inherit the Baskerville estate and thus had a compelling interest in bringing about the death of Sir Charles. This transformed view of Stapleton leads Holmes to secure the evidence needed to convict Stapleton of the earlier murder and to prevent the murder of Holmes's client. It is the turning point in the story.

There is yet another Gestalt shift that is much harder to see; in fact, it may first have been seen shortly before 2008 by a prominent professor of literature at University of Paris VIII, Pierre Bayard, who some years earlier had published a book titled *Who Killed Roger Ackroyd?* In this volume, Bayard dissects Agatha Christie's novel *The Death of Roger Ackroyd* to show that the evidence indicates that the person found guilty in the novel is not in fact the murderer! Then in 2008 Bayard came forth with *Sherlock Holmes Was Wrong: Reopening the Case of The Hound of the Baskervilles*, in which he argues that the person actually intending murder is none other than Beryl Stapleton whom Jack Stapleton claims is his sister, but who is actually his wife. Moreover, Bayard provides substantial evidence that the intended murder victim was Jack Stapleton. In particular, Beryl's method is to convince people that Henry Baskerville had been murdered, that the murderer was Jack Stapleton, and that recognition of him as the murderer of Charles would lead to the execution of Jack Stapleton, which would allow her to marry Charles Baskerville. Critics of Bayard's book recognize that he has made an interesting if not fully convincing case, backing up his claims by abundant evidence drawn from Doyle's text.

I offer two suggestions about this situation. First, at one point in Doyle's *Hound* narrative, Holmes remarks to Watson: "I shall soon be in the position of being able to put into a single connected narrative one of the most singular and sensational crimes of modern times."[12] Such an accomplishment is certainly an important step in efforts to get at the truth. On the other hand, success at constructing such a narrative entails also establishing that no other narrative can fit the evidence available. This is a

[11] Doyle, *Holmes*, II, 880.
[12] Doyle, *Holmes*, II, 884.

more demanding challenge, but it is a necessary criterion for establishing the truth. If Bayard's narrative also fits with the empirical information, then Holmes himself has more work to do. To put it differently, if Bayard's reconstruction fits the facts, then we have a situation similar to a two-element Gestalt shift. If this is true, then the claims that Holmes makes for the correctness of his deductions and solutions are problematic.[13] My second point is to suggest that there may be cases where Gestalt shifts are in other Holmes stories, and we fail to see them. This should not happen often, however, because we have Sherlock Holmes helping us!

[13] As mentioned in the Preface, I developed this book while teaching over the last seven years a course for senior citizens at Forever Learning Institute in South Bend, Indiana. This was a challenge because a substantial number of the enrollees had advanced training; for example, they held a doctoral degree in medicine, law, or an academic subject. I co-taught the course with Denis Burke, a distinguished lawyer, who contributed in numerous ways to the course and to this book. In the 2018 version of the course we treated *The Hound of the Baskervilles*, which led me to mention Bayard's book. The heart of the presentation that day consisted of Denis Burke, J.D., in a judicial robe and barrister's wig, making the case that Bayard had proposed *against* Stapleton as the murderer. To do this, he interrogated three enrollees in the class, one wearing a deerstalker, another brandishing a butterfly net, and the third wearing a women's hat. This twenty-five-minute presentation was the highlight of the course. Totally on her own initiative, one person pulled out her iPhone and made a video recording of the performance, which we now cherish. Denis has agreed to allow me to include his email address (dpb999@hotmail.com), should any Sherlockian wish to request his script for a Sherlockian event.

Part Four: *The Valley of Fear* (Novel, 1914–1915)

Of the four Sherlock Holmes novels that Doyle published, the last to appear was *The Valley of Fear*. It was first published as a serial in the *Strand*, but later as a book. Its merits are disputed. For example, Steven Doyle and David Crowder remarked: "Of the four novels, *The Valley of Fear* has always been ranked last in popularity polls. It even ranks pretty low overall. Objectively speaking, it's an underrated masterpiece, a perfect amalgam of classic Holmes with hard-boiled detective story, with both halves succeeding."[14] Another expert, Chris Redmond, adopts a very different position: "This novel may just be Doyle's masterpiece; it may even be two *Masterpieces*...."[15] The well-known writer of detective fiction and also the author of a biography of Doyle, John Dickson Carr, noting that some critics are prone to dismiss *The Valley of Fear* as below par, adopted a very different view, stating that "the first part, a separate unit called *The Tragedy of Birlstone*, is a very nearly perfect piece of detective-story writing."[16] Perhaps the most meaningful evaluation of it came from no less a figure than T. S. Eliot (1888–1965), one of the most distinguished literary figures of the twentieth century. Eliot was at the Wednesday Club in 1956 when friends asked him what his favorite passage in English prose was. Eliot not only answered them but also recited from memory the following passage, which no one at the party could identify.

> "Well," cried Boss McGinty at last, "is he here? Is Birdy Edwards here?"
>
> "Yes," McMurdo answered slowly. "Birdy Edwards is here. I am Birdy Edwards."[17]

As Sherlockians will recognize, this passage is from *The Valley of Fear*. We shall return to the question of the quality of the story and also to this passage.

As is well known, *The Valley of Fear* is in two parts. My thesis is that each part fits the structure of a bipolar Gestalt shift and that these two

---

[14] Steven Doyle and David A. Crowder, *Sherlock Holmes for Dummies* (Hoboken, NJ: Wiley, 2010), 349.

[15] Christopher Redmond, *Sherlock Holmes Handbook*, 2nd ed. (Toronto: Dundurn, 2009), 29–31.

[16] John Dickson Carr, *The Life of Sir Arthur Conan Doyle: The Man Who Was Sherlock Holmes* (New York: Vintage, 1975), 349.

[17] For details, see http://www.jot101.com/2013/06/the-table-talk-of-ts-eliot.html. Viewed October 3, 2014.

bipolar Gestalts produce a higher-level bipolar Gestalt. All that I mean by this is that after finishing the novel, readers recognize that they have read two stories that are vastly different, but ultimately strikingly parallel in structure and definitely historically linked.

The first half of the novel, "The Tragedy of Birlstone," recounts the story of the death of Jack Douglas, a wealthy American with an estate in England, who has been brutally murdered; in fact, a double-barreled shotgun blew away his face. When Holmes and Watson arrive, they meet Douglas's grieving wife and his good friend Cecil Barker as well as the astute Inspector MacDonald. Holmes, Watson, and MacDonald investigate a wide array of clues, including some anomalies, the significance of which they judge rather differently. The reader encounters the information that MacDonald has turned up, including his success in arresting a suspect elsewhere in England. The reader receives strong hints that Mrs. Douglas and Barker may somehow be involved in the death. Holmes, however, hesitates to adopt any of these scenarios, but provides little explanation of his reticence. Then in a scene near the end of the story, he urges MacDonald to abandon his efforts and when MacDonald protests, Holmes makes a remarkable statement, which within five minutes totally turns the case on its head. It is the shift moment when an almost totally new Gestalt appears (Fig. 2.2) and convinces the assembled group that Holmes is a genius. Holmes tells Mrs. Douglas:

> [A]t that time I had every reason to believe that you were directly concerned in the crime. Now I am assured that this is not so. At the same time, there is much that is unexplained, and I should strongly recommend that you ask Mr. Douglas to tell us his own story."
>
> Mrs. Douglas gave a cry of astonishment at Holmes's words. The detectives and I must have echoed it, when we were aware of a man who seemed to have emerged from the wall, who advanced now from the gloom of the corner in which he had appeared. Mrs. Douglas turned, and in an instant her arms were round him. Barker had seized his outstretched hand.
>
> "It's best this way, Jack," his wife repeated; "I am sure that it is best."
>
> "Indeed, yes, Mr. Douglas," said Sherlock Holmes, "I am sure that you will find it best."
>
> The man stood blinking at us with the dazed look of one who comes from the dark into the light. It was a remarkable face, bold gray eyes, a strong, short-clipped, grizzled moustache, a square, projecting chin, and a humorous mouth. He took a good look at us all, and then to my amazement he advanced to me and handed me a bundle of paper.[18]

[18] Doyle, *Holmes*, II, 953–954.

Fig. 2.2 Wiles's drawing of Douglas emerging.

We'll return to the bundle of papers later, but I should first explain that what Holmes had concluded was that an intruder had indeed come, that he and Douglas struggled over the shotgun, that the gun had fired into the face of the intruder, who was approximately the same build and height as Douglas, and that Douglas was quick-witted enough to realize that if he switched clothes with the intruder, left a few misleading clues, and secured the cooperation of both his wife and Barker, there was a good chance that this would convince everyone, including the bad guys who wished to murder him, that the murderous attack on Douglas had succeeded. Holmes also realized that there was a good hiding place at hand into which Douglas could disappear for a period. It was from this hiding place that Douglas had emerged, or as it seemed, come back from the dead.

Douglas's appearance meets all four criteria of a Gestalt switch. The images of Douglas as dead and alive are certainly distinct. Moreover, the shift is rapid, unexpected (dead men do not often show up in a room), and global. In fact, the reader begins to recall incident after incident, statement after statement from the earlier parts of the story that change their meaning. A few examples among many: Earlier in the story Holmes finds out that before the shooting, a suspicious fellow had spent the night in a local inn. He gets even a description of the fellow. He comments: "'Well, bar the expression, that might almost be a description of Douglas himself,' said Holmes. 'He is just over fifty, with grizzled hair and moustache, and about the same height.'"[19] Note also that the reader's images, not only of Douglas but also of his wife and of Barker, now greatly change. The assumed murder has become a case of self-defense. Lastly, and most globally, even the title of this portion of the book—"The Tragedy of Birlstone"—has become just the opposite of appropriate; it could have been called "The Victory of Jack Douglas" or perhaps "The Rescue at Birlstone."

Let us now turn to the second part of *The Valley of Fear*, labeled "The Scowrers," which is a Scottish term for scarers, people who frighten us. We immediately encounter a mystery about this mystery; we do not know who wrote it or why it is included. It is set not in Britain, but in the Pennsylvania coal region. It focuses on a thoroughly wicked brash young Irishman, Jack McMurdo, who has just arrived in town, having fled Chicago, where he had been accused of murder. He seeks to join the Scowrers, headed by Boss McGinty, a ruthless leader who rules the area by having members beat up or kill people who oppose him. McMurdo joins the lodge, goes through its painful initiation, takes part in a number of raids, and simultaneously becomes romantically involved with a local young lady, who loves him despite his reputation for brutality and crime. Toward the end of the story, McMurdo gets word that in an effort to convict the lodge of its many wrongdoings, the railroads have hired a prominent Pinkerton detective named Birdy Edwards to come to the town and master the mob. When McMurdo reports this to McGinty, the Scowrers decide to ambush Edwards, McMurdo (who claims that he can recognize Edwards) being appointed the chief organizer. The leading Scowrers gather at a house, McMurdo leaves the room to open the door of the house for Edwards, and then returns to the inner room, where the following exchange takes place.

[19] Doyle, *Holmes*, II, 945.

"Well!" cried Boss McGinty at last. "Is he here? Is Birdy Edwards here?"
"Yes," McMurdo answered slowly. "Birdy Edwards is here. I am Birdy
Edwards!"[20]

Moreover, at this instant the police arrive, rifles raised, and by arresting the
leaders of the Scowrers end their lawless ways. Scowrers, up to now ruthless rulers of the region, become jailed criminals fearing for their lives.
With the five short sentences just quoted McMurdo is totally transformed:
formerly seen as an enemy of the law, he has become the embodiment of
it. Nearly every statement he has made takes on a new meaning. Moreover,
the reader realizes that Birdy Edwards aka Jack McMurdo is also the
author of this entire text and in fact is Jack Douglas, who had handed
Watson a packet of papers that he had composed while in hiding. And with
this revelation, the two very different parts of *The Valley of Fear* all of a
sudden become two parts of one story; a new whole has appeared and fits
together very effectively.

Doyle has exhibited extraordinary skill in giving McMurdo lines that
on first reading show him to be a criminal and that on second reading
reveal McMurdo to be a shrewd detective and actor, who manages to
appear the worst of the worst when in fact he has consistently worked
toward the good of the people. Holmesian expert Ian McQueen recognizes the skill on Doyle's part exhibited in his presentation of Edwards:
Doyle has employed "all his artistic skill to create an unforgettable scene
with superb effect." Doyle has created "a word-picture so brilliantly con-
ceived that it must remain for all time one of the great English literary
experiences."[21] And readers recognize that the sharp exchanges McMurdo
has with the policeman Captain Marvin are really choreographed exchanges
that they had designed to fool the Scowrers into believing that these men
are bitter enemies, when in fact we now see them as detectives outsmart-
ing the criminals. Moreover, we see that this section rather than being
titled "The Scowrers" could now be renamed "The Saviors."

In Doyle's *The Valley of Fear*, there are two huge Gestalt shifts, and in
fact a third when the two parts merge into one, when the reader recognizes
that Jack Douglas is Birdy Edwards. Whatever its level of overall quality
(which I suggest is very high), it seems indisputable that the story was
crafted with extraordinary attention to detail, dialogue, and dramatic effect.

[20] Doyle, *Holmes*, II, 1014.
[21] Ian McQueen, *Sherlock Holmes Detected* (New York: Drake, 1974), 180.

BIBLIOGRAPHY

PRINTED SOURCES

Carr, John Dickson. *The Life of Sir Arthur Conan Doyle: The Man Who Was Sherlock Holmes* (New York: Vintage, 1975).

Doyle, Arthur Conan. *The Complete Sherlock Holmes,* 2 vols. (New York: Doubleday, 1953).

Doyle, Steven. and David A. Crowder. *Sherlock Holmes for Dummies* (Hoboken, NJ: Wiley, 2010).

McQueen, Ian. *Sherlock Holmes Detected* (New York: Drake, 1974).

Redmond, Christopher. *Sherlock Holmes Handbook*, 2nd ed. (Toronto: Dundurn, 2009).

INTERNET SOURCE

http://www.jot101.com/2013/06/the-table-talk-of-ts-eliot.html. Viewed 3 October 2014.

CHAPTER 3

The Adventures of Sherlock Holmes (1892)

"A Scandal in Bohemia" (1891)

At the beginning of "A Scandal in Bohemia," we encounter Sherlock Holmes, the King of Bohemia, and Irene Adler. Watson describes the first as "the most perfect reasoning and observing machine the world has seen"[1] and a misogynist who avoids the softer emotions, the second as a "man of strong character,"[2] and Adler as an "adventuress"[3] and "of dubious and questionable memory."[4] By a few pages later, Holmes has seen through the King's disguise and also fully recognized the seriousness of the situation. He reveals this recognition by ironically remarking, after the King states that his marriage will take place in three days: "That is very fortunate, as I have one or two matters of importance to look into at the present."[5] Shortly thereafter, Holmes sees Irene, whom he describes with his typical analytical acuteness as "a woman with a face that a man might die for."[6] And very little later, Holmes is trying to talk Watson (these two committed opponents of crime) into aiding him in committing a crime, which may lead to their arrest, a plan to which Watson makes

---

[1] Doyle, *Holmes*, I, 177.
[2] Doyle, *Holmes*, I, 181.
[3] Doyle, *Holmes*, I, 182.
[4] Doyle, *Holmes*, I, 177.
[5] Doyle, *Holmes*, I, 183.
[6] Doyle, *Holmes*, I, 186.

© The Author(s) 2018
M. J. Crowe, *The Gestalt Shift in Conan Doyle's Sherlock Holmes Stories*, https://doi.org/10.1007/978-3-319-98291-5_3

no objection.[7] Seven pages further on, Holmes, filled with confidence that he will be able to secure the photograph that the King is seeking, meets with the King who remarks concerning Irene: "I wish she had been of my own station! What a Queen she would have made!" As matters unfold very differently from what Holmes had expected, the King remarks: "Would she not have made an admirable queen? Is it not a pity that she was not on my level?"[8] Holmes ironic response is: "From what I have seen of the lady she seems indeed to be on a very different level from your Majesty."[9] And the story ends with Watson commenting that "the best plans of Mr Sherlock Holmes were beaten by a woman's wit. He used to make merry over the cleverness of women, but I have not heard him do it of late. And when he speaks of Irene Adler ... it is always under the honourable title of *the* woman."[10] In short, Doyle has transformed Irene from being "a woman of dubious and question-able memory" into being, for Sherlock Holmes, "*the* woman" and a beauty of queenly dignity who outwitted Holmes both in plotting and in imperson-ation. Moreover, Doyle has unmasked the King as an oaf. We now see Holmes as a man who has learned his limitations and whose view has changed not only of Irene, but of women in general. Doyle has once again illustrated Holmes's message to Watson "You see, but you do not observe"[11] by showing us how differently situations and people may appear when they are properly observed. In short, we have experienced a whole set of Gestalt shifts.

Addendum: Before leaving this story, it will prove useful to mention a dramatic development that occurred only a matter of days before the dead-line for delivering my manuscript to Palgrave Macmillan. For five or more years, I have searched unsuccessfully to see whether any other scholar on this planet has explored the connections between the Gestalt approach and Doyle's Sherlockian stories. I located a very impressive book titled *Vision, Science, and Literature, 1870–1920: Ocular Horizons* (University of Pittsburgh Press, 2016), written by Professor Martin Willis of the University of Cardiff in England. A key topic in his seventh chapter is the strong link-age between Conan Doyle and Sherlock Holmes, especially on matters of vision. Of course, I wondered whether this gifted author had scooped my message, but checking his book's index for the word Gestalt relieved my concern: the word "Gestalt" does not appear. Nonetheless, the book was rich in discussions, many relevant to what I have been writing. Careful

[7] Doyle, *Holmes*, I, 187.

[8] Doyle, *Holmes*, I, 194.

[9] Doyle, *Holmes*, I, 194.

[10] Doyle, *Holmes*, I, 194.

[11] Doyle, *Holmes*, I, 179.

reading of the appropriate chapters showed me that while pursuing a parallel course, Professor Willis had developed information relevant to the approach I have been attempting in this book. One of his central points is that Conan Doyle was strongly interested in optical (including ophthalmological) issues. Most authors whom I have used as sources portray Doyle's chief interest from January 1891 to March 1892, when he was living mainly in Vienna receiving training in ophthalmology, as actually being a time when Doyle above all sought to develop his career as an author. Professor Willis provides solid evidence that Doyle was seriously interested in ophthalmology; for example, that for three years earlier he had been spending three hours per day treating patients with eye problems. Willis also provides details on the depth of Doyle's contacts with a leading Parisian ophthalmologist, Edmund Lundolt, with whom Doyle had spent two weeks in Paris.[12] Willis does this in order to set that stage for his claim that Doyle in his Holmes writings drew heavily on optical, visual effects. Willis's first and fullest example is "A Scandal in Bohemia," which he notes "attests to the influence of vision on narrative content." He notes that Vienna is located in Bohemia and that the story "is suffused with visual and optical referents: disguises and misdirections, lenses, lighting and silhouette, modes of observation and perception, and visual evidence; Holmes is described in the first paragraph as an 'observing machine.'"[13] He stresses that "the central object of the story is a photograph" and that the key scene in the story "is an elaborate illusion designed to force Irene Adler ... to reveal the hiding place of the photographic evidence that Holmes has been charged to uncover."[14] This fits with Willis's theme that Holmes repeatedly appears as a sort of magician who makes objects appear or disappear. As he states: "Holmes controls the events like a stage magician, employing the techniques of misdirection and sleight of hand as a grand *coup de theatre.*"[15] Willis further develops this perspective by briefly analyzing a dozen or more other Holmes stories. Moreover, he stresses in much detail the interest that Conan Doyle took in the career and methods of the magician Harry Houdini, whom Doyle first met in 1920.

---

[12] Martin Willis, *Vision, Science, and Literature, 1870–1920: Ocular Horizons* (University of Pittsburgh Press, 2016), 167–169.
[13] Willis, *Vision*, 169.
[14] Willis, *Vision*, 170.
[15] Willis, *Vision*, 170.

All this seems significantly related to my book, which I had initially titled *Now You Don't See It; Now You Do: The Gestalt Shift in Conan Doyle's Sherlock Holmes Writings*, which I discarded because of its length. The phenomena associated with Gestalt shifts are in many ways magical and in most cases involve vision. In researching our different approaches, we read with special interest many of the same passages but saw them somewhat differently but by no means, I believe, in a contradictory fashion. All this was a wonderful discovery, which led me to email Professor Willis, who is a distinguished academic; in fact, he is not only a prolific author but also former Chair of the British Society for Literature and Science and Editor of the *Journal of Literature and Science*. His response, which appears below and with his permission, led me to conclude that he is also a very gracious gentleman.

I read with interest your own account of my account and how both mine and yours might be said to be complementary. I agree with you that they are. My own consideration of Holmes's practice as a magician was to elucidate, historically, his close association with magical traditions and with the ways in which magicians contemporary with Conan Doyle were conscious appropriators of optical knowledge emerging in the sciences. However, it is certainly possible, and indeed adds to the richness of the Sherlock Holmes canon, to consider Holmes's visual manipulations as textual forms of what psychology would see as Gestalt experimentation with shifting visual images and our interpretation of them. There is no doubt that thinking of Holmes as issuing forth perceptual challenges that in turn interrogate the psychology of his interlocutors is a very useful way to think about the active role of the short stories. I would also add, and I imagine this is equally of interest to you, that the Kuhnian paradigm change, as reconsidered by Kuhn, owes a lot to a kind of inclusive Gestalt shift, and that this can usefully inform a more conceptual approach to the Sherlock Holmes stories and their involvement with catastrophic change.

I hope this helps, and I wish you the best of luck with your book.

Martin Willis

"The Red-Headed League" (1891)

This story begins with a pawnbroker, Jabez Wilson, who seeks help from Holmes regarding why Wilson lost his part-time job. In discussing the employment problem he has faced, Wilson describes his pawn shop and his assistant, whom Wilson characterizes as good-natured, diligent, lower-class young man with a peculiar but harmless hobby (photography). One wonders why Holmes would bother about such unimportant people and the trivial matter of the loss of a part-time job, which Wilson had secured solely by having bright red hair. Holmes alerts Watson that this seemingly almost trivial problem may actually be so serious that it is "quite a three pipe problem."[16] This marks the beginning of Gestalt shifts: After visiting Wilson's shop and meeting his assistant, Holmes remarks to Watson that Wilson's innocuous assistant is rather a "smart fellow." Holmes adds: "He is, in my judgment, the fourth smartest man in London, and for daring I am not sure that he has not a claim to be third. I have known something of him before."[17] Later Holmes reveals the real problem they face, when he has Watson join him on an evening's excursion with Inspector Peter Jones and Mr. Merryweather, a bank manager, who bemoans the fact that he is missing for the first time his Saturday night rubber of bridge. Holmes consoles Merryweather by remarking:

> I think you will find that you will play for a higher stake to-night than you have ever done yet, and that the play will be more exciting. For you, Mr. Merryweather, the stake will be some £30,000; and for you, Jones, it will be the man upon whom you wish to lay your hands.
>
> John Clay, the murderer, thief, smasher, and forger. He's a young man, Mr. Merryweather, but he is at the head of his profession, and I would rather have my bracelets on him than on any criminal in London. He's a remarkable man, is young John Clay. His grandfather was a royal duke, and he himself has been to Eton and Oxford. His brain is as cunning as his fingers, and though we meet signs of him at every turn, we never know where to find the man himself.[18]

Holmes also reveals that he had determined that Clay is head of a gang that on this evening plans to break into the basement of the Saxe Coberg

[16] Doyle, *Holmes*, I, 205.
[17] Doyle, *Holmes*, I, 205.
[18] Doyle, *Holmes*, I, 207.

Bank to rob it of 30,000 French florins stored in its basement vault, accomplishing this by means of a tunnel that Clay has been digging from Wilson's pawn shop to the nearby bank. He had done this digging while supposedly in the basement working on photography.

They succeed in foiling the criminals, capturing Clay (Fig. 3.1), and saving the bank holdings, which greatly pleased Merryweather: "I do not know how the bank can thank you or repay you. There is no doubt that you have detected and defeated in the most complete manner one of the most determined attempts at bank robbery that have ever come within my experience."[19]

Fig. 3.1 "It's no use, John Clay."

[19] Doyle, *Holmes*, I, 211.

Holmes view of the matter was rather different: "It saved me from ennui." Watson disagreed, stressing to Holmes that he "is a benefactor of the race."[20] Overall, as this indicates, we have seen that Holmes has transformed what at first appears to be an inconsequential difficulty faced by a rather insignificant shopkeeper into a crime and capture of national notoriety.

[20] Doyle, *Holmes*, I, 212.

"A Case of Identity" (1891)

Some cases in the Holmes canon fit better than others with the idea that they are interpretable in terms of a Gestalt shift. "A Case of Identity" fits very well indeed, but there is a problem that will be discussed later.

This story centers on Miss Mary Sutherland, a young, near-sighted woman whose fiancé, Hosmer Angel, had disappeared on the way to the church for their wedding. She comes to Holmes and Watson to hire Holmes to find Hosmer. Mary recounts in some detail how Hosmer had courted her, with the approval of Mary's mother as well as her stepfather. She describes Hosmer as well as mentioning a few mild peculiarities in his behavior; for example, his letters to her were always typewritten. After her departure, Watson and Holmes discuss her and her story. Watson runs over many of the details he had observed; Holmes proceeds to tell Watson that the case is "trite" and to suggest that Watson had missed most of the important clues. Their conversation, which is too long to quote, is very similar to what one might witness when one person (unsuccessfully) tries to help another person see a Gestalt; for example, the Dalmatian Gestalt. Watson does not get it, nor does Holmes tell him what the Gestalt is. The next day Watson arrives at Holmes's rooms, hoping to "assist at the dénouement of the little mystery." He immediately asks whether Holmes had solved the mystery, Holmes responding: "There was never any mystery in the matter."[21] Watson asks, "Who was he?"[22] Just at this point Mary's stepfather, Mr. Windibank, arrives, having agreed to meet with Holmes. Windibank expresses his delight at Holmes's report that he is quite certain he will find Hosmer. But his enthusiasm disappears when Holmes explains how he has come to know that Hosmer is in fact Windibank, who by such disguises as tinted glasses, false mostache and whiskers, and sending letters entirely typewritten had fooled his stepdaughter and thereby created a situation that would keep her inheritance within his household. The case made by Holmes is convincing enough that Windibank responds by stammering: "It—it's not actionable."[23] Their conversation concludes when Holmes reaches for a horsewhip and Windibank runs out the door.

[21] Doyle, *Holmes*, I, 222.
[22] Doyle, *Holmes*, I, 222.
[23] Doyle, *Holmes*, I, 223.

To the reader, by this point, the new Gestalt has become fully clear. The only problem is that some Sherlockian commentators on this story find it insufficiently challenging—they report seeing the shift rather too early. Having first read the story over five decades ago, my recollections of my reaction to it are too dim to dispute their report. Nonetheless, it seems that solving a case upon first hearing it and securing confirmation from the offender without ever leaving one's room reveal a detective with special gifts for detecting and revealing Gestalts.

"The Boscombe Valley Mystery" (1891)

This story centers on four characters: two older men, Charles McCarthy and John Turner, who had spent part of their lives in Australia; two younger persons, McCarthy's son James and Turner's daughter Alice, both eighteen years old. And investigating are Holmes, Watson, and Inspector Lestrade. The elder McCarthy, as Holmes and Watson learn, has just been murdered, his head bashed in by a blunt instrument, possibly a gun butt. Much evidence points to James McCarthy as the murderer; he had earlier argued with his father, was known to be in the area of the killing, and his gun and hat were on the ground. This evidence leads Watson to remark: "I could hardly imagine a more damning case.... If ever circumstantial evidence pointed to a criminal it does so here."[24] Holmes's commentary on circumstantial evidence sounds very much like language used in discussing Gestalts: "Circumstantial evidence is a very tricky thing.... It may seem to point very straight to one thing, but if you shift your own point of view a little, you may find it pointing in an equally uncompromising manner to something entirely different. It must be confessed, however, that the case looks exceedingly grave against the young man."[25] Nonetheless, Holmes decides that in this case he will adopt an approach fitting very well with what he declared regarding circumstantial evidence: "I shall approach this case from the point of view that what this young man says is true, and we shall see whither that hypothesis will lead us."[26]

Holmes carefully examines the evidence, including discussing the case with James McCarthy and also Alice Turner, the latter defending McCarthy. After examining the scene of the crime, Holmes shares with Lestrade the information that the murderer is "a tall man, left-handed, limps with the right leg, wears thick-soled shooting-boots and a grey cloak, smokes Indian cigars, uses a cigar-holder, and carries a blunt pen-knife in his pocket. There are several other indications, but these may be enough to aid us in our search."[27] Lestrade is not impressed, nor does he believe Holmes when shortly afterwards Holmes remarks regarding the mystery: "It is solved."[28]

---

[24] Doyle, *Holmes*, I, 228.
[25] Doyle, *Holmes*, I, 228.
[26] Doyle, *Holmes*, I, 231–232.
[27] Doyle, *Holmes*, I, 238.
[28] Doyle, *Holmes*, I, 239.

Later, at a local inn, Holmes and Watson discuss the case, which leads Watson eventually to conclude: "The culprit is—"[29] Just at this moment a waiter announces an arrival: "Mr. John Turner." And Turner walks into the room. The drama of his entrance (he had come at Holmes's request) is rivaled by the drama of Turner's confessing that he had been a highwayman in Australia, accumulating fortune enough to return to England, where he reformed, married, and cherished his daughter Alice. The elder McCarthy had for years been blackmailing him and recently was insisting that Alice marry his son, who had not as yet shown himself to be a person of responsibility. Turner, who was dying of diabetes, decides that Holmes has sufficient evidence to prove him to be the murderer of his blackmailer. Holmes takes pity on him after hearing his statement but requires that he sign a full confession to be used if, and only if, James McCarthy were to be convicted. Although Turner prepares a full confession, it proves unnecessary, partly because Holmes helps McCarthy be cleared. Alice and James, Watson relates, later married without ever learning of the checkered pasts of their fathers. The Gestalt shift feature was certainly evident in reversing what the circumstantial evidence indicated, and perhaps it is not too much to join with Holmes and Watson in seeing a reformation shift in the elder Turner.

[29] Doyle, *Holmes*, I, 241.

"THE FIVE ORANGE PIPS" (1891)

We saw in "The Red-Headed League" a case in which a client seeks Holmes help on what appears to be a nearly trivial matter. Holmes's gifts show up not least in recognizing that a far more serious issue is at stake: robbery of a major bank. If the events of a story are judged only from Jabez Wilson's perspective, one could conclude that Holmes had failed; Holmes did nothing to restore Wilson's lost income. A similar situation and shift occurs in this story. John Openshaw comes to Holmes asking him whether he should be worried about having received five dried orange seeds in an envelope with its sender identified only by three letters (K.K.K.). Holmes's shows his brilliance by proceeding from the fact of the five orange pips to explain to Openshaw that this is an international matter that involves murder. Thus Holmes has taken a small object (the five orange pips) and correctly read into them an international assassination attempt. Moreover, Holmes proceeds from the pips and the envelopes in which they arrived to identify who earlier had managed to murder Openshaw's uncle and father. Doyle, who delighted in presenting contrasts, managed to instill contrasts even within the nature of this case. He highlighted the contrast in this instance by indicating that Openshaw's uncle, who had earlier received a set of pips, viewed them as some "preposterous practical joke,"[30] whereas when John contacted the police after having received pips, they also viewed them as a joke and attributed the deaths of his uncle and father to accidents.[31] Holmes, upon hearing the story, has a very different reaction: "You must act, man, or you are lost."[32] And he tells Watson that "of all our cases we have had none more fantastic than this."[33] It is an interesting and perhaps relevant point that Ronald Knox in famously setting out the eleven parts of an ideal Holmes story misses this part (Holmes's report on what the real issue is).[34]

---

[30] Doyle, *Holmes*, I, 249.

[31] Doyle, *Holmes*, I, 251.

[32] Doyle, *Holmes*, I, 250.

[33] Doyle, *Holmes*, I, 252.

[34] Knox wrote: "The first part is the Prooimion, a homely Baker Street scene, with invaluable personal touches, and sometimes a demonstration by the detective. Then follows the first explanation, or Exegesis ... that is, the client's statement of the case, followed by the Ichneusis, or personal investigation, often including the famous floor-walk on hands and knees. No. I is invariable, Nos. 2 and 3 almost always present." Quoted from Michael J. Crowe (ed.). *Ronald Knox and Sherlock Holmes: Five Writings by Ronald Knox* (Indianapolis: Gasogene Books, 2010), 43.

After Openshaw leaves, Holmes reveals to Watson the reason for his concern, explaining that K.K.K. stands for the notorious American group known as the Ku Klux Klan. From the seaports from which the three mailings had been sent and from the dates of the letters, Holmes infers that the assassin must be from a specific ship, leading Holmes to arise early the next morning to determine the boat bearing the assassin, only to learn from Watson reading the newspaper report the sad news that Openshaw had died after having fallen (been thrown from) from Waterloo Bridge that night and had drowned. Holmes proceeds to seek revenge, using the dates and portstops on the three envelopes to determine that the murderer must have come from the "Captain James Calhoun, Bark Lone Star, Savannah, Georgia."[35] When Holmes later learns that this ship had been shipwrecked during its return to the United States, Holmes is saved from carrying the case further.

[35] Doyle, When Holmes ... case further. I, 257.

"THE MAN WITH THE TWISTED LIP" (1891)

Sometimes it is difficult to tell when the Gestalt moment (the time of the occurrence of the Gestalt shift) occurs in a Holmes story; in fact, at times it is hard even to identify a Gestalt in a story. Neither is the case in this story. The time of the Gestalt shift can be specified to the second, and it seems similarly easy to specify that this story features a bipolar Gestalt shift.

The central character in the story is Neville St. Clair, a young prosperous businessman with a loving wife and growing family. Holmes's client is Mrs. St. Clair whose husband has disappeared. In particular, Mrs. St. Clair happened to be in one of the less seemly parts of London when she saw him in a second story window, from which he disappeared. She gained entrance to the house, went to the second floor, and found him gone, the only occupant being a deformed miserable beggar named Hugh Boone, who was of no help. Further developments, such as the locating of St. Clair's coat in the Thames, point toward the conclusion that the beggar had murdered St. Clair. The police arrest him and deposit him in a jail cell. The next morning Holmes, helped by spending the night smoking an ounce of shag, awakens Watson telling him that they must go to the jail, Holmes carrying with him some unidentified item of detective paraphernalia in a bag. They gain entrance to the cell, Holmes opens the bag, goes to the beggar Hugh Boone, and with a few swipes of his hand makes him disappear and Neville St. Clair appear (Fig. 3.2).

Fig. 3.2 "He is a professional beggar."

The magic material used by Holmes: soap and a sponge. We learn that St. Clair, who had background in theater and in newspaper writing, some years ago had done a story pretending (with the help of face paint and tape) to be a beggar, whose gift for gab and solicitation was such that he found that he could make more money as a beggar than as a businessman. And from this career he and his family (totally unaware of St. Clair's way of bringing home the bacon) had prospered. The metamorphosis undergone by the duck/rabbit pair was scarcely more rapid. St. Clair of course realizes that he must no longer support his lifestyle in this manner and turns his talents in a proper direction.

There is at least one other very small Gestalt shift that appears in this story, which can be noted but needs little comment (though it has received extensive attention among Sherlockians). This is a shift that occurs when the wife of John Watson called him James.[36]

---

[36] Doyle, *Holmes*, I, 259.

"THE ADVENTURE OF THE BLUE CARBUNCLE" (1892)

In the *Adventures* series of cases, we have at least twice encountered a story in which the client does not know what the real crime is; Holmes has to determine this, and does. A yet more unusual pattern appears in this story, where it turns out that there is no client and for an extended period there appears to be no crime. But there is a puzzle. Watson visits Holmes to wish him a good Christmas and finds him investigating a hat, which Peterson the commissionaire has brought him. The owner of the hat had abandoned it along with a goose after some ruffians had accosted the owner. Holmes describes his investigation of the hat as "a perfectly trivial one." Watson, no doubt recalling the "The Red-Headed League" and the "The Five Orange Pips," suggests that Holmes's hat investigation may lead to some crime, but Holmes dismisses this: "No, no. No crime."[37] Holmes then rolls out one deduction after another (fifteen by my count) about the owner of the hat, leaving Watson and the reader amazed. One deduction especially deserves mention: Holmes reports that the hat's owner must be very intelligent. Watson asks Holmes to explain.

> For answer Holmes clapped the hat upon his head. It came right over the forehead and settled upon the bridge of his nose. "It is a question of cubic capacity," said he; "a man with so large a brain must have something in it."[38]

One wonders why Watson did not doubt Holmes's rule that intelligence correlates with hat size, especially since Holmes's action would imply that Holmes's intelligence was less than impressive.

Immediately after Holmes had deeply impressed Watson by his deductive skills, especially on such a trivial matter, Petersen excitedly returns, informing Holmes that Petersen's wife had discovered a gem in the goose's crop (never mind that geese do not have crops). Holmes reports that this is no garden-variety gem: "This is the Countess of Morcar's blue carbuncle," even the reward for which was £1000.[39] At this point, the significance of Holmes's hat investigation escalates to a remarkable degree; or to put it in psychological terms, a Gestalt shift has occurred.

The significance of Holmes's "trivial" investigation of the hat advances to yet another level when Holmes mentions that the police had evidence

---

[37] Doyle, *Holmes*, I, 277.
[38] Doyle, *Holmes*, I, 279.
[39] Doyle, *Holmes*, I, 280.

based on the testimony of a James Ryder that a plumber, John Horner, was the perpetrator of the robbery of the blue carbuncle. Holmes locates Horner, who is terrified because if convicted he would be sentenced to "seven years' penal servitude."[40] Holmes, however, becomes convinced of Horner's innocence. Having by this point traced the path that led to the blue carbuncle being placed in the crop of a goose sold by a particular vendor, Holmes meets up with James Ryder, who claims that he knows nothing about how the carbuncle ended up in the goose's crop. Holmes then transforms Ryder by stating "Excuse me, I know everything of it"[41] and by explaining exactly how this occurred. In particular, he convinces Ryder that Holmes knew of Ryder's involvement in the robbery (he shows Ryder the Gestalt that Holmes had come to see), and thereby gets Ryder to confess that he had hidden the carbuncle in the crop of a goose, but then lost track of the goose. Ryder's distress at having been found out combined with Holmes's sensitivity to the Christmas season leads him to let Ryder go free, provided that Ryder withdraws his evidence against Horner. In a sense, Holmes, like a magician, has pulled all this out of an empty hat![42]

[40] Doyle, *Holmes*, I, 285.

[41] Doyle, *Holmes*, I, 286.

[42] Sherlockians have pointed out that Doyle himself did a bit of magic in this story. They have uncovered that geese do not have crops (Arthur Conan Doyle, *The New Annotated Sherlock Holmes*, annotated by Leslie S. Klinger, vol. 1 (New York: W. W. Norton, 2005), 224); that carbuncles come in many colors, but not blue (Klinger, *Holmes*, I, 203), and that geese could not be sold at Covent Gardens at that time, though vegetables, flowers, and fruit were. See D. Martin Dakin, *A Sherlock Holmes Commentary* (Newton Abbot: David & Charles, 1974), 74.

"The Adventure of the Speckled Band" (1892)

More than one Gestalt may make an appearance in a Holmes story, but it seems that there can be only one Gestalt point, which is the point when Holmes and possibly the reader come to see a particular Gestalt that is central to the story and that changes the tale's direction or brings it to a culmination. The central Gestalt in this story concerns a widower, Dr. Grimesby Roylott, who comes from an old and distinguished family, although a family that has gone into decline. Holmes's client is Helen Stoner, Roylott's stepdaughter, who fears that Roylott may have killed her sister Julia, and now Helen fears that Roylott plans to murder her. Roylott's motive seems to be that if his stepdaughters marry, he will lose the inheritance from his deceased wife, which is destined for her daughters. Helen's sister in fact had died mysteriously some time ago after she had become engaged. The circumstances were strange: Dr. Roylott had moved the sister into a bedroom next to his. Then one night she ran screaming from her locked bedroom, and before she died had uttered the words "speckled band." But no one could tell what this meant.

Helen herself has now become engaged, which brings on fears that Roylott will be planning her death, a fear generated partly by the unusual aspects of her sister's demise. So she hires Holmes, who takes her fears very seriously. Part of the problem of course is to determine how the sister had died and what the "speckled band" clue may mean. This is made all the more pressing because Roylott had recently asked Helen to move into the same room where the sister had been attacked. In hopes of saving Helen and determining the cause of Julia Stoner's death, Holmes and Watson rush to the Roylott estate. In a number of ways, Holmes situation is comparable to a person examining what we have called the Dalmatian Gestalt, where one may be told that a dog can be seen in the picture, but one has not as yet discerned its image. In this instance, it appears rather clear that Roylott is the probable murderer, if there is one; what is mysterious is what his murder method might be.

After arriving and inspecting the house (Roylott not being around), Holmes and Watson inspect Helen's room, and arrange to spend the night there. Holmes's inspection of the room produces various clues, including that the bed is attached to the floor, that the bell rope is not attached to any ringer, and that the ventilator does not ventilate. All this is enough to lead Holmes to abandon an early theory that local gypsies were involved in Julia's murder; nonetheless, the "locked room" puzzle remains.

After some hours of waiting, Holmes cries out "You see it, Watson?"[43] What Holmes has seen is a snake (the speckled band) crawling down the bell rope and heading toward Helen. Holmes strikes at it (Fig. 3.3), causing it to retreat and exit through the ventilator, returning thereby to Roylott's room and in its frenzy fatally striking Roylott himself.

Fig. 3.3 Holmes lashes the speckled band.

The Gestalt moment is when Holmes realizes that the method of murder used by Roylott is this snake. This not only explains all the key questions that beset the investigation, but because the snake turns on Roylott himself, leads to the murderous Roylott receiving his punishment.

---

[43] Doyle, *Holmes*, I, 309. The verb used by Holmes seems significant. In one sense, Holmes is asking not only whether Watson can see the snake, but also whether Watson can *understand* the plan for the murder worked out by Roylott.

Holmes's client now understands how her sister had been killed and who the murderer was, how her stepfather planned to murder her, and sees that her suspicions of him are fully justified. Moreover, to the annals of fictional crime, this story has contributed a new and distinctive murder instrument, a snake that can climb a bell rope.

"THE ADVENTURE OF THE ENGINEER'S THUMB" (1892)

As noted in the introduction, a Gestalt shift must meet four conditions: the images must be distinct and the shift must be rapid, unexpected, and global. Not all these characteristics need be at the same level of prominence in every instance. Moreover, there will typically be a shift point associated with the Gestalt shift. These criteria are best fulfilled in this story when late in the narrative, Holmes, Watson, Inspector Bradstreet, a "plain-clothes man," and the engineer Victor Hatherly have come to Eyford, the train stop where the criminals had earlier picked up Hatherly and brought him to a location ten to twelve miles away (judging by the fact that the trip had taken about an hour). Their hope is to locate the house containing the hydraulic press used in the counterfeiting operation and to arrest the criminals. The difficulty is that they do not know the direction in which the house was located. They draw a circle centered on Eyford and each of the participants recommends a direction and offers justification for his choice: Bradstreet recommends south, Hatherly east, the plain-clothes man west, and Watson north. This leaves Holmes to break the tie, but instead he unexpectedly suggests: "You are all wrong."[44] They respond: "But we can't *all* be." Holmes replies: "Oh, yes, you can." Holmes then places his finger in the center of the circle and assures them "This is where we shall find them."[45] He explains that Hatherly had noticed when they picked him up that the horse for the carriage had a "fresh and glossy" coat, indicating that the criminals must have come from near the train stop but then attempted to mislead Hatherly regarding the location of the house by driving the horse six miles away and then six miles back. Holmes's claim proves to be correct, which enables them to find the house near the station; in fact, they find it ablaze. Although by then the counterfeiters had fled, this confirms Hatherly's account of what had happened and brings a resolution to the case. This development meets all four criteria and is marked by a shift point.

Before leaving this story, it may be useful to suggest that the account of it provided here supports a claim that the author makes in the first paragraph of the story. Here he compares his account with another, remarking that his story is

> so strange in its inception and so dramatic in its details that it may be the more worthy of being placed upon record, even if it gave my friend fewer

[44] Doyle, *Holmes*, I, 325.
[45] Doyle, *Holmes*, I, 325.

openings for those deductive methods of reasoning by which he achieved such remarkable results. The story has, I believe, been told more than once in the newspapers, but, like all such narratives, its effect is much less striking when set forth en bloc in a single half-column of print than when the facts slowly evolve before your own eyes, and the mystery clears gradually away as each new discovery furnishes a step which leads on to the complete truth. At the time the circumstances made a deep impression upon me, and the lapse of two years has hardly served to weaken the effect.[46]

It seems probable that the account of the discussion of how to find the house where the counterfeiters worked is the most dramatic part of the story, but also an element that would not make it into a press account.

---

[46] Doyle, *Holmes*, I, 311.

"The Adventure of the Noble Bachelor" (1892)

When approaching a work of literature in terms of the idea of a Gestalt shift, especially when taking a holistic perspective, one must search for Gestalts even in the title. In this case, many indications point to the conclusion that Doyle may have intended "Noble" as ironic, so much so that the title could have been "The Ignoble Bachelor." Nonetheless, the concluding paragraphs indicate that even though Watson favors the view of Lord St. Simon as ignoble, Holmes is less judgmental.[47] Thus another more global Gestalt must be sought.

In this story, which recounts the dramatic disappearance of Hattie Doran within an hour of marrying Lord St. Simon, the most likely Gestalt shift point occurs after Holmes has listened to Lord St. Simon's recounting the disappearance of Hattie Doran. Holmes, after his prominent guest has departed, remarks to Watson: "I have solved it."[48] And somewhat later he makes an even more extraordinary statement to Inspector Lestrade: "Lady St. Simon is a myth. There is not, and there never has been, any such person."[49] The explanation of this is that Doran, while walking up the aisle in the ceremony, sees in the church a man to whom she knows she is married, but who she had good reason to believe was dead. In fact, Doran apparently accidently drops her bouquet near this man, which allows him to give her a message. Holmes reaches his conclusion by making inferences from her behavior and information derived from others and then by ingeniously locating her husband. At the end of the story, Holmes makes a remark to Watson, which Holmes intends to be taken as a major lesson about how one should understand criminal action and the investigation of it. Holmes suggests:

> The case has been an interesting one ... because it serves to show very clearly how simple the explanation may be of an affair which at first sight seems to be almost inexplicable. Nothing could be more natural than the sequence of events as narrated by this lady, and nothing stranger than the result when viewed, for instance by Mr. Lestrade, of Scotland Yard.[50]

Thus the Gestalt shift in the story that Holmes detects and that clarifies what has happened is his recognition that Lady St. Simon does not exist.

[47] Doyle, *Holmes*, I, 343.
[48] Doyle, *Holmes*, I, 335.
[49] Doyle, *Holmes*, I, 337.
[50] Doyle, *Holmes*, I, 342.

"THE ADVENTURE OF THE BERYL CORONET" (1892)

This story has an abundance of Gestalts. It opens with Watson seeing a "madman coming along" Baker Street.[51] Holmes takes a look and correctly sees a client, who turns out to be Alexander Holder, who is "the senior partner in the second largest banking concern in the City of London."[52] Holder's problem is that he very recently loaned £50,000 for a few days to a person whose "name ... is one of the highest, noblest, most exalted names in England,"[53] taking as security the "Beryl Coronet [which is one] of the most precious public possessions of the empire."[54] What has Holder so upset is that he took home the beryl coronet to protect it, but woke up that night to find his son Arthur holding the coronet, which had three of its thirty-nine gems removed.

Arthur was Holder's only child, but he was spoiled, addicted to gambling, and influenced by his talented if somewhat dissolute friend, Sir George Burnwell. Holder's twenty-four-year-old niece, Mary, also lives at the house and in effect manages it. After the robbery, Holder calls the police and has his son, who would not confess, taken into custody, but a search of the house fails to find the three missing beryls. Holmes's comment on the case at this point is that though to Holder, it appears to be "a simple case; to me it seems to be exceedingly complex."[55] In fact, Holmes shows himself skeptical of Arthur's guilt.

Holmes and Watson go to Holder's estate and meet Holder's niece Mary and inspect the beryl coronet, Holmes shocking the group by trying to tear off a coronet, which he fails to do, which is indicative of his hesitancy in attributing the crime to Arthur. He and Watson depart, asking that Holder provide whatever funds Holmes needs to get back the missing gems. Holder agrees and arranges to meet Holmes at nine the next morning. After returning to Baker Street, Holmes emerges, having switched into the attire of a "common loafer."[56] A few hours later he returns in an excellent mood and swinging "an old elastic-sided boot."[57] And then departs again.

[51] Doyle, *Holmes*, I, 343.
[52] Doyle, *Holmes*, I, 344.
[53] Doyle, *Holmes*, I, 345.
[54] Doyle, *Holmes*, I, 346.
[55] Doyle, *Holmes*, I, 351.
[56] Doyle, *Holmes*, I, 355.
[57] Doyle, *Holmes*, I, 356.

The next morning Holder arrives, but experiences anguish; his dear, dependable niece has left his household, leaving this note:

> My dearest Uncle:
>   I feel that I have brought trouble upon you, and that if I had acted differently this terrible misfortune might never have occurred. I cannot, with this thought in my mind, ever again be happy under your roof, and I feel that I must leave you forever. Do not worry about my future, for that is provided for; and, above all, do not search for me, for it will be fruitless labour and an ill-service to me. In life or in death, I am ever
>   Your loving
>   Mary.[58]

Whereas Holder fears it may be a suicide note, Holmes suggests that the note may be "the best possible solution"[59] and may lead to the end of Holder's troubles. And I suggest that this is a Gestalt shift moment, and that with it nearly every major character goes through a significant shift. Holmes first produces the missing gems and then explains that George Burnwell stole them with help from Mary, who has now fled with Burnwell. He explains that Burnwell is "one of the most dangerous men in England—a ruined gambler, an absolutely desperate villain, a man without heart or conscience."[60] He further explains that Arthur saw Mary pass the coronet to Burnwell, chased him, struggled with him over the coronet, and believed that he had recovered it, only to find three gems missing. Arthur, having behaved heroically in trying to save his father's property but finding himself accused of robbery and also out of concern for Mary whom he loved, refused to tell what had happened until Holmes came to him and urged him to come forward with his part of the story. Thus all the principals were changed: Arthur was freed and recognized by his father for his heroic actions, Mary would get her punishment through her involvement with Burnwell, and Alexander recognized the qualities of his son, and found himself in a situation where both he and his country were spared a horrible scandal.

---

[58] Doyle, *Holmes*, I, 357.
[59] Doyle, *Holmes*, I, 357.
[60] Doyle, *Holmes*, I, 358.

"The Adventure of the Copper Beeches" (1892)

In this story, Violet Hunter takes up a new position with the Rucastle family as a governess, with more than ample pay for relatively mild if somewhat odd duties. She is to watch over one six-year-old boy, wear certain dresses that had been worn by Rucastle's daughter who is currently living in Philadelphia, cut her long hair, and read by a window with her back to it. Finding the latter duties strange, she turns to Holmes who has just engaged with Watson in an unresolved discussion of whether the Holmes stories should primarily focus on sensational events or on the extraordinary deductions that Holmes makes in solving his cases. As in the previous story, this story involves apparently innocuous details leading to major issues, and this in turn produces a very significant Gestalt shift. The shift is prefigured in Holmes's surprising comments to Watson as they travel to the location where Hunter is employed. Holmes informs Watson that the level of criminality in rural areas of England is beyond what occurs in London itself. As they drive by various old rural homesteads and Watson admires their beauty, Holmes remarks: "They always fill me with a certain horror. It is my belief, Watson, founded upon my experience, that the lowest and vilest alleys in London do not present a more dreadful record of sin than does the smiling and beautiful countryside."[61] This revelation is illustrated by what they find at Hunter's place of employment. What they discover led Sherlockian Christopher Redmond to describe this story as "an admirable venture into the Gothic genre, with its isolated house, intimations of madness in the attic, feminine fear, and final bloodshed."[62]

In particular, Holmes, helped by Hunter, determines that the "daughter in Philadelphia" was imprisoned in a remote wing of the estate and that Hunter had been hired chiefly to engage in activities that would convince the daughter's suitor that she no longer lives on the estate. When Rucastle becomes aware of Hunter's suspicions, he threatens "I'll throw you to the mastiff."[63]

Soon Holmes and Watson arrive in response to Hunter's request. When Rucastle is away, they gain entrance to the house and seek to release the daughter. Their efforts fail because the daughter's suitor had already aided her escape. Rucastle soon arrives and finding Holmes and Watson turns his mastiff on them, but in fact the mastiff turns upon Rucastle himself. As

---

[61] Doyle, *Holmes*, I, 369.

[62] Christopher Redmond, *Sherlock Holmes Handbook*, 2nd ed. (Toronto: Dundurn Press, 2009), 19.

[63] Doyle, *Holmes*, I, 375.

readers witness how this story unfolds, they come to see the plausibility of Holmes's suggestions about criminality in rural England, having seen that the Rucastle home was in fact a "sinister house,"[64] or to put it differently, they experiences a Gestalt shift not only in this story, but possibly also in their view of the Victorian English countryside.[65]

[64] Doyle, *Holmes*, I, 375.

[65] It is worth mentioning that some months after finishing the first draft of this book, I reread every chapter hoping to improve the book and check it central thesis. I found that in the first draft I had listed this story as not conforming to the Gestalt shift pattern! One factor that especially pointed me away from this analysis was my recognition of the importance of Holmes's comments on the criminality of the countryside, especially when linked with my belief that it is vital to see the stories in a holistic manner.

BIBLIOGRAPHY

PRINTED SOURCES

Crowe, Michael J. (ed.). *Ronald Knox and Sherlock Holmes: Five Writings by Ronald Knox* (Indianapolis: Gasogene Books, 2010).

Dakin, D. Martin, *A Sherlock Holmes Commentary* (Newton Abbot: David & Charles, 1974).

Doyle, Arthur Conan. *The Complete Sherlock Holmes,* 2 vols. (New York: Doubleday, 1953).

Doyle, Arthur Conan. *The New Annotated Sherlock Holmes*, annotated by Leslie S. Klinger, vol. 1 (New York: W. W. Norton, 2005).

Redmond, Christopher, *Sherlock Holmes Handbook*, 2nd ed. (Toronto: Dundurn Press, 2009).

Willis, Martin. *Vision, Science, and Literature, 1870–1920: Ocular Horizons* (University of Pittsburgh Press, 2016).

CHAPTER 4

The Memoirs of Sherlock Holmes (1894)

"THE ADVENTURE OF SILVER BLAZE" (1892)

"Silver Blaze" exhibits an A grade Gestalt shift. Here's the story, summarized so as to help readers assess this claim. King's Pylands stable in the Dartmoor area has suffered a double loss. The head trainer, John Straker, has been found dead having suffered a knife wound in his thigh but also a fatal blow to the head made with a heavy weapon (Fig. 4.1).

Fig. 4.1 Silver Blaze.

© The Author(s) 2018
M. J. Crowe, *The Gestalt Shift in Conan Doyle's Sherlock Holmes Stories*, https://doi.org/10.1007/978-3-319-98291-5_4

Moreover, King's Pylands's best horse, Silver Blaze, has disappeared, all this occurring just a few days before the big race in which Silver Blaze was the favorite. Colonel Ross, owner of the stable, asks Holmes to investigate. Inspector Gregory, a capable man, is also working on the case. The chief suspect in the murder is Fitzroy Simpson, a racing tout who was seen near the stables on the night before Straker's death and who, according to some evidence, had drugged the stable boy in order to allow Simpson to lead the racehorse away. Simpson's walking stick appears to be the likely weapon. Holmes, however, describes the evidence as circumstantial and focuses on finding the horse by tracking across the moor the impressions made by its horseshoes, which eventually leads him to Mapleton, the other horse stable in the area. Here he meets Silas Brown, head trainer of the stables, and describes how tracks he had followed over the moor indicated that Silver Blaze had wandered near to Mapleton and that Brown had taken him into his stables and camouflaged him by blackening a distinctive white streak on Silver Blaze's head. Brown admits this and agrees to bring Silver Blaze to King's Pylands on the day of the race. Holmes then tells Ross that he and Watson are returning to London, but would return in four days for the race. He also tells Ross that he should have his jockey ready for the race, which surprises Ross because he has no horse and because he was becoming convinced that Holmes was unreliable. Before leaving, however, Holmes gives Ross and Gregory some enigmatic but now famous advice. Holmes points to what he believes is an important clue:

[Gregory] "Is there any point to which you would wish to draw my attention?"
    [Holmes] "To the curious incident of the dog in the night-time."
    [Gregory] "The dog did nothing in the night-time."
    [Holmes] "That was the curious incident," remarked Sherlock Holmes.[1]

When the day of the race arrives, Ross confronts Holmes:

"I have seen nothing of my horse," said he.
    "I suppose that you would know him when you saw him?" asked Holmes.

---

[1] Doyle, *Holmes*, I, 397.

The Colonel was very angry. "I have been on the turf for twenty years, and never was asked such a question as that before," said he. "A child would know Silver Blaze, with his white forehead and his mottled off-foreleg."[2]

The six horses scheduled for the race then pass them by, one carrying Ross's colors. Ross, by this point infuriated, comments: "That's not my horse.... That beast has not a white hair upon its body. What is this that you have done, Mr. Holmes?"[3]

The race is then run, with Ross's horse winning the prize. Ross is pleased but totally puzzled, until Holmes suggests that Ross wash the horse's head. When this action produces Silver Blaze, Ross remarks: "You take my breath away!"[4] More surprises follow in the text:

"My dear sir, you have done wonders. ... You would do me a greater still if you could lay your hands on the murderer of John Straker."

"I have done so," said Holmes quietly.

The Colonel and I stared at him in amazement. "You have got him! Where is he, then?"

"He is here."

"Here! Where?"

"In my company at the present moment."

The Colonel flushed angrily. "I quite recognize that I am under obligations to you, Mr. Holmes," said he, "but I must regard what you have just said as either a very bad joke or an insult."

Sherlock Holmes laughed. "I assure you that I have not associated you with the crime, Colonel," said he. "The real murderer is standing immediately behind you." He stepped past and laid his hand upon the glossy neck of the thoroughbred.

"The horse!" cried both the Colonel and myself.

"Yes, the horse. And it may lessen his guilt if I say that it was done in self-defence, and that John Straker was a man who was entirely unworthy of your confidence."[5]

This sketch of the story shows the high level of drama in Doyle's narrative. Each of the two dramatic developments takes place rapidly, almost magically: Now you do not see the horse, now you do! Moreover, note

---

[2] Doyle, *Holmes*, I, 397.
[3] Doyle, *Holmes*, I, 398.
[4] Doyle, *Holmes*, I, 398.
[5] Doyle, *Holmes*, I, 398–399.

that this horse unknown to Ross was rapidly transformed into his prize horse. Even more dramatically, the murderer of Straker turns out not to be Simpson, but an entity distinctly different, in particular, a horse defending itself. Similarly, Straker goes from being Ross's close friend and head trainer to someone who had acted criminally. In fact, the changes can be described as global. Which is in one sense to suggest that this story, which the Sherlock Holmes Society ranked as the fourth best Holmes story, draws much of it drama from in effect following the format of a Gestalt shift.[6]

[6] For an excellent analysis of this story, see Gilbert K. Chesterton, "How to Write a Detective Story," on the internet at http://www.chesterton.org/how-to-write-detective/. Viewed March 21, 2015. For example, Chesterton notes that it is a "story of theft in which the horse plays the part of the jewel until we forget that the jewel can also play the part of the weapon." Chesterton's essay is also available in John Peterson (ed.), *G. K. Chesterton on Detective Fiction* (Sauk City, Wisconsin: The Battered Silicon Dispatch Box: 2010), 74–79.

"The Adventure of the Yellow Face" (1893)

Many Holmes stories take the form that the great detective manages to be the first to attain a surprising view or analysis of some series of events, typically involving crime. Late in the story Holmes shares his view or analysis with others—to their great astonishment and sometimes delight or horror. We are usually informed when Holmes himself goes through the Gestalt shift, but at other times we are not. In this story, there are at least two Gestalt shifts, one of which greatly surprises Holmes (and perhaps helps him with humility) and the second, which delights not only Holmes but also the central characters in the story, and possibly nearly all readers. This is a reminder that it is not only the drama but also the diversity of the stories that makes them so engaging.

Grant Munro is a client who, deeply distressed by the actions of his wife who was a young widow, comes to Holmes seeking advice. The actions of Effie Munro that distress her husband include her request for £100 without providing any explanation of why she needs a sum that would be perhaps one third of the annual earnings of a middle-class Brit, her disappearance in the middle of night, her appearances at a nearby home, which she begs her husband not to enter, and the appearance at the window of that house of a yellow-faced person of indeterminate gender. The husband, who dearly loves Effie, can bear it no longer. After much thought, Holmes suspects that blackmail may be involved and forms a "provisional hypothesis": "This woman's first husband is in that cottage."[7] Very possibly some readers favor the idea that Effie was having an affair.

Resolution occurs only when Munro, Holmes, and Watson come to the mystery house and demand that Effie admit them to the upstairs room in the window of which Munro had seen the strange yellow face. Watson narrates not only the surprise the three men encounter, but also the Gestalt shift they experience; they see a "little girl."

> Her face was turned away as we entered, but we could see that she was dressed in a red frock, and that she had long white gloves on. As she whisked ⅰⅰⅰⅰⅰⅰⅰ ⅰⅰⅰ ⅰⅰⅰ, ⅼ ⅾⅰⅰⅰ ⅰⅰ ⅰⅰⅾ ⅰⅰ ⅰⅰⅰⅰⅰⅰⅰ ⅰⅰⅰⅼ ⅰⅰⅰⅰⅰⅰⅰ ⅰⅰⅼ ⅼⅰⅰⅰ ⅰⅰⅼⅰⅰ ⅰⅰ ⅰⅰⅰⅰⅰⅰⅼ towards us was of the strangest livid tint, and the features were absolutely devoid of any expression. An instant later the mystery was explained. Holmes, with a laugh, passed his hand behind the child's ear, a mask peeled off from her countenance, and there was a little coal black negress, with all

[7] Doyle, *Holmes*, I, 411–412.

her white teeth flashing in amusement at our amazed faces. I burst out laughing, out of sympathy with her merriment; but Grant Munro stood staring, with his hand clutching his throat.[8]

The little girl, Effie explains, is her daughter by her deceased husband. She had come to miss her to the extent that she needed to bring her from Atlanta to England for a visit. She had never mentioned the girl's existence to Grant Munro, nor had she revealed that her first marriage was biracial. Ten minutes later (the text is quite specific on this), a second, hardly less dramatic Gestalt shift occurs:

It was a long ten minutes before Grant Munro broke the silence, and when his answer came it was one of which I love to think. He lifted the little child, kissed her, and then, still carrying her, he held his other hand out to his wife and turned towards the door.

"We can talk it over more comfortably at home," said he. "I am not a very good man, Effie, but I think that I am a better one than you have given me credit for being."[9]

A few lines later Watson ends the story by recording one of the effects that the events had on Holmes:

Not another word did [Holmes] say of the case until late that night, when he was turning away, with his lighted candle, for his bedroom.

"Watson," said he, "if it should ever strike you that I am getting a little over-confident in my powers, or giving less pains to a case than it deserves, kindly whisper 'Norbury' in my ear, and I shall be infinitely obliged to you."[10]

[8] Doyle, *Holmes*, I, 414.
[9] Doyle, *Holmes*, I, 415.
[10] Doyle, *Holmes*, I, 415.

"THE ADVENTURE OF THE STOCK-BROKER'S CLERK"
(1893)

The structure of this story involves a major complicated Gestalt shift, much of which Holmes detects, and the rest of which probably does not come to him as a complete surprise. Hall Pycroft, a clerk who fills his language with Cockney colloquialisms and whose new employment opportunity strikes him as possibly too good to believe, consults Holmes in a story that in some ways resembles "The Red-Headed League." Doyle, who loved contrasts, has Pycroft explain to Holmes that Arthur Pinner, a leading executive of the new "Franco-Midland Hardware Company [with] a hundred and thirty-four branches in the towns and villages of France, not counting one in Brussels and one in San Remo,"[11] has hired him. His position is to be a clerk at an excellent salary working in the company's Birmingham branch under the supervision of Arthur's brother, Harry Pinner, managing director. Although the brothers describe the company in lavish terms, the Birmingham office contains only a dusty desk and a few chairs. Moreover, one little problem especially troubles Pycroft; it is that both Arthur and Harry (who never appear together) seem to have an essentially identical poorly filled gold front tooth complicating their smiles. This, and the contrast between the grandeur of the image they draw of the company compared to the unimpressive office in which Pycroft is assigned his duties, send Pycroft to Holmes.

This produces a minor transformation in the detective and physician: Holmes and Watson travel to Birmingham to apply for jobs at the company, Holmes as an accountant, Watson as a clerk. Pycroft takes them to Pinner, who for some reason seems deeply distressed, but listens to them and then excuses himself to go into a second room, from which worrisome noises soon resound. Holmes and Watson break down the door to find that Pinner has tried to hang himself, but sufficiently ineffectually that Dr. Watson can bring him around. They correctly infer that nothing they had said or done could have produced this effect, leading them to note that when they entered, Pinner was reading a newspaper, which they find carried a report of an unsuccessful attempt to rob a major London stock broking company of nearly £100,000 in securities. This, it turns out, is a firm in which Pycroft had been offered a position, but decided he preferred the Pinners's great firm. Moreover, the robber (who had imperson-

[11] Doyle, *Holmes*, I, 420.

ated Pycroft) had been killed, and turns out to be a one of a pair of well-known crooks, the Beddington brothers, who on this occasion had adopted the name Pinner. Thus within a short period of time, a major financial firm has been saved from robbery and the Franco-Midland startup with all its branches has evaporated as well as Pycroft's position, Moreover, one of the chief executives of the company has been fatally shot by the police and the other has been exposed and brought back from a nearly successful attempt at suicide, and then delivered to the police as a surprise gift from Holmes. We are left to imagine the transformation in Pycroft.

"THE ADVENTURE OF THE *GLORIA SCOTT*" (1893)

This story features a small but very important Gestalt shift and also a larger but relatively less significant shift. First, the second shift. The setting is that Holmes shares with Watson an account of an adventure that Holmes had before the two had met. Holmes's tale begins with a mystery. Holmes recounts that while he was visiting his college friend Victor Trevor, Trevor's father received a short, apparently meaningless letter that struck the elder Trevor "dead with horror when he read it."[12] The message was "The supply of game for London is going steadily up…. Head-keeper Hudson, we believe, has been now told to receive all orders for fly-paper and for preservation of your hen-pheasant's life."[13] After examining the letter, Holmes explains to Victor that if, beginning with the first word, every third word is read, the message is transformed from nonsense into a desperate warning: "The game is up Hudson has told all fly for your life." Knowing that Hudson was a ne'er-do-well who had a strange power over the elder Trevor and his closest friend (the author of the note), Victor understood why this note had so terrified his father. And he understood this all the more when, after his father's death, he read his father's account of his earlier life, which had involved a conviction for failing to pay a debt, sentencing to deportation to Australia, and a mutiny on the journey, in which only his father, his friend Beddoes, and Hudson had survived. Beddoes and Trevor prospered in the Australian gold fields, then returned to England, but were hounded and blackmailed by Hudson. In fact, the public did not it seems learn of the elder Trevor's misdeeds whereas Beddoes successfully fled, but the image that Victor had of his father changed very significantly.

The elder Trevor was the source of another smaller but ultimately more influential shift. At one point, impressed by the deductions that his son's school chum had made, he comments to Holmes (who was still engaged in his university studies): "I don't know how you manage this, Mr. Holmes, but it seems to me that all the detectives of fact and of fancy would be children in your hands. That's your line of life, sir, and you may take the word of a man who has seen something of the world."[14] Immediately after this is quoted, Holmes reveals to Watson: "And that recommendation, with the exaggerated estimate of my ability with which he prefaced it, was, if you will believe me, Watson, the very first thing which ever made me feel that a profession might be made out of what had up to that time been the merest hobby."[15]

---

[12] Doyle, *Holmes*, I, 429.
[13] Doyle, *Holmes*, I, 429.
[14] Doyle, *Holmes*, I, 432.
[15] Doyle, *Holmes*, I, 432.

"The Adventure of the Musgrave Ritual" (1893)

In this case, which Holmes describes as his third earliest case, Reginald Musgrave, who owned an extensive estate in Sussex, asks Holmes for his assistance in dealing with two problems that had recently occurred. One is that Brunton, his family's longtime head butler, had disappeared shortly after Musgrave had dismissed him for secretly reading family documents, including a seventeenth-century document called the Musgrave Ritual. The other problem is that a few days later one of the maids, Rachel Howells, had also disappeared, her footprints having been traced to the lake on the estate, which when dragged produced no body but a sack containing some rusty metallic objects and pebbles. Holmes immediately suspects that the issue is composed not of two, but actually three linked mysteries, the third being the meaning of the Musgrave Ritual.[16]

Holmes sets off for Musgrave's estate and begins by seeking to decipher the Ritual document, which he takes to be some sort of treasure map referring to objects on the estate. This proves a success in leading them to an underground chamber near the house, covered by a large stone slab, too heavy for one person to remove without help. After he and a policeman succeed in removing the slab, they find an empty box and the dead body of Brunton in the chamber (Fig. 4.2).

Fig. 4.2   Holmes and Watson find the dead butler.

[16] Doyle, *Holmes*, I, 452.

This is the Gestalt moment. Holmes thus succeeds in deciphering the Musgrave Ritual, confirms his suspicion that Brunton had earlier solved the Musgrave ritual, and with the aid of Rachel Howells, with whom Brunton had earlier had a relationship, had opened the chamber, but that Howells had decided to release the cover before Brunton had exited. Having caused the death of Brunton, Howells experiences hysteria and ultimately decides to leave the estates, throwing the "treasure" into the lake. Thus Holmes's success at detecting the links relating the three mysteries and deciphering the Ritual leads to clarity concerning the other issues. Moreover, upon examining the metallic structure and stones recovered from the lake, Holmes shows that they were the "the ancient crown of the kings of England,"[17] left there by Charles I, who entrusted them to one of Musgrave's ancestors when Charles fled from England.

Thus Holmes's investigation has not only resolved the disappearance of the two servants and revealed their wicked ways, but also deciphered the meaning of what appeared to be a meaningless document and established that the rubble found in the lake was a historically very significant crown.

[17] Doyle, *Holmes*, I, 457.

"The Adventure of the Reigate Puzzle"[18] (1893)

Two parts of this story are candidates for being labeled Gestalt shifts. The first relates to Holmes's health, which he had taxed solving an internationally significant case. For example, for two months he had devoted fifteen or more hours per day to the case and at one point had gone five days without sleep. The gradualness of his slide and of his recovery disqualifies this change as a Gestalt shift.

A better candidate for Gestalt shift status is Holmes's taking up another case, which he encounters while spending time in a rural home near Reigate in Surrey, where he solves a "little country crime ... which must seem too small for your attention."[19] In fact, the crime began with a burgled house from which thieves had stolen such objects as a few candlesticks and a ball of twine. A second crime (central to the Gestalt) occurs on the day after Holmes came to relax at the home of Watson's friend Colonel Hayter. This crime is another burglary, but in this instance it is more serious, because it involves the murder of William Kirwan, the coachman at the estate of the Cunninghams. Inspector Forrester comes by to see Holmes regarding the case, but their only evidence consists of a torn scrap of paper found in the dead man's hand, which scrap contains eight handwritten words: "at quarter to twelve learn what may be."[20] Holmes's reaction to this is the chief candidate for a Gestalt moment. Dr. Watson, who tells us that Holmes stared at the scrap for a number of minutes, reports: "When he raised his face again I was surprised to see that his cheek was tinged with colour, and his eyes as bright as before his illness."[21] This appears to be the beginning of a Gestalt shift. Shortly thereafter, Holmes, Watson, and Inspector Forrester set off to examine the crime scene, which is the Cunningham home, an estate where Alec Cunningham and his father resided. After learning some details from them and the father asking whether they have any clues, Forrester states: "There is only one. We thought if we could only find—"[22] at which point Holmes falls to the ground and experiences con-

---

[18] The usual name for this story in American editions of the stories is "The Reigate Puzzle," whereas English editions use the name "The Reigate Squires." Arthur Conan Doyle's original name for it was "The Adventure of the Reigate Squire." See https://www.facebook.com/video.php?v=479669702579. Viewed December 24, 2014.

[19] Doyle, *Holmes*, I, 459.

[20] Doyle, *Holmes*, I, 462.

[21] Doyle, *Holmes*, I, 462.

[22] Doyle, *Holmes*, I, 464.

vulsions. They carry him into the kitchen, where he recovers, explaining his fall as a carryover from his recent illness. At the conclusion of the conversation, Holmes requests the elder Cunningham to offer a reward for the capture of the perpetrator of the crime. Holmes drafts the statement but specifies the time incorrectly, which leads him to ask the elder Cunningham to correct his mistake, thereby getting a sample of his handwriting. Holmes also asks the Cunninghams for a tour of their house.

Shortly after entering the son's room, Holmes deliberately knocks over a table with fruit and a water carafe on it, blaming this on Watson, and then while the people are cleaning up the mess, Holmes disappears. Soon Watson and the Inspector find him in the room of the elder Cunningham, the two Cunninghams attacking him. What Holmes had done was to conclude correctly that the remainder of the scrap of paper was probably in the Cunningham closet. After the arrest of the Cunninghams, Holmes explains that from the eight words on the scrap of paper, he had made four major deductions, all of which pointed to the two Cunninghams. Moreover, Holmes explains to the group that he had faked a fit to prevent Forrester from telling the Cunninghams about the scrap of paper they had found. Similarly, Holmes admits that he had deliberately knocked over the table so as to distract the group while he examined the pockets of the elder Cunningham's coat. And finally, he explains that the motive for the Cunninghams's actions must have been that their coachman had learned that it was they who had burgled Acton's home, the reason being that they wanted to recover a document that gave Acton claims over half their estate.

Overall, I place this story among the three stories ranking lowest in degree of "shiftiness." This ranking seems to fit with materials in a recent book: Christopher Redmond (ed.), *About Sixty: Why Every Sherlock Holmes Story Is the Best*.[23] Redmond asked each of his sixty authors to make a case that one story was the best, Ashley Polasek serving as champion of this story. The author begins by admitting that among five well-known rankings of Holmes stories, "The Adventure of the Reigate Squires" is the only story that fails to make every list, even though it ranks twelfth in a ranking made by Conan Doyle. Dr. Polasek defends this story because of the attention given to the friendship of Holmes and Watson. My comment is to suggest that it ranks low among the sixty stories because of its failure to feature a major Gestalt shift, because Doyle wished to highlight the friendship of his two main characters.

[23] (Wildside Press, 2016).

"THE ADVENTURE OF THE CROOKED MAN" (1893)

Three closely related Gestalt shifts occur in this story, one of which comes very, very early in the text, but will be treated last. In this case, Holmes travels to a military base at Aldershot to help officials investigate the apparent murder of Colonel James Barclay, who famously had risen from being a private to be commander of the Royal Munsters, an Irish regiment. Greatly admired for his bravery, especially during the time of the Indian uprising, Barclay was also known for being somewhat moody and suffering at times from depression. He and his beautiful wife Nancy were a well-known couple; in fact, they were viewed "as the very model of a middle-aged couple."[24]

On the evening in question, Mrs. Barclay returned at 9:30 from a meeting and went to the morning room in their home, where her husband joined her. Soon the servants overheard a "fierce altercation"[25] between them, followed by screams from Mrs. Barclay. Because the door was locked, the servants entered through French doors, finding the Colonel dead with a gash to his head and Mrs. Barclay hysterical. An unsuccessful search was made for the key to the door.

When Holmes arrives, he infers from the key's absence that a third person must have been in the room, an inference that Holmes supports by finding footprints on the lawn. What Holmes finds remarkable is that some were of a person, but others were of a strange animal, which, as we shall see, turns out to be a mongoose. Holmes also infers that something must have happened when Nancy Barclay had been out earlier in the evening. Holmes consequently presses Nancy's companion on the excursion, Jane Stewart, for information. Aware that Mrs. Barclay, who by then was suffering with brain fever, might be accused of killing her husband, Jane reveals that while they were out,

> "they saw a man coming towards them with his back very bent and a box slung over one of his shoulders. He appeared to be deformed, for he carried his head low and walked with his knees bent. They were passing him when he looked up at them ... screamed out in a dreadful voice, 'My God, it's Nancy!' Mrs. Barclay turned as white as death, we are told, and would have fallen down had the dreadful-looking creature not caught hold of her."
>
> "I was going to call for the police, but she, to my surprise, spoke quite civilly to the fellow."

[24] Doyle, *Holmes*, I, 476.
[25] Doyle, *Holmes*, I, 477.

"'I thought you had been dead this thirty years, Henry,'" said she, in a shaking voice.

"'So I have,' said he, and it was awful to hear the tones that he said it in."[26]

Holmes, finding this report very interesting, comments that "it was like a light on a dark night. Everything that had been disconnected before began at once to assume its true place, and I had a shadowy presentiment of the whole sequence of events."[27] Note how well Holmes's description fits the pattern of a Gestalt shift. Note also that this event had a powerful impact on Nancy and Henry, who were also seeing their world greatly changed (Fig. 4.3).

Fig. 4.3   Mrs. Barcley encounters Henry Wood.

[26] Doyle, *Holmes*, I, 481–482.
[27] Doyle, *Holmes*, I, 482.

Securing Jane's information on this crippled and deformed person helps Holmes to locate the individual and to learn the details of the death of Major Barclay. At his meeting with Henry Wood, which includes Watson as a witness, Holmes explains that they knew that the man was present at the death of Barclay and that it was probable that Nancy would be charged with murder. Deeply distressed, Henry agrees to tell his story. He recounts that about thirty years earlier he had been a corporal in the British army in India. The belle of his regiment was Nancy whom he loved, but she was also sought by Sergeant James Barclay. At one point, their group, finding itself surrounded by Indian mutineers, focused its chief hope on getting word to other troops requesting that they be rescued. Wood volunteered to sneak through enemy territory to transmit this message, following a route worked out with Barclay. Soon after departing, Wood was apprehended by the enemy and before long discovered that Barclay had betrayed him in hopes that he could thereby secure Nancy's hand. Barclay's plan in fact succeeded, whereas Wood experienced numerous hardships, leaving him crippled and deformed. He kept himself alive by performing conjuring tricks, which included a mongoose and a defanged cobra. Only recently had he secured funds to return to England, where he happened to cross paths with his beloved Nancy. Regarding what happened at the Barclay home, Wood admits to following Nancy and overhearing her violent argument with her husband when she confronted him about his treachery. Wood then entered the room and Barclay, his life crashing down on him, keeled over and died of a stroke. Wood then left, taking the key to the room with him, while Nancy screamed at the tragedy. Wood agrees to come forward if Nancy were to be put on trial. This proves unnecessary when Major Murray reports that the doctors had found that Barclay died from apoplexy, not from the wound, which was not the cause but a result of his collapse.

With Wood's story, readers come to see a drastically different view of the events and persons involved in the story. The initial issue that brought Holmes into the case was finding the murderer of the highly respected Major Barclay. Allied to this, who caused the great grief of Mrs. Barclay? Soon we encounter the prime suspect: Out of the evening emerges Henry Wood, the "Crooked Man" of the story's title. It appears that Holmes, by carefully questioning Mrs. Barclay's maid, has succeeded in solving the case and locating the criminal. On reflection, however, we come to see a drastically different reality. Holmes has discovered the actual crime, criminal, and victim. He has learned that the highly respected Barclay had in fact built his life and marriage on a despicable act of treachery, ruining in the process the life of brave Henry Wood, endangering thereby the people Barclay was responsible for protecting, not least the life of the woman whom he married. We see that Barclay died not from a physical blow from Wood, but from Barclay's recognition that the story of his own infamy had been exposed to his wife and very possibly would soon be exposed to the world. In short, we see that the "Crooked Man" of the title is not Wood, but Barclay. We see also that the crime uncovered by Holmes occurred not in the previous week but thirty years earlier.

"The Adventure of the Resident Patient" (1893)

This case begins when a physician, Percy Trevelyan, asks Holmes to investigate a problem. After graduating from medical school a few years earlier, Trevelyan hoped to open a practice near Trafalgar Square, but lacked capital to do this. Then he was visited by a Mr. Blessington, who had offered to buy a house in which the two of them might live. Trevelyan would practice medicine on the premise, treat Blessington as a "resident patient," and give Blessington three fourths of the income resulting from his practice. This arrangement had worked well for some years, but recently Blessington seemed unduly worried about a robbery in the neighborhood and was especially concerned when he found evidence that one of Trevelyan's patients had entered his room while he was away. Trevelyan explained that this must have been when an elderly Russian man and his adult son arranged for Trevelyan to treat the elder for catalepsy while the son supposedly stayed in the waiting room. Blessington was extremely upset at this intrusion. Holmes visited Blessington, but when Blessington insisted that he had no idea of the identity of the intruders, Holmes walked out, believing that he was not telling the truth. The next morning Trevelyan informed Holmes that Blessington had hung himself during the night.

Arriving at Blessington's house, Holmes meets Inspector Lanner, who describes the death as a suicide. Holmes, on the other hand, based on objects such as various cigar stubs found in the room and footprints that he had traced, concludes that the death was "a very deeply planned and cold-blooded murder"[28] by three men who had conducted a sort of trial after having been admitted to the house by a confederate. Holmes asks to borrow a photograph of Blessington, promising to return later in the day. He also urges the police to arrest the pageboy, who had recently been hired.

The core of what Holmes reports at the later meeting is contained in the following interchange between the Holmes and Inspector Lanner, the latter speaking first:

> "We have got the boy, sir."
> "Excellent, and I have got the men."
> "You have got them!" we cried, all three.

[28] Doyle, *Holmes*, I, 499.

"Well, at least I have got their identity. This so-called Blessington is, as I expected, well known at headquarters, and so are his assailants. Their names are Biddle, Hayward, and Moffat."

"The Worthingdon bank gang," cried the inspector.

"Precisely," said Holmes.

"Then Blessington must have been Sutton."

"Exactly," said Holmes.

"Why, that makes it as clear as crystal," said the inspector.[29]

In short, Holmes totally transforms the situation; not only is the suicide in fact a murder, but also Trevelyan's housemate Blessington, rather than being an upstanding if reclusive "resident patient," is actually a prominent bank robber named Sutton using the arrangement to hide out from three other criminals who together with Sutton had earlier perpetrated an infamous bank robbery. More recently, the three had murdered Sutton for having ratted them out.

Thus a major Gestalt shift has occurred, although it has happened in two parts separated by only a few hours.

[29] Doyle, *Holmes*, I, 501.

"The Adventure of the Greek Interpreter" (1893)

It is easy in this story to identify a number of small Gestalt shifts. For example, very early in the story we learn that Sherlock Holmes is not the earthling most gifted with observational and deductive skills; in fact, in that category he ranks second in his family! First is Mycroft Holmes, who a few people know works as a clerk in the British government, whereas Sherlockians who have read "The Adventure of the Bruce-Partington Plans" are aware that "occasionally he *is* the British government."[30] Also, Mr. Meles, the Greek Interpreter, learns that the men who came to hire him as an interpreter for a Greek speaker want him to help force a marriage on Sophy Kratides and thereby steal money from her family. Sophy's brother, Paul, who recently came from Greece because he worried that a person who supposedly loves and hopes to marry Sophy, may in fact be above all concerned to steal the family fortune. Moreover, he had not only confirmed his suspicion, he himself had become a prisoner. It is in Meles's presence that Sophy learns that her fiancé has captured and is holding her brother, that the person whom she had believed loves her is in fact her worst enemy. And Meles himself comes to see that a supposedly legitimate client is a criminal, ready not only to kidnap him but also possibly to kill him. On one level, the most significant Gestalt shift occurs when Meles realizes that because the kidnappers knew no Greek, he could gain valuable information from Paul by attaching to the questions that their captors wanted answered other questions that they definitely did not want answered. If there is a Gestalt moment in the story, it is when Meles puts this trickery into play. Surprises there are in this story and drama as well, but overall this story derives less of its dramatic impact from Gestalt shifts than most other Holmes stories.

"THE ADVENTURE OF THE NAVAL TREATY" (1893)

"The Adventure of the Naval Treaty," the longest of Doyle's fifty-six Holmes short stories, features one major Gestalt shift, which can be described as of the Dalmatian form; in other words, it features a shift in which Holmes, faced with a variety of clues, some of them contradictory, manages to detect a plot that explains all that has happened in the crime and this leads to the recovery of the precious stolen document.

Percy Phelps, a school chum of Watson, a nephew of England's Foreign Minister, and himself a clerk in England's Foreign Office, has been given the task of spending an evening transcribing a very important secret naval treaty between England and Italy. Around 9:45 p.m., at a late stage in the transcription, Phelps leaves his office to get coffee available elsewhere in the building. Although this takes little time, Phelps returns to his office to find that someone has stolen the precious document, which if sold to the French or German governments would have major implications. Phelps, aided by the commissionaire in the building and by the police, immediately seeks to recover the document. When these efforts fail, Phelps, aware of the gravity of the situation, has a fit, which leads to a mental breakdown and to his confinement in his home in Woking for nine weeks, gradually recovering, partly through help supplied by his very capable fiancé, Annie Harrison, who was living in the house along with her older brother, Joseph Harrison. In fact, Phelps has been moved to Joseph's room, where a nurse watches over him every night. It is at this time and location that Holmes begins to investigate, Phelps having requested this through Watson. Having discussed the case with Phelps and the Harrisons, Holmes and Watson return to London promising to be back the next day.

Faced with a vast assortment of clues, Holmes focuses on three: (1) the fact that as yet there is no indication that any foreign power had reacted to this controversial treaty, (2) the evidence that no one besides Phelps and the Foreign Minister knew of the important task that Phelps had apparently bungled and this had caused him to lie in his bed for nine weeks "unconscious and raving with brain-fever,"[31] nursed during the day by Annie and at night by a hired nurse, and (3) the fact that although the theft had occurred on a rainy evening, no tracks appeared on the floor, which suggests that the person who stole the treaty had arrived in a cab.[32]

[31] Doyle, *Holmes*, I, 525.
[32] Doyle, *Holmes*, I, 527–529.

Following the third clue, Holmes contacts London newspapers, offering a reward for any information on a cab that had dropped a passenger at the Foreign Office on the night in question. Returning to London, Holmes discusses the case with Inspector Forbes and Lord Holdhurst, and the next day he and Watson return to Phelps in Woking.

There they find Phelps improved in condition to the point that for the first time since his confinement, he has no need of a nurse to watch over him during the night. On the other hand, during the night an intruder had attempted to break into the house, entering through Phelps's room! This information excites Holmes, who proposes that they search the grounds for evidence, but he privately asks Phelps's fiancé to remain in his room while they are gone. Moreover, he mysteriously asks her to remain in the room continuously, and if leaving, to lock its door. In addition, Holmes requests that Phelps return with Watson and him to London for the night. The astute Annie, thoroughly baffled, nonetheless trusts Holmes; even when her brother asks her to join them on the lawn, she excuses herself because of a headache.[33] Watson himself is greatly puzzled by Holmes's behavior, all the more so when, after the three had set off for the train station, "Holmes had a still more startling surprise for us, however, for, after accompanying us down to the station and seeing us into our carriage, he calmly announced that he had no intention of leaving Woking."[34] Watson and Phelps return to London filled with bafflement

The next morning Holmes joins them, with "his left hand … swathed in a bandage and … face … very grim and pale." Disappointed, Phelps comments: "He looks like a beaten man."[35] When they ask him if he has made any progress regarding the case, he refuses to answer them until breakfast. At breakfast, after Holmes requests the dejected Phelps to uncover one of the dishes Mrs. Hudson had served, pandemonium ensues:

> Phelps raised the cover, and as he did so he uttered a scream, and sat there staring with a face as white as the plate upon which he looked. Across the centre of it was lying a little cylinder of blue-gray paper. He caught it up, devoured it with his eyes, and then danced madly about the room, pressing it to his bosom and shrieking out in his delight. Then he fell back into an arm-chair so limp and exhausted with his own emotions that we had to pour brandy down his throat to keep him from fainting.

[33] Doyle, *Holmes*, I, 534–535.
[34] Doyle, *Holmes*, I, 535.
[35] Doyle, *Holmes*, I, 537.

"There! there!" said Holmes, soothing, patting him upon the shoulder. "It was too bad to spring it on you like this, but Watson here will tell you that I never can resist a touch of the dramatic."[36]

Rapidly, unexpectedly, and distinctively, with this Gestalt shift, the world has changed (Fig. 4.4).

Fig. 4.4   Holmes shows Phelps the Naval Treaty.

What had happened the night before is that Holmes returns to Phelps's house to watch for a second burglary attempt. His suspicions are confirmed when in the middle of the night Joseph Harrison, Annie's brother, breaks into the room. As Holmes suspects, the treaty had been hidden there, but Joseph had to surrender the room when Percy's illness necessitated its use. Because the room had been occupied 24/7 by Phelps and those caring for him, Harrison had no possibility of retrieving the treaty. This changes first when on the previous night Phelps no longer needs the nurse, and again when the room is unoccupied because Phelps had gone

[36] Doyle, *Holmes*, I, 538.

to London. Thus Holmes foils Joseph's plan and recovers the treaty, thereby saving Phelps's career and protecting England's efforts to keep the treaty secret. Holmes learned that Harrison had lost a lot of money in securities and so hoped to recover this by selling the treaty. The Gestalt shift central to the story is that Holmes finds a new way of viewing the central facts of the case, which not only accounts for them but also results in the restoration of the precious document. Doyle has embellished the shift by the dramatic way in which he restores the document to Phelps.

"THE FINAL PROBLEM" (1893)

Many Gestalt shifts, some smaller than others, appear in this story. We experience lesser shifts when we learn that a bulky cabman, Mycroft, turns out to be the most brilliant man in London and when we see an elderly priest metamorphose into Sherlock Holmes. Later, we recognize that a young lad delivering a compassionate plea that Watson return to the inn to minister to a dying English lady is actually one of Moriarty's minions. Reichenbach Falls appears to be a beautiful resort area; for Holmes and Moriarty it is above all a site for a duel to death. All these appear to be one thing, but they prove to be something very different. One of the more important but less apparent Gestalt patterns is in the very language itself. For example, when Moriarty visits Holmes in his lodgings, the tone has the gentlemanly character of two friends sitting down for a game of chess, whereas the reality is that each is hoping to bring on the death of the other. Holmes and Watson appear to be two friendly travelers on an excursion; in fact, their goal is extermination. Understatements appear repeatedly, but the Victorian reader who had read earlier Holmes stories knows how to read them. The presence of pistols makes clear that this is an exchange about life and death. Similarly, as Holmes and Watson travel to Europe, sometimes their language is such as one would expect between two friends on an excursion, but the reader knows that they are headed for a killing field. Again and again we see Doyle's attraction to contrasts: Holmes in this story encounters for the first time a true rival in cunning and intelligence. And neither flinches. Moreover, Doyle had taught his readers how to read between the lines of his story. Think of Watson's comment on his return to the lodge to minister to the expiring English lady:

> When I was near the bottom of the descent I looked back. It was impossible, from that position, to see the fall, but I could see the curving path which winds over the shoulder of the hills and leads to it. Along this a man was, I remember, walking very rapidly.
>
> I could see his black figure clearly outlined by the green behind him. I noted him, and the energy with which he walked, but he passed from my mind as I hurried on upon my errand.[37]

---

[37] Doyle, *Holmes*, I, 553.

Doyle's readers may have been more observant; possibly on their first, definitely on their second reading, they would supply the name of that distant walker (Fig. 4.5).

Fig. 4.5   Holmes and Moriarty in a fatal struggle.

The major Gestalt contrast is of course between these two men of surpassing intelligence, resourcefulness, and power, but totally different relations to law and order. Doyle has constructed the story as a conflict between good and evil and between law and criminality. Moreover, at the end, we do not know which side has prevailed. For all we can know, the shift has been between two brilliant and powerful men engaged in a fierce struggle but ending up as two battered, water soaked corpses. Doyle will tell us years later what actually happened, but no clue appears in the story, though it is made clear that Holmes would have died happy had he been assured that Moriarty had died as well. It is a battle between "the best and wisest man"[38] that Watson had ever known and the "organizer of half that is evil and all that is undetected"[39] in London.

One final point before leaving this story: It is important to note how Holmes comes to see an image that had been invisible to everyone else.

As you are aware, Watson, there is no one who knows the higher criminal world of London so well as I do. For years past I have continually been conscious of some power behind the malefactor, some deep organizing power which forever stands in the way of the law, and throws its shield over the wrong-doer. Again and again in cases of the most varying sorts—forgery cases, robberies, murders—I have felt the presence of this force, and I have deduced its action in many of those undiscovered crimes in which I have not been personally consulted. For years I have endeavored to break through the veil which shrouded it, and at last the time came when I seized my thread and followed it, until it led me, after a thousand cunning windings, to ex-Professor Moriarty of mathematical celebrity.[40]

This process seems very similar to the process by which we eventually see a Gestalt, where before we saw a scattering of unrelated objects.

[38] Doyle, *Holmes*, I, 555.
[39] Doyle, *Holmes*, I, 544.
[40] Doyle, *Holmes*, I, 544.

BIBLIOGRAPHY

PRINTED SOURCES

Chesterton, G. K. "How to Write a Detective Story," in John Peterson (ed.). *G. K. Chesterton on Detective Fiction* (Sauk City, Wisconsin: The Battered Silicon Dispatch Box, 2010), 74–79.

Doyle, Arthur Conan. *The Complete Sherlock Holmes,* 2 vols. (New York: Doubleday, 1953).

Redmond, Christopher (ed.). *About Sixty: Why Every Sherlock Holmes Story Is the Best* (Wildside Press, 2016).

INTERNET SOURCES

Chesterton, Gilbert K. "How to Write a Detective Story," on the internet at http://www.chesterton.org/how-to-write-detective/. Viewed 21 March 2015.

https://www.facebook.com/video.php?v=479669702579. Viewed 24 December 2014.

CHAPTER 5

The Return of Sherlock Holmes (1905)

"THE ADVENTURE OF THE EMPTY HOUSE" (1903)

In discussing this story, it is wise to keep in mind its place in the chronology of the canon. In December 1893, Doyle had published "The Final Problem," which most readers understood as containing the sad news that Holmes had died in 1891. Then in 1902, Doyle published *Hound of the Baskervilles*, but the time period for this novel was before the events at Reichenbach Falls. In September 1903, Doyle resurrected Holmes in "The Adventure of the Empty House," which reports events that occurred in 1894.

"The Empty House" contains arguably the most important Gestalt shift that occurs in the canon. It begins when Watson, out for a walk, bumps into an "elderly, deformed … bibliophile."[1] This strange creature causes some slight surprise when later in the day he shows up at Watson's door and soon produces in Watson a surprise of sufficient magnitude to make Watson faint. Such is his response to this aged bibliophile revealing himself as Sherlock Holmes, whom Watson believed had died three years earlier.[2] An allied but unwelcome surprise occurs when members of Moriarty's gang discover that Holmes has returned to London. This resulted in a major disruption in the life of Colonel Sebastian Moran, who goes from being a prominent retired military man who had distinguished himself in India to being unmasked as the "most cunning and dangerous

---

[1] Doyle, *Holmes*, II, 561.
[2] Doyle, *Holmes*, II, 562.

© The Author(s) 2018
M. J. Crowe, *The Gestalt Shift in Conan Doyle's Sherlock Holmes Stories*, https://doi.org/10.1007/978-3-319-98291-5_5

criminal in London."[3] By the end of the story, Holmes has turned Moran over to Lestrade, which makes Moran the least dangerous man in London because he is confined to jail awaiting trial.[4] After Holmes, with minor help from Lestrade, captures Moran, the two discuss what they have achieved. This reveals how little Lestrade has understood what has just happened. After talking about the air gun and its bullets, Lestrade has the following remarkable interchange with Holmes:

> "You can trust us to look after that, Mr. Holmes," said Lestrade, as the whole party moved towards the door. "Anything further to say?"
>
> "Only to ask what charge you intend to prefer?"
>
> "What charge, sir? Why, of course, the attempted murder of Mr. Sherlock Holmes."
>
> "Not so, Lestrade. I do not propose to appear in the matter at all. To you, and to you only, belongs the credit of the remarkable arrest which you have effected. Yes, Lestrade, I congratulate you! With your usual happy mixture of cunning and audacity you have got him."
>
> "Got him! Got whom, Mr. Holmes?"
>
> "The man that the whole force has been seeking in vain—Colonel Sebastian Moran, who shot the Honourable Ronald Adair with an expanding bullet from an air-gun through the open window of the second-floor front of No. 427, Park Lane, upon the 30th of last month. That's the charge, Lestrade. And now, Watson, if you can endure the draught from a broken window, I think that half an hour in my study over a cigar may afford you some profitable amusement."[5]

Doyle's love of contrasts is especially evident in these developments: (1) Watson rejoices that Holmes is alive; (2) Moran, thought to be an honored citizen, is exposed as a card cheat, thief, and murderer on his way to jail; and (3) Lestrade recognizes that he will soon be lauded for capturing a notorious criminal, when in fact Holmes deserves all the credit. And on another level, readers of the stories celebrated that Holmes, who had never existed, had returned to life.

---

[3] Doyle, *Holmes*, II, 568.
[4] Doyle, *Holmes*, II, 568.
[5] Doyle, *Holmes*, II, 571–572.

"THE ADVENTURE OF THE NORWOOD BUILDER" (1903)

The four criteria for a Gestalt shift (distinct images and that the shift be rapid, unexpected, and global) must all appear, but they can appear with different intensities. The Gestalt shift in this story is of the bipolar type, is in two strongly related parts, and Holmes brings it about in a masterful fashion. The contrast is between what can be labeled the Lestrade view (McFarlane has killed Jonas Oldacre) and the Holmes view (McFarlane is innocent). In a sense there is a reference to a number of other Gestalts or theories of the crime. For example, immediately after Lestrade has laid out, with an abundance of evidence, his theory that McFarlane murdered Oldacre, Holmes claims:

> I could very easily give you half-a-dozen [theories].... Here, for example, is a very possible and even probable one. [Oldacre] is showing documents which are of evident value. A passing tramp sees them through the window, the blind of which is only half down. Exit the solicitor. Enter the tramp! He seizes a stick, which he observes there, kills Oldacre, and departs after burning the body.[6]

One reason why this is possible is that in every case there are dozens, if not hundreds, of clues. It would be instructive to count the number of possibly relevant clues in one of Holmes's cases.

From this point on, Doyle traces Holmes's efforts to find clues that go against Lestrade's claim and that point toward McFarlane's innocence. This presents challenges; before long, Holmes laments to Watson:

> It's all going wrong, Watson—all as wrong as it can go. I kept a bold face before Lestrade, but, upon my soul, I believe that for once the fellow is on the right track and we are on the wrong. All my instincts are one way and all the facts are the other, and I much fear that British juries have not yet attained that pitch of intelligence when they will give the preference to my theories over Lestrade's facts.[7]

After devoting three pages to Holmes's search for evidence, Doyle has Holmes say: "'So, my dear Watson, there's my report of a failure. And yet—and yet—' he clenched his thin hands in a paroxysm of conviction—'I know it's

---

[6] Doyle, *Holmes*, II, 582.
[7] Doyle, *Holmes*, II, 583.

all wrong. I feel it in my bones.'"[8] Doyle, however, does not stop; in fact, he reports a telegram from Lestrade: "Important fresh evidence to hand. McFarlane's guilt definitely established. Advise you to abandon case."[9] The new evidence is that Lestrade reported the discovery of a bloody thumbprint of McFarlane on the wall in Oldacre's house. As they discuss this, Watson despairs: "It was evident that our unfortunate client was lost."[10] Lestrade pronounces his evidence final and chides Holmes for not seeing that it is. Holmes, however, agrees that it is final, but Watson reports Holmes's strange reaction by remarking that "his whole body gave a wriggle of suppressed excitement."[11] We eventually learn why Holmes was so excited by Lestrade's new evidence; it was that he saw it as proving McFarlane innocent:

> "The fact is that there is one really serious flaw in this evidence to which our friend attaches so much importance."
> "Indeed, Holmes! What is it?"
> "Only this: that I know that that mark was not there when I examined the hall yesterday."[12]

The problem then becomes to find the criminal. Again Holmes can oblige, and in a most dramatic manner. In preparing for the capture, Holmes, according to Watson, "stood before us with the air of a conjurer who is performing a trick."[13] Holmes's trick is to make the supposed dead Oldacre appear before the police. He accomplishes this by starting a small but smoky fire in Oldacre's house and having police and others present shout "Fire!" The result, in Watson's words, is that "an amazing thing happened. A door suddenly flew open out of what appeared to be solid wall at the end of the corridor, and a little, wizened man darted out of it, like a rabbit out of its burrow."[14] This is Oldacre, the "Norwood Builder," who as a builder was able to equip his house with a secret room. A deeply impressed Lestrade tells Holmes "this is the brightest thing that you have done yet…. You have saved an innocent man's life, and you have prevented a very grave scandal, which would have ruined my reputation in the

---

[8] Doyle, *Holmes*, II, 585.
[9] Doyle, *Holmes*, II, 586.
[10] Doyle, *Holmes*, II, 587.
[11] Doyle, *Holmes*, II, 587.
[12] Doyle, *Holmes*, II, 588.
[13] Doyle, *Holmes*, II, 589.
[14] Doyle, *Holmes*, II, 590.

Force."[15] Thus Holmes has succeeded at his job by saving McFarlane from a murder charge and also rescuing Lestrade's reputation. Holmes unmasks Oldacre as a criminal seeking to avoid paying just debts and reveals that Oldacre's housekeeper has been his accomplice. In one sense, the Gestalt moment occurs when Holmes turns Lestrade's best evidence on its head by showing that it proves his client's innocence; in another sense, it occurs slightly later when Holmes produces Oldacre from out of nowhere as dramatically as later he would resurrect the supposedly murdered Jack Douglas in *The Valley of Fear*.[16]

[15] Doyle, *Holmes*, II, 590.
[16] Doyle, *Holmes*, II, 953–954.

"THE ADVENTURE OF THE DANCING MEN" (1903)

To solve this mystery, Holmes must find a way to solve two puzzles (or Gestalts). Hilton Cubitt presents Holmes with the first mystery by reporting that various messages in a strange code have disturbed his wife; all the messages consist of collections of stick figures of dancing men, which Holmes correctly concludes stand for letters of the alphabet. The second mystery is that a few days later Cubitt and his wife, Elsie, are found shot in a room in their house with both the door and window locked, the husband being dead, and the wife severely wounded and unable to communicate. A reasonable account of what happened in this locked room mystery is that Cubitt's wife had shot him and then tried to take her own life. Holmes, who mentions that he had carefully studied the interpretation of codes, succeeds in breaking the dancing men code; in fact, by this method, he gains enough knowledge of the code that he can send a message to the person, Abe Slaney, who signed (in code) the messages, and moreover Holmes sends an inquiry by cable to Chicago, which brings him the information that Slaney is the "most dangerous crook in Chicago."[17] Regarding his reconstruction of what happened in the room, Holmes explores the possibility that the two shots that people had reported hearing consisted in fact of two simultaneous shots followed by a third shot. Slaney, when captured, admits that he had come to the house on the night in question to try to convince Elsie, who years earlier had rejected him, to come away with him. Cubitt finds them and fires at Slaney, who simultaneously fires at Cubitt; Slaney kills Cubitt whereas Cubitt's bullet goes amiss. Holmes finds it by reconstructing the events so as to entail the possibility of the bullet being lodged in the wall. After Slaney flees the crime scene taking his pistol with him, Elsie Cubitt shuts the window and attempts to take her own life. This story shares one of its most dramatic features with the "Norwood Builder." By sending a note to Slaney written in the code and supposedly sent by Elsie, Holmes succeeds in getting Slaney to return to the crime scene, where the police easily arrest him. Moreover, Holmes manages to receive direct confirmation from Slaney for Holmes's reconstruction of the murder.

[17] Doyle, *Holmes*, II, 608.

"The Adventure of the Solitary Cyclist" (1903)

Who was the Solitary Cyclist? It is very important in analyzing the structure of this story to be clear that it was not Violet Smith. It is true that she was a cyclist and also that she typically rode her bicycle as a solitary person. But there is good evidence that she is not *the* solitary cyclist. For example, an examination of the original manuscript reveals that Doyle originally titled his story "The Solitary Man."[18] This is an important issue because the central question in the story is: Who is the solitary cyclist? This is what Violet Smith wants to know and this is the question that Holmes and Watson successfully answer. In other words, Smith wants to know who has been following her and what his intentions are. The assumption readers naturally make is that a man with evil intentions is following her. Thus we can say that one Gestalt is the image of the rider as a man who may harm Smith. As the story develops, Holmes and Watson determine that this is quite the reverse of the truth. They conclude that the bearded man following her is trying to protect her, not harm her. We learn that the cyclist is Bob Carruthers, the widower who hired her to instruct his daughter and who falls in love with her and late in the story proposes marriage. Moreover, it becomes clear that someone is out to force himself on her; in particular, this person wishes to marry her so as to get access to the fortune left her (but unbeknownst to her) by her recently deceased uncle, Ralph Smith, who had made a fortune in the South African gold fields. In fact, what launches the plot is that Carruthers and Jack Woodley had known Smith's uncle when they were in South Africa. When the uncle was near death, Carruthers and Woodley devised a plan to return to England and to acquire the fortune by one of them marrying his heir.

Late in the story Holmes and Watson come to the road where Violet had been followed and watch for her as she leaves for the train station riding in a dog cart. Then Violet disappears and they find the dogcart empty. Just then *the* Solitary Cyclist arrives and accuses them of having removed Violet Smith. Soon they realize that the person who had seized her must be Woodley. It appears that Holmes had already suspected that the Solitary Cyclist's goal is probably protection, especially from Woodley, whom Holmes had encountered in the local pub. This makes it understandable that the three would join forces in searching for Smith.

---

[18] D. Martin Dakin, *A Sherlock Holmes Commentary* (Newton Abbot: David & Charles, 1976), 169.

The Gestalt point in the story occurs just after Woodley captures Violet Smith and prepares to have Williamson, a defrocked clergyman, force a marriage to Woodley on her. During this period the Cyclist identifies himself as Carruthers, who follows Holmes's leadership in capturing Woodley and Williamson and freeing Violet Smith from them.

"The Adventure of the Priory School" (1904)

Arthur Conan Doyle was not only very skillful in writing his Holmes stories, he also excelled at promoting the stories by stressing the importance
of those involved or by noting the uniqueness of a story. In fact, an examination of the sixty stories shows that in a quite high percentage of them
Doyle informs his readers that this story is unique or that it has one or
more unique features. Such is certainly the case in "The Adventure of the
Priory School." For example, Watson begins the story by stating: "I cannot recollect anything more sudden and startling than the first appearance
of Thorneycraft Huxtable,"[19] Headmaster of the Priory School, "the best
and most select preparatory school in England,"[20] who though "pomp-
ous" and "dignified" promptly fainted upon appearing before Holmes and
Watson.[21] What so upset Huxtable was that a student at his school had
been abducted. This was no ordinary student; it was the ten-year-old son
of the Duke of Holdernesse, "the greatest, and perhaps the wealthiest"
subject of the Crown.[22] So concerned was the Duke that he had offered a
"check for five thousand pounds to the person who can tell him where his
son is, and another thousand to him who can name the man or men who
have taken him."[23] The crime was more than a kidnapping; the German
master at the school seems to have followed on a bicycle the person who
kidnapped the young man, which cost this tutor his life. The Duke's residence, it turns out, is just a few miles from the Priory School. Holmes and
Watson meet the Duke, and also the Duke's personal secretary, James
Wilder, and learn that the Duchess now lives in France, which is a sadness
to Lord Saltire, the Duke's young son.

Holmes manages some shrewd deductions; for example, he notices that
cow tracks along the route of the abduction and murder are positioned as
they would be were a horse moving along the path; as he states: "It is a
remarkable cow which walks, canters, and gallops."[24] From this he infers
that a horse was used for the abduction. Holmes also meets with Reuben
Hayes, the proprietor of the Fighting Cock Inn, located nearby. Hayes's
behavior puts him under suspicion. Moreover, after leaving, Holmes sees

[19] Doyle, *Holmes*, II, 627.
[20] Doyle, *Holmes*, II, 629.
[21] Doyle, *Holmes*, II, 627.
[22] Doyle, *Holmes*, II, 628.
[23] Doyle, *Holmes*, II, 643.
[24] Doyle, *Holmes*, II, 629.

Wilder riding a bicycle to the Inn, and later a second man in a cart arrives for a short visit. All this leads to the most dramatic moment in the story (and the Gestalt shift moment) when Holmes meets with the Duke himself. Holmes immediately asks him to write out the check for the reward.

"Is this a joke, Mr. Holmes? It is hardly a subject for pleasantry."
"Not at all, your Grace. I was never more earnest in my life."
"What do you mean, then?"
"I mean that I have earned the reward. I know where your son is, and I know some, at least, of those who are holding him."
The Duke's beard had turned more aggressively red than ever against his ghastly white face.
"Where is he?" he gasped.
"He is, or was last night, at the Fighting Cock Inn, about two miles from your park gate."
The Duke fell back in his chair.
"And whom do you accuse?"
Sherlock Holmes's answer was an astounding one. He stepped swiftly forward and touched the Duke upon the shoulder.
"I accuse *you*," said he. "And now, your Grace, I'll trouble you for that cheque."
Never shall I forget the Duke's appearance as he sprang up and clawed with his hands like one who is sinking into an abyss. Then, with an extraordinary effort of aristocratic self-command, he sat down and sank his face in his hands. It was some minutes before he spoke.
"How much do you know?" he asked at last, without raising his head.[25]

Holmes makes it clear that he knows that James Wilder had organized the abduction, but that Hayes had been the person who abducted Saltire. Another striking exchange occurs, where it is the Duke who surprises Holmes. After Holmes tells the Duke that Hayes has been arrested, the Duke comments: "I am right glad to hear it, if it will not react upon the fate of James." Holmes replies: "Your secretary?" and the Duke responds "No, sir, my son."[26] Holmes expresses astonishment at this information, which leads the Duke to explain that Wilder is his illegitimate son, whom the Duke admits he has badly spoiled and who has always resented that the Duke's estate will pass to Saltire. This resentment is what led Wilder to organize the abduction, hoping to use it to persuade his father to give him

[25] Doyle, *Holmes*, II, 646–647.
[26] Doyle, *Holmes*, II, 648.

a large portion of the inheritance. When Wilder learned of the murder of the German teacher, he became exceedingly distressed, to the point that his father had concluded that Wilder was responsible for the abduction. This leads the father to tell Wilder that he must make plans to leave for Australia. Thus a global shift has occurred: Wilder's wickedness has become evident, his true nature revealed, and he has fled; the Duke has realized his failings as a father; Lord Saltire has been rescued as has Huxtable and the reputation of his school; Hayes has been arrested; and Holmes has demonstrated his prowess, improved his financial situation, and taught some important lessons at the Priory School.

"THE ADVENTURE OF BLACK PETER" (1904)

One feature of the Gestalt model is that it points the reader toward the wholeness of the story. This is evident in "The Adventure of Black Peter," which begins with Holmes informing Watson of the apparently bizarre activity in which he had engaged that morning: investigating whether he could throw a harpoon with sufficient force that it would penetrate a hog hung on a hook at a butcher shop. This seems irrelevant but later proves to be a key factor in determining who killed Peter Carey, aka Black Peter, an angry alcoholic retired sea captain. Inspector Hopkins had requested Holmes's help in investigating this crime

Two opposing Gestalts are central in this narrative. One is a Gestalt developed by Hopkins; the other is Holmes's preferred Gestalt. After Holmes and Hopkins gather extensive evidence about the killing of Carey, they find John Hopley Neligan breaking into the cabin where someone had earlier killed Carey by impaling him with a harpoon. Hopkins concludes that Neligan was the murderer. Neligan had a motive: He believed that Carey had stolen securities from Neligan's deceased father, a banker, whom Carey may actually have killed. On the other hand, Holmes repeatedly stresses to the young and promising Hopkins that a detective "should always look for a possible alternative. It is the first rule of criminal investigation."[27] Holmes shares other objections to Hopkins's view; for example, he questions whether a tobacco pouch with the letters P.C. on it that was found at the scene of the crime belongs to Carey because there was no evidence that Carey had a pipe or indulged in smoking.

Late in the story Watson reports on a climactic conversation between Hopkins and Holmes, the latter having invited the former to join Watson and Holmes for breakfast.

> Sharp at the hour named Inspector Stanley Hopkins appeared…. The young detective was in high spirits at his success.
>
> "You really think that your solution must be correct?" asked Holmes.
>
> "I could not imagine a more complete case."
>
> "It did not seem to me conclusive."
>
> "You astonish me, Mr. Holmes. What more could one ask for?"
>
> "Does your explanation cover every point?"
>
> [Hopkins then lays out much of the evidence he has regarding Neligan's guilt, concluding] "Surely that is all simple and obvious?"

[27] Doyle, *Holmes*, II, 662.

Holmes smiled and shook his head.

"It seems to me to have only one drawback, Hopkins, and that is that it is intrinsically impossible." [Holmes then reminds Hopkins that Neligan was too frail to have harpooned Black Peter.]

The detective's face had grown longer and longer during Holmes's speech. His hopes and his ambitions were all crumbling about him. But he would not abandon his position without a struggle.

"You can't deny that Neligan was present that night, Mr. Holmes. The book will prove that. I fancy that I have evidence enough to satisfy a jury, even if you are able to pick a hole in it. Besides, Mr. Holmes, I have laid my hand upon *my* man. As to this terrible person of yours, where is he?"

"I rather fancy that he is on the stair," said Holmes, serenely. "I think, Watson, that you would do well to put that revolver where you can reach it." He rose, and laid a written paper upon a side-table. "Now we are ready," said he.[28]

Within minutes Holmes has the murderer in handcuffs, using a technique reminiscent of Holmes's capture of Jefferson Hope in *Study in Scarlet*. He then explains to the amazed Hopkins, Watson, and the murderer how he had pulled off this extraordinary achievement. Relying on his analysis of the harpoon murder, Holmes set out to find a harpooner fitting the evidence. Posing as a sea captain (Captain Basil), Holmes advertises that because he will shortly be sailing for Arctic locations, he needs to hire a harpooner. He also checks crew records for sailings of Peter Carey's ship in the period when Neligan's father had disappeared. This search leads him to a husky harpooner named Patrick Cairns (initials P.C.), who arrives at Holmes's lodgings when Hopkins is present. Holmes succeeds in handcuffing the unsuspecting Cairns, who admits that he had killed Carey, but claims that he had acted in self-defense. Hopkins expresses his amazement when he recognizes that Holmes's methods had led him not only to identify the criminal but also to success in apprehending him. Holmes's achievement not only amazes Hopkins but also produces numerous effects. It leads to the imprisonment of Cairns, the freeing of Neligan from confinement, and may restore the reputation of Neligan's father. It also provides a lesson to Hopkins, who recognizes the superiority of Holmes's analysis of the crime by exclaiming "Wonderful! ... Wonderful!"[29] It seems easy to see this expression of emotion as fully comparable to what we regularly experience when witnessing a Gestalt shift.

[28] Doyle, *Holmes*, II, 662–663.
[29] Doyle, *Holmes*, II, 667.

"THE ADVENTURE OF CHARLES AUGUSTUS MILVERTON" (1904)

As noted earlier, Doyle delighted in pointing to the uniqueness of many of his stories. Within the first two pages of this story, he uses a superlative or labels something unique no less than six times! Not only does he describe this case as "unique" but as "an absolutely unique experience" in Holmes's and Watson's career.[30] Not only does he describe Milverton as wicked, but as the "worst man in London."[31] This being apparently insufficient to do justice to Milverton's character, Holmes comments "I've had to deal with fifty murderers in my career, but the worst of them never gave me the repulsion which I have [for Milverton]."[32] Holmes employs another form of superlative when he describes Milverton as "the king of all the blackmailers."[33] After elaborating further on Milverton's level of cunning and criminality, he repeats that he is "the worst man in London."[34] And who is Holmes's client: "the most beautiful débutante of last season."[35] Immediately after this introduction, Watson for the first time meets Milverton, whom he describes as "a small, stout man ... of fifty ... with something of Mr. Pickwick's benevolence in his appearance."[36] Milverton, whose powers, influence, and wickedness were very great, goes through an immense shift in this narrative: at its end, not only is he dead, but also Holmes has destroyed all the evidence that not only so worried his client but that also made many dozens so fearful of Milverton.

Another unique feature of this story is that Holmes and Watson risk not only their careers to save Holmes's client, but also their lives. After Milverton has left Holmes's rooms, Holmes himself departs. Some days later Holmes shocks Watson by telling him that he has become a "plumber with a rising business"[37] and, even more surprising, has done this as a step toward becoming the fiancé of Milverton's housemaid. Moreover, Holmes goes to this extent as a way to get information that would help him burglarize Milverton's house. Such was the respect that Watson had for

[30] Doyle, *Holmes*, II, 667.
[31] Doyle, *Holmes*, II, 667.
[32] Doyle, *Holmes*, II, 668.
[33] Doyle, *Holmes*, II, 668.
[34] Doyle, *Holmes*, II, 668.
[35] Doyle, *Holmes*, II, 668.
[36] Doyle, *Holmes*, II, 668.
[37] Doyle, *Holmes*, II, 671.

Holmes that he offers to join the detective as a fellow burglar. After their nocturnal break-in of Milverton's mansion, Holmes's carefully prepared plan goes awry. A woman arrives for a meeting with the blackmailer, but rather than delivering the money he had demanded, she fires numerous bullets into Milverton's chest and then flees. As a result of this complication, Holmes has only moments to destroy Milverton's cache of blackmailing materials by transferring them from safe to fireplace. The two then, but just barely, make a successful escape. The closeness of their escape is evident in the most humorous passage in the story, which occurs when Lestrade visits them the next day and confidently recounts what Scotland Yard had learned of Milverton and of the villains involved:

> "We have had our eyes upon this Mr. Milverton for some time, and, between ourselves, he was a bit of a villain. He is known to have held papers which he used for blackmailing purposes. These papers have all been burned by the murderers. No article of value was taken, as it is probable that the criminals were men of good position, whose sole object was to prevent social exposure."
>
> "Criminals?" said Holmes. "Plural?"
>
> "Yes, there were two of them. They were as nearly as possible captured red-handed. We have their footmarks, we have their description, it's ten to one that we trace them. The first fellow was a bit too active, but the second was caught by the under-gardener, and only got away after a struggle. He was a middle-sized, strongly built man—square jaw, thick neck, moustache, a mask over his eyes."
>
> "That's rather vague," said Sherlock Holmes. "My, it might be a description of Watson!"
>
> "It's true," said the inspector, with amusement. "It might be a description of Watson."[38]

The story ends with Holmes revealing (sort of, and only to the reader) the identity of the person who dispatched Milverton. At lunch, after Holmes had (for some reason!) declined Lestrade's request to work on the case, Holmes, after seemingly struggling with some issue, leaps up and leads Watson to a location on Oxford Street. As Watson reports:

> Here, on the left hand, there stands a shop window filled with photographs of the celebrities and beauties of the day. Holmes's eyes fixed themselves

---

[38] Doyle, *Holmes*, II, 679.

upon one of them, and following his gaze I saw the picture of a regal and stately lady in Court dress.... Then I caught my breath as I read the time-honoured title of the great nobleman and statesman whose wife she had been. My eyes met those of Holmes, and he put his finger to his lips as we turned away from the window.[39]

We see in this story Holmes himself go through a Gestalt shift. He moves from being a paragon of lawfulness to committing breach of promise, breaking and entering, burglary, fleeing from the scene of a crime, failing to report the person who murdered Milverton, and inciting his closest associate to criminality. It is true that he explains that he did all this because of his belief that "there are crimes which the law cannot touch, and which therefore, to some extent, justify private revenge."[40]

In Holmes stories, we typically see a Gestalt shift point marked by Holmes reporting: "I have solved it." Finding such a point in this story may seem something of a challenge. My conclusion is that it may be when Watson says, as they enter Milverton's house: "An instant afterwards he had closed the door behind us, and we had become felons in the eyes of the law." Another candidate is earlier in the story when after Holmes has told Watson of all the wild things he has done (e.g., committing "breach of promise") and plans to do (e.g., breaking and entering, theft), that Watson, after having pointed out all the difficulties involved in what Holmes proposes to do, says: "When do we start?" And it is worth adding that the actions they take involve even more problems than they foresaw, such as declining the chance to prevent the murder of Milverton.

[39] Doyle, *Holmes*, II, 680.
[40] Doyle, *Holmes*, II, 679.

"THE ADVENTURE OF THE SIX NAPOLEONS" (1904)[41]

Two competing Gestalts are fundamental to the structure of this story. One of the Gestalts can be labeled the Lestrade Gestalt and centers around Lestrade's claim that the reported smashing of a Napoleonic bust indicates that the perpetrator must be a maniac. At this stage, Holmes takes no interest. When, however, two more Napoleonic busts are smashed as part of a burglary, Holmes becomes more interested, noting that "some of my most classic cases have had the least promising commencement."[42] When a fourth bust smashing involves a murder, both Lestrade and Holmes conclude it is time for Holmes to become engaged in the case. Holmes, who (unlike Lestrade) directs his efforts to investigating the source of the busts, has the good fortune of having the distributor of the busts identify the person in a picture found in the dead man's pocket. This is Beppo, whom Holmes learns had worked part time for the distributor of the busts. Holmes then contacts Morse Hudson, the manufacturer of the busts, and learns that all four of the smashed busts were part of a set of six identical busts produced by his firm. Moreover, Hudson reports that Beppo had been at one time an employee; in fact, Beppo may have worked on the production of the busts. By this time, Lestrade's maniac theory has morphed into a Mafia theory, spurred by finding that Beppo is Italian.

Holmes, learning that six busts had been manufactured simultaneously and that one of the two that had not yet been smashed was located at Chiswick, determines to watch this property. Holmes and Lestrade conceal themselves outside the house of the owner of this bust. When Beppo arrives and smashes the bust, they seize him. This can be characterized as a secondary Gestalt moment. Whereas Lestrade focuses on the criminal, Holmes is concerned about the smashed bust; he examines the shards carefully, finding nothing of interest. Holmes then contacts the owner of the sixth and last bust in the set, promising him good money if he agrees to sell it. The man arrives, takes Holmes's money, gives Holmes the bust, and departs. Then comes the main Gestalt moment, derived from Holmes's conviction that the reason for smashing the busts must be that at least one of them contains some valuable object. Having secured the last of the six busts, Holmes duly smashes it, which reveals that it contains a beautiful black pearl. In fact, Holmes proclaims: "Gentlemen, let me introduce you

---

[41] I am especially indebted to Denis Burke for parts of my analysis of this story.
[42] Doyle, *Holmes*, II, 695.

to the famous black pearl of the Borgias," which Holmes announces is "the most famous pearl now existing."[43] Moreover, Holmes succeeds in showing that the pearl had been stolen about a year ago, that Beppo was probably involved in the robbery, and that he probably had taken the stone and hidden it by pushing it into the soft plaster of a Napoleonic bust on which he had been working.

Lestrade, duly impressed, speaks in terms of superlatives: "Well, I've seen you handle a good many cases, Mr. Holmes, but I don't know that I ever knew a more workmanlike one than that."[44] Watson reports on this incident, also in terms of uniqueness: "'Thank you!' said Holmes. 'Thank you!' and as he turned away, it seemed to me that he was more nearly moved by the softer human emotions than I had ever seen him."[45]

"Six Napoleons" is ranked among the best of the Sherlock Holmes stories. Its structure features a contrast between two Gestalts, corresponding to the methods of Lestrade and of Holmes. It also has two Gestalt shift points, but neither is as striking or as rapid as, for example, those in *Valley of Fear* or in "Twisted Lip." It seems clear that Holmes was correct when he used two superlatives in telling Watson that "Six Napoleons" "presents some features which make it *absolutely* original in the history of crime. If ever I permit you to chronicle any more of my little problems, Watson, I foresee that you will enliven your pages by an account of the singular adventure of the Napoleonic busts."[46]

[43] Doyle, *Holmes*, II, 694.
[44] Doyle, *Holmes*, II, 696.
[45] Doyle, *Holmes*, II, 696.
[46] Doyle, *Holmes*, II, 692.

"The Adventure of the Three Students" (1904)

Sometimes one can examine a Holmes story in terms of a Gestalt point of view in more than one way, with one image being more revealing than the other. This story provides a good illustration.

1. The story can be interpreted as featuring three Gestalts, corresponding to the three students competing for the prize. The question is: Who was it that had inappropriately examined the Thucydides text selected for the competition? Was it good-natured Gilchrist, who was both an athlete and a scholar, was it Daulet Ras, an Indian student who was seen nervously pacing in his room, or was it grumpy McLaren, a brilliant but dissipated student?

2. A second approach centers the question of *how* to solve this mystery and how to *prove* this solution. Let us first focus on locating the Gestalt shift point. It seems to occur the morning of the exam when Watson and Holmes have the following exchange:

"Have you anything positive to tell him?"
"I think so."
"You have formed a conclusion?"
"Yes, my dear Watson, I have solved the mystery."[47]

This seems problematic as a shift point if the key question is which student is guilty, but it makes sense if one thinks of a bipolar Gestalt centering on the question: *How* should one investigate this mystery? To most readers, the answer is obvious: Investigate the three students. Holmes's procedure embodies a different approach: he focuses on Bannister, the servant of the college tutor, Soames, whom Soames describes in the words "his honesty is absolutely above suspicion."[48] What leads Holmes to focus on Bannister is not that Bannister was so upset (he nearly fainted when he learned of the problem) nor the fact that Bannister had made the viewing of the exami-

---

[47] Doyle, *Holmes*, II, 705.
[48] Doyle, *Holmes*, II, 687.

nation possible by leaving his key in Soames's door; it was rather that Holmes early on had concluded that when Soames and Bannister entered Soames's study and found the examination papers disturbed, the culprit must have fled into Soames's bedroom and that Bannister was very probably aware of this. In other words, Holmes believes that "honest" Bannister was lying. Later Holmes and Watson speak to the three students and then set off to visit various stationers. During their search, Watson asks Holmes which of the three students seems the most likely culprit. In that context Holmes comments:

> "[T]hat fellow *does* puzzle me."
> "Who?"
> "Why, Bannister, the servant. What's his game in the matter?"
> "He impressed me as being a perfectly honest man."
> "So he did me. That's the puzzling part. Why should a perfectly honest man—"[49]

At this point they arrive at their destination, which keeps Holmes from finishing his sentence by such words as "repeatedly lie." Shortly after this, Holmes makes a significant remark to Watson in defining the problem they have been confronting as "the problem of the nervous tutor, the careless servant, and the three enterprising students."[50]

By the morning of the examination, Holmes has solved part of his problem; he has become convinced that Gilchrist was the intruder. This leaves a major issue unsolved: How is he to prove Gilchrist's guilt? He reveals his solution to this problem on the morning of the exam when Holmes and Watson meet with Soames.

Holmes proceeds to have the three arrange their chairs as a sort of court (Fig. 5.1) and then calls in not one of the students, but rather Bannister, to whom Holmes addresses the question:

> "Now, Bannister, will you please tell us the truth about yesterday's incident?"

---

[49] Doyle, *Holmes*, II, 705.
[50] Doyle, *Holmes*, II, 705.

The man turned white to the roots of his hair.
"I have told you everything, sir."[51]

Fig. 5.1   Bannister appears before the "court."

Bannister, showing increasing nervousness, repeats his denials, which leads
Holmes to tell Bannister to seat himself elsewhere in the room and to ask
Bannister to summon Gilchrist. Holmes then asks Gilchrist, "We want to
know, Mr. Gilchrist, how you, an honourable man, ever came to commit
such an action as that of yesterday?" This issues in a highly dramatic
moment, a sort of second Gestalt moment:

[51] Doyle, *Holmes*, II, 706.

The unfortunate young man staggered back, and cast a look full of horror and reproach at Bannister.

"No, no, Mr. Gilchrist, sir, I never said a word—never one word!" cried the servant.

"No, but you have now," said Holmes. "Now, sir, you must see that after Bannister's words your position is hopeless, and that your only chance lies in a frank confession."

For a moment Gilchrist, with upraised hand, tried to control his writhing features. The next he had thrown himself on his knees beside the table, and burying his face in his hands, he had burst into a storm of passionate sobbing.[52]

The remainder of the story details the actions of Bannister and Gilchrist and helps readers be sympathetic to their misdeeds. Moreover, it shows the correctness of Soames's comment to Holmes early in the story: "Your discretion is as well known as your powers,...."[53]

Before leaving this story, it seems appropriate to ask why Doyle put "Three Students" in its title and why he so stressed Bannister's honesty? We have a suggestion in the statement made by Doyle when he was asked how to write a good detective story. He advised: "Having got [the] key idea, one's next task is to conceal it and lay emphasis upon everything which can make for a different explanation."[54] I suspect that his motive in composing this story was not so much to deceive the reader as to create striking contrasts, and above all to instruct the reader that the most effective way of solving various cases may involve proceeding from an oblique direction.[55]

---

[52] Doyle, *Holmes*, II, 706.

[53] Doyle, *Holmes*, II, 696.

[54] Arthur Conan Doyle, *Memories and Adventures and Western Wanderings* (Newcastle on Tyne: Cambridge Scholars Publishing, 2009), 75.

[55] An example may illustrate this point. It is well known that Dr. Gregory House, the lead character in the highly successful TV series *House, M.D.* is based on Doyle's Sherlock Holmes. One of the most famous statements about medical practice made by Gregory House, the genius diagnostician at the center of this medical drama series, is: "Everybody lies." In other words, he is stressing the point, which many physicians would endorse, that a substantial portion of what patients say to their physicians is not to be trusted. This does not entail that the skillful medical diagnostician should pay no attention to what his or her patients say; rather, it means that the physician needs skillfully to interpret and decode what the patient is reporting. Dr. House also repeatedly listens to what relatives and other associates state about the patient's problems, but these comments must be decoded. Doyle was illustrating a parallel point: the skillful detective needs sophistication and insight into what clients tell them. On this overall point, see, for example, Henry Jacoby (ed.),

"The Adventure of the Golden Pince-Nez" (1904)

The main Gestalt shift in this story is of the Dalmatian type; in other words, confronted with confusion, one somehow suddenly sees an image that is clear and distinct. In this story the process is in two steps. The first shift occurs during Holmes's meeting with Inspector Stanley Hopkins, who lays out the clues that he has found concerning the death of Willoughby Smith, the assistant of Professor Coram. One of the chief clues is that before dying, Smith had uttered the words: "The Professor, it was she,"[56] which Hopkins did not take very seriously. Holmes is disappointed by Hopkins's report. Hopkins, however, nonchalantly shows Holmes another source: a golden pince-nez found in the dead man's hand. After a careful examination of it, Holmes presents Hopkins with a note containing his deductions concerning the person who killed Smith, commenting that this note is "the best that I can do for you." The note says:

> Wanted, a woman of good address, attired like a lady. She has a remarkably thick nose, with eyes which are set close upon either side of it. She has a puckered forehead, a peering expression, and probably rounded shoulders. There are indications that she has had recourse to an optician at least twice during the last few months. As her glasses are of remarkable strength and as opticians are not very numerous, there should be no difficulty in tracing her.[57]

This astonishes Hopkins and leads him to listens intently to Holmes's explanation, labeling it "marvelous."[58] And as experienced Sherlockians will expect, it turns out to be spot on. Detailed as this description is, it offers no clear method of apprehending the person, especially because no one in the household is forthcoming about whom this may be.

Success in locating the guilty person comes in a later part of the story, a part in which Holmes and Coram twice discuss the mystery. In these parts, Coram's Alexandrian cigarettes prove crucial. During this section of the story Coram asks Holmes:

> "Well, Mr. Holmes, have you solved this mystery yet?" He shoved the large tin of cigarettes which stood on a table beside him towards my companion.

House and Philosophy: Everybody Lies (Hoboken, N.J.: John Wiley & Sons, c. 2009) and also Donna Andrews, "Sex, Lies, and MRIs" in Leah Wilson, *House Unauthorized: Vasculitis, Clinic Duty, and Bad Bedside Manner* (Dallas: BenBella Books, 2007), 221–234.

[56] Doyle, *Holmes*, II, 712.

[57] Doyle, *Holmes*, II, 715.

[58] Doyle, *Holmes*, II, 716.

132 M. J. CROWE

Holmes stretched out his hand at the same moment, and between them they tipped the box over the edge. For a minute or two we were all on our knees retrieving stray cigarettes from impossible places. When we rose again I observed that Holmes's eyes were shining and his cheeks tinged with colour. Only at a crisis have I seen those battle-signals flying.

"Yes," said he, "I have solved it."

Stanley Hopkins and I stared in amazement. Something like a sneer quivered over the gaunt features of the old Professor.

"Indeed! In the garden?"

"No, here."

"Here! When?"

"This instant."

"You are surely joking, Mr. Sherlock Holmes...."

"I have forged and tested every link of my chain, Professor Coram, and I am sure that it is sound."[59]

How were the cigarettes crucial? Holmes in an earlier session chain-smoked a number of Coram's cigarettes while pacing the floor of Coram's study. What Holmes was actually doing was laying down a blanket of ash to see whether someone else, presumably the murderer, was concealed in Coram's study. Then when Holmes returns a few hours later to the study, he spills the cigarettes all over the floor and in picking them up detects footprints in the ash. Holmes then tells Coram that the woman came into his study yesterday after the killing and has remained in the study. Coram responds:

"And you mean to say that I could lie upon that bed and not be aware that a woman had entered my room?"

"I never said so. You WERE aware of it. You spoke with her. You recognised her. You aided her to escape."

Again the Professor burst into high-keyed laughter. He had risen to his feet and his eyes glowed like embers.

"You are mad!" he cried. "You are talking insanely. I helped her to escape? Where is she now?"

"She is there," said Holmes, and he pointed to a high bookcase in the corner of the room.

I saw the old man throw up his arms, a terrible convulsion passed over his grim face, and he fell back in his chair. At the same instant the bookcase at which Holmes pointed swung round upon a hinge, and a woman rushed out into the room. "You are right!" she cried, in a strange foreign voice. "You are right! I am here."[60]

---

[59] Doyle, *Holmes*, II, 722.
[60] Doyle, *Holmes*, II, 723.

Holmes had once again[61] made a culprit appear almost as from nowhere (Fig. 5.2). We learn that the woman had been married to Coram in Russia, when Coram years ago turned over false information on her and her "dear friend" to the government, which led to the friend's being sent to Siberia. She had come to England, hoping to find Coram (not his real name) and get the evidence she needed to free her friend, and had accidently killed Smith when he detected her opening Coram's files.

Fig. 5.2   Coram's wife suddenly appears.

With this exposure, major changes occur: Coram is revealed as an international rogue Russian and traitor to his wife. The woman is revealed as his wife and she dies by having taken poison just before leaving her hiding place. And Holmes is again seen as a detective who performs feats that might challenge a magician.

---

[61] As in *Study in Scarlet*, "Black Peter," "Norwood Builder," and later in *Valley of Fear*.

"The Adventure of the Missing Three-Quarter"
(1904)

This story opens with Holmes receiving a cryptic telegram: "Please await me. Terrible misfortune. Right wing three-quarter missing, indispensable to-morrow. Overton."[62] Soon the sender arrives, coming from a world that frequently rivals if it does not surpass the stage in dramatic intensity: sport. Cyril Overton, somewhat surprised that Holmes and Watson do not recognize his name, is flat out amazed that they do not know the name Godfrey Staunton, whom Overton describes as "skipper of the Rugger [rugby] team of Cambridge 'Varsity' [Trinity College of Cambridge University]."[63] Regarding Staunton, Overton remarks, "I didn't think there was a soul in England who didn't know Godfrey Staunton, the crack three-quarter, Cambridge, Blackheath, and five Internationals. Good Lord! Mr. Holmes, where *have* you lived?"[64] Problem is: Staunton has disappeared just before their big match with Oxford University. Overton explains that Staunton is an orphan and also heir of Lord Mount-James, one of the richest men (and tightest misers) in England. The image readers get of Staunton from this introductory section is that he is an athletic powerhouse, but somewhat unreliable. Nonetheless, Holmes begins to investigate, attaining some success by visiting a telegraph office from which Staunton had sent a message.

Soon Holmes makes contact with two difficult men, the first being Lord Mount-James, who fears that Holmes will uncover information that will hurt Staunton's reputation and, perhaps worse, result in Mount-James's having to pay Holmes a fee. Holmes tactfully pacifies Mount-James by mentioning the possibility of a kidnapping, and what this might cost him. The other difficult man is Leslie Armstrong, a physician in Cambridge, who had sent Staunton a telegram and who now fears that Holmes may discover and reveal some of Staunton's secrets. Holmes makes various efforts, nearly all unsuccessful, to determine Armstrong's relation to Staunton, all of which efforts Armstrong foils. Finally, Holmes succeeds by spraying the wheels of Armstrong's carriage with aniseed and employing a bloodhound to trace his travels.

[62] Doyle, *Holmes*, II, 727.
[63] Doyle, *Holmes*, II, 729.
[64] Doyle, *Holmes*, II, 728.

This succeeds, leading Holmes and Watson to a cottage from which comes "a low sound … a drone of misery and despair which was indescribably melancholy."[65] Entering they see a "woman, young and beautiful, lying dead upon the bed. Her calm, pale face, with dim, wide-opened blue eyes, looked upward from amid a great tangle of golden hair. At the foot of the bed, half sitting, half kneeling, his face buried in the clothes, is a young man, whose frame was racked by his sobs."[66] This is Staunton. Soon Dr. Armstrong arrives and explains that Staunton had married the young woman a year earlier, but she had developed a virulent strain of consumption, which Dr. Armstrong had been treating. Staunton had kept the marriage secret, fearing that his miserly uncle would disinherit him.

With this the image of Staunton as world-class athlete who would desert those around him at their time of greatest need totally changes. Now readers recognize that Staunton has priorities far higher than those of sport; he is a person of great compassion who shows intense loyalty to the person nearest and dearest to him. Also, Holmes recognizes Armstrong as a physician dedicated to helping Staunton and his wife and to preserving their secret, whereas Armstrong sees Holmes as a fellow professional who shares these priorities and in fact can do more than Livingston to preserve Staunton's secret commitments and reputation. This story, like so many other Holmes stories, exhibits the feature that at its end readers realize that various views they may have adopted about most of the characters need almost total revision (Lord Mount-James is an exception). Moreover, what appears at first to be a story of competition turns out to be a story of compassion.

[65] Doyle, *Holmes*, II, 742.
[66] Doyle, *Holmes*, II, 742.

"THE ADVENTURE OF THE ABBEY GRANGE" (1904)

Two competing Gestalts are central in this story, but the situation in quite complex. On the one hand, there is a Gestalt story (account of the murder of Sir Eustace Brackenstall) that Lady Brackenstall and her maid present to Hopkins and Holmes along with an ample amount of evidence. Their account even names the culprits (the Redding gang). It has the good feature that it leaves Lady Brackenstall and her maid as fully innocent. Inspector Hopkins throughout the story accepts this account. Initially Holmes does as well. Gradually, however, Holmes begins to see some of the evidence as anomalous and possibly contradictory to the account supplied to them. In fact, Holmes sets off from Abbey Grange with Watson to return to London still accepting this theory, but near the end of the journey Holmes announces to Watson that they must return to Abbey Grange because he has seen that the case will not hold up. The evidence that triggers this change of mind consists of a seemingly trivial fact: the amount of bee's wax in one of the three wine glasses from which the alleged murderers had drunk. As Watson reports to his readers, Holmes states:

> I am sorry to make you the victim of what may seem a mere whim, but on my life, Watson, I simply *can't* leave that case in this condition. Every instinct that I possess cries out against it. It's wrong—it's all wrong—I'll swear that it's wrong. And yet the lady's story was complete, the maid's corroboration was sufficient, the detail was fairly exact. What have I to put up against that? Three wine-glasses, that is all.[67]

At this stage, we can describe Holmes as having discarded the first Gestalt after having glimpsed only portions of a second Gestalt, which eventually attributes the murder to a tall, agile, and strong man with a naval background (who later turns out to be Captain Jack Crocker) and whose existence was hidden by a false account that Lady Brackenstall and her maid presented to the detectives. Gradually, such evidence leads Holmes to begin to see another Gestalt story, at first having only second-rate clues. It turns out (at least such is Captain Crocker's claim) that Brackenstall died in a fight with the thoroughly honorable Crocker, that the maid and Lady Brackenstall aided in covering this up, but that they had good reasons for doing what they did. The problem was that in the first year of his marriage Sir Eustace already had shown himself to be alcoholic and abusive.

[67] Doyle, *Holmes*, II, 751.

A key development in the story consists of Holmes locating the tall, agile, and strong man with a naval background, Holmes having inferred the last attribute from the naval knots used in tying up Lady Brackenstall. This is Captain Crocker, who was in love with Lady Brackenstall even before her marriage. Holmes confronts Crocker, who admits having taken Brackenstall's life, but in self-defense. Another key development against Hopkins's construal was that on the day after Brackenstall's death the leading suspects (Redding gang) were arrested in New York, which proved their innocence.

A significant complexity of the story is that, although Holmes had full knowledge that Crocker had killed Brackenstall and that Lady Brackenstall had collaborated in his efforts to conceal this from the police, Holmes with Watson's support had decided that he was morally justified in keeping this information from Hopkins because he had acquired it as a private person. In addition, after nearly reporting his results to Scotland Yard, he decides against this action, explaining to Watson:

> "No, I couldn't do it, Watson," said he, as we reentered our room. "Once that warrant was made out, nothing on earth would save him. Once or twice in my career I feel that I have done more real harm by my discovery of the criminal than ever he had done by his crime. I have learned caution now, and I had rather play tricks with the law of England than with my own conscience."[68]

This creates a situation in which the reader may fully agree with Holmes's conclusions as to what happened, but strongly disagree with Holmes's decision to keep his conclusions and its evidence from Hopkins and the British courts. One curious feature of the story is that it was published only seven years after the events occurred. One can imagine that Hopkins upon reading the story would decide to prosecute Crocker and Lady Brackenstall, and possibly even Holmes.

[68] Doyle, *Holmes*, II, 756.

"The Adventure of the Second Stain" (1904)

This story offers excellent illustrations of the fact that two or more persons can look at the same entity but see it very differently. Consider the letter and envelope so central to this story. One observation of it is that it is on high quality paper, but it may be as insignificant as most letters. A fire can totally destroy it in seconds; a toss toward a waste can will no doubt have the same effect. To Lord Bellinger, "twice Premier of Britain" and to Trelawney Hope, Britain's "Right Honorable Secretary of European Affairs," the letter from an unnamed "foreign Potentate" seems

> of such immense importance that its publication might very easily—I might almost say probably—lead to European complications of the utmost moment. It is not too much to say that peace or war may hang upon the issue. Unless its recovery can be attended with the utmost secrecy, then it may as well not be recovered at all, for all that is aimed at by those who have taken it is that its contents should be generally known.[69]

Holmes shows his distinguished clients that he understands their message by stating that failure to recover this letter "may well mean the expenditure of a thousand millions and the lives of a hundred thousand men."[70] To the lovely Lady Hilda Hope, wife of the European Secretary, the letter can lead to nothing less than the recovery of an indiscreet letter she had written before her marriage. To her husband, his loss of the letter would almost certainly lead to his disgrace and cost him his career. To Watson, the letter is the centerpiece of Holmes's "most important international case."[71] To spy Eduardo Lucas, who had secured the letter, its sale or ransom would probably have brought a fortune, had he survived beyond the first few hours after securing it. Holmes also is aware of the importance of this case; in fact, he realizes that the recovery of the letter would "certainly represent the crowning glory of my career."[72]

It is not only objects but also people who can appear very different. Consider Lucas: The English public views him as a prominent and successful bachelor of "charming personality" and "one of the best amateur ten-

---

[69] Doyle, *Holmes*, II, 762.
[70] Doyle, *Holmes*, II, 764.
[71] Doyle, *Holmes*, II, 761.
[72] Doyle, *Holmes*, II, 772.

ors in the country."[73] To Scotland Yard, his murder seems a tragedy to which they should devote their attention, which certainly would not have occurred had they known of the internationally important crime he had committed shortly before his death. Lady Hilda saw him as despicable, but also the savior of her reputation. His wife, who stabbed him, saw him as an adulterer and viewed Lady Hilda as an adulteress. To Holmes, who had a wide-angle view, Lucas and his death offer very possibly the path to a recovery of the stolen letter. After Watson suggests that Scotland Yard may now become central, Holmes responds:

> Not at all. They know all they see at Godolphin Street [Lucas's address]. They know—and shall know—nothing of Whitehall Terrace. Only *we* know of both events, and can trace the relation between them. There is one obvious point which would, in any case, have turned my suspicions against Lucas. Godolphin Street, Westminster, is only a few minutes' walk from Whitehall Terrace. The other secret agents whom I have named live in the extreme West End. It was easier, therefore, for Lucas than for the others to establish a connection or receive a message from the European Secretary's household—a small thing, and yet where events are compressed into a few hours it may prove essential.[74]

Holmes was not surprised that three days after the murder of Lucas, Lestrade sought his help regarding the murder. Hoping that such contact might have bearing on the major crime, although Scotland Yard knew nothing of it, Holmes obliges, and is rewarded for doing so. This contact leads to a second Gestalt moment, when Holmes while in Lucas's residence notices the significance of the fact that the position of the bloodstain on Lucas's rug is different from the bloodstain on the floor. Lestrade see this as a "mere trifle,"[75] but Holmes views it with great excitement and manages to get Lestrade out of the room long enough to search for a hiding place in the floor, which he finds contains NOTHING. At first disappointed, Holmes soon realizes the significance of this: It indicates that Lady Hilda had made a second visit to Lucas's lodging, this time succeeding in locating and removing the letter of international importance. Soon Holmes and Watson set off for the home of the European Secretary, Holmes assessing the situation and its global significance:

[73] Doyle, *Holmes*, II, 766–767.
[74] Doyle, *Holmes*, II, 767.
[75] Doyle, *Holmes*, II, 773.

Come, friend Watson, the curtain rings up for the last act. You will be relieved to hear that there will be no war, that the Right Honourable Trelawney Hope will suffer no setback in his brilliant career, that the indiscreet Sovereign will receive no punishment for his indiscretion, that the Prime Minister will have no European complication to deal with, and that with a little tact and management upon our part nobody will be a penny the worse for what might have been a very ugly incident.[76]

Arriving at the Trelawney Hope residence, Holmes persuades Lady Hilda to admit that she has the letter and also to agree to a method by which she can restore it without having to admit her actions to her husband. The claim would be that it had simply been overlooked in the box. Just then, the European Secretary and Premier arrive. Although stressing their belief that a search of the box would be fruitless, they finally agree. When this search turns up the letter, the Premier exclaims in delight "Mr. Holmes, you are a wizard, a sorcerer!"[77] A final, if smaller and subtler Gestalt shift follows, as the Premier with "twinkling eyes" asks Holmes privately what actually happened. When Holmes responds, "We too must have our diplomatic secrets,"[78] the Premier graciously lets the matter drop. Thus Holmes had found a method to avoid war not only on the international front, but also in Britain's government and in the Hope family.

In short, this discussion has attempted to show that a Gestalt shift approach can effectively be used to describe this case, where entities—persons, objects, activities—all undergo major changes in how the characters conceive them.

---

[76] Doyle, *Holmes*, II, 775.
[77] Doyle, *Holmes*, II, 780.
[78] Doyle, *Holmes*, II, 780.

Bibliography

Printed Sources

Andrews, Donna. "Sex, Lies, and MRIs" in Leah Wilson, *House Unauthorized: Vasculitis, Clinic Duty, and Bad Bedside Manner* (Dallas: BenBella Books, 2007), 221–234.

Dakin, D. Martin. *A Sherlock Holmes Commentary* (Newton Abbot: David & Charles, 1976).

Doyle, Arthur Conan. *The Complete Sherlock Holmes,* 2 vols. (New York: Doubleday, 1953).

Jacoby, Henry, ed. *House and Philosophy: Everybody Lies* (Hoboken, N.J.: John Wiley & Sons, c. 2009).

CHAPTER 6

His Last Bow (1917)

"The Adventure of Wisteria Lodge" (1908)

Let us begin near the end of this story when Holmes comments to Watson:

> "A chaotic case, my dear Watson," said Holmes over an evening pipe. "It will not be possible for you to present in that compact form which is dear to your heart. It covers two continents, concerns two groups of mysterious persons, and is further complicated by the highly respectable presence of our friend, Scott Eccles, whose inclusion shows me that the deceased Garcia had a scheming mind and a well-developed instinct of self-preservation. It is remarkable only for the fact that amid a perfect jungle of possibilities we, with our worthy collaborator, the inspector, have kept our close hold on the essentials and so been guided along the crooked and winding path."[1]

Conan Doyle, in writing this story, faced some serious problems. The case involved his client (Scott Eccles) and three people: Inspector Baynes, a rural, unimpressive looking detective; Garcia, a somewhat shady friend of his client, who had a home in rural England served by some strange staff; and Henderson, a respectable neighbor about whom little was known. This does not seem to be the making of an engaging and memorable story. Let us see what Doyle does with these characters.

---

[1] Doyle, *Holmes*, II, 1042–1043.

© The Author(s) 2018
M. J. Crowe, *The Gestalt Shift in Conan Doyle's Sherlock Holmes Stories*, https://doi.org/10.1007/978-3-319-98291-5_6

1. Inspector Baynes: In previous stories, Doyle had contrasted Holmes with various police figures, most from Scotland Yard—for example, Gregson, Jones, and Lestrade—all of whom Doyle presents as basically bunglers or at least defective detectives when compared to Holmes. Readers encountering Inspector Baynes would naturally expect Baynes to be of comparable competence to his predecessors, especially after Watson described this "county detective" as "a stout, puffy, red man, whose face was only redeemed from grossness by two extraordinarily bright eyes, almost hidden behind the heavy creases of cheek and brow."[2] In fact, by the end of the story, Baynes has managed to match Holmes at every step, sometimes reaching the same result by a different approach. Late in the story Holmes discovers that Baynes was after Henderson just as Holmes had been. Holmes's surprise is evident when he asks: "What, you were after Henderson?" And Baynes replies: "Why, Mr. Holmes, when you were crawling in the shrubbery at High Gable I was up one of the trees in the plantation and saw you down below. It was just who would get his evidence first."[3]

2. Henderson: Henderson is reclusive but also a prosperous occupant of one of the best houses in the area. Late in the story, after Garcia had attempted to murder him, Holmes turns to Baynes with a key question: "But tell me, Baynes, who is this man Henderson?" "Henderson," the inspector answered, "is Don Murillo, once called the Tiger of San Pedro."[4] This leads Holmes to predict to Baynes: "You will rise high in your profession. You have instinct and intuition."[5]

3. Garcia: We first see Garcia acting suspiciously; for example, he devises a method of using Holmes's client, Eccles, as an alibi in Garcia's efforts to murder Henderson. Moreover, Garcia's servants at his home are a very suspicious group, who seem also to be involved in the murder attempt. By the end of the story, we see that Garcia "is the noble, chivalrous Garcia who has fallen, while the monster [Henderson] goes safe."[6] These are the words of Miss Burnet, whose husband Henderson had murdered and who bravely aided Garcia by getting a job as governess of

[2] Doyle, *Holmes*, II, 1026.
[3] Doyle, *Holmes*, II, 1039.
[4] Doyle, *Holmes*, II, 1026. D. Martin Dakin states that he was unable to identify a Central American city or country that has the name San Pedro. See Dakin's *A Sherlock Holmes Commentary* (Newton Abbot: David and Charles, 1972), 219.
[5] Doyle, *Holmes*, II, 1026.
[6] Doyle, *Holmes*, II, 1040.

Henderson's children. She forcefully describes not only Henderson's character but also the difficulties of preventing him from further atrocities, when she explains to Holmes and Baynes why she had participated in the plot:

> I join in it because there is no other way in the world by which justice can be gained. What does the law of England care for the rivers of blood shed years ago in San Pedro, or for the shipload of treasure which this man has stolen? To you they are like crimes committed in some other planet. But we know. We have learned the truth in sorrow and in suffering. To us there is no fiend in hell like Juan Murillo, and no peace in life while his victims still cry for vengeance.[7]

And a bonus: As the last quotation, especially in conjunction with the first quotation in this analysis, suggests, a central contrast in the story is between England and the Central America of the Tiger of San Pedro. The citizens and police of San Pedro were unable to bring Murillo to justice. England, on the other hand, has a magnificent police force that seems helpless in ridding the planet of this monster. He is simply a resident whom the police would protect as much as they would protect Eccles. Watson reminds them of this dilemma by stating: "A plausible lawyer could make [Henderson's killing of Garcia] out as an act of self-defense. There may be a hundred crimes in the background, but it is only on this one that they can be tried."[8] Baynes responds from the other side by suggesting: "Come, come, ... I think better of the law than that. Self-defense is one thing. To entice a man in cold blood with the object of murdering him is another, whatever danger you may fear from him. No, no, we shall all be justified when we see the tenants of High Gable at the next Guildford Assizes."[9]

---

[7] Doyle, *Holmes*, II, 1040.
[8] Doyle, *Holmes*, II, 1042.
[9] Doyle, *Holmes*, II, 1042.

"THE ADVENTURE OF THE CARDBOARD BOX" (1893)

Introductory Note: The publishing history of this story is somewhat complicated. It was first published in January 1893 in *The Strand Magazine*. It then appeared in the American edition of *The Memoirs of Sherlock Holmes* (1893), but at Doyle's initiative was not included in the British version of *Memoirs*. It later appeared in America as the second story of *His Last Bow* (1917) and eventually in British editions of *The Memoirs of Sherlock Holmes*.[10]

This story centers on the reception by Susan Cushing, a fifty-year-old unmarried woman who was the eldest of three sisters, of a mailed cardboard box containing two non-matching human ears preserved in salt. The reader is offered two Gestalt accounts as to how this package should be perceived: (1) Lestrade's view, which was that the package was a joke sent by medical students who had formerly been roomers at Susan Cushing's house until their behavior led her to ask them to move elsewhere; and (2) Holmes's view, which interpreted the package as evidence of criminal action that should be investigated.[11] Note the striking contrast: For Lestrade, the box is a sort of prank; for Holmes, the box points to a horrific double murder.

The structure of the story is more complicated than this. In particular, Holmes, after investigating what seems a paucity of evidence, surprises Watson and Lestrade by what he claims in the following conversation, which began immediately after Holmes received an answer to a telegram that he has sent, and which can be described as the Gestalt moment in the story:

"Have you found out anything?"
"I have found out everything!"
"What!" Lestrade stared at him in amazement. "You are joking."
"I was never more serious in my life. A shocking crime has been committed, and I think I have now laid bare every detail of it."
"And the criminal?"

[10] On this matter, see Leslie S. Klinger, "The Textual Problem of the Resident Patient" at http://www.sherlockian.net/canon/klinger.html. Viewed December 31, 2014, and http://en.wikipedia.org/wiki/The_Adventure_of_the_Cardboard_Box. Viewed December 31, 2014.
[11] Doyle, *Holmes*, II, 1048.

Holmes scribbled a few words upon the back of one of his visiting cards and threw it over to Lestrade.

"That is the name," he said. "You cannot effect an arrest until to-morrow night at the earliest. I should prefer that you do not mention my name at all in connection with the case, as I choose to be only associated with those crimes which present some difficulty in their solution."[12]

Of course, there are many stories in which Holmes finds evidence that leads to the apprehension of the criminal. It is to be noted that this conversation enhances the contrast between the situation before and after Holmes's arrival. What Lestrade viewed as a prank Holmes has interpreted as a double murder that demands attention. Having adopted this view, Holmes builds on it to identify not only the murdered persons but also the criminal, why the criminal acted as he did, and how Lestrade could apprehend him.

The clues Holmes uses to attain these results are in most cases *as clues* invisible to Lestrade and probably to readers. For example, from the lack of embalming fluid in the ears, Holmes infers that medical students were not involved. From the knots in and the nature of the twine around the package, Holmes concludes that the culprit was a seaman and supported this idea by noting that the package had been mailed from Belfast, a port town. Moreover, Holmes's detailed knowledge of the structure and configurations of human ears enables him to recognize that one of the ears must have been cut from one of Susan's two sisters. And from seemingly irrelevant information supplied by Susan, he concludes that Susan's sister, Mary, must have been one of the victims. From learning that Mary had been married to a strong and willful sailor named James Browner who was addicted to alcohol, Holmes infers that he was the murderer. Moreover, from realizing that the other sister was Sara and from learning that she, like Susan, was living in Croydon, Holmes plausibly concludes that the package addressed to "S. Cushing" must have been mistakenly sent to the wrong sister. The male ear Holmes infers came from Alec Fairburn. He was a man who had had (as a result of efforts made by Sara) an adulterous affair with Mary. This led to Browner's anger at both Fairburn and Mary.

---

[12] Doyle, *Holmes*, II, 1052.

"The Adventure of the Red Circle" (1911)

At its beginning this story about a lodger in a boarding house seems rather insignificant; in fact, at one point, Holmes describes it as "Mrs. Warren's whimsical problem."[13] The story begins with a report from Mrs. Warren that a bearded man has sought lodging under unusual conditions. These include that food be brought to him and left outside his door, which entails that he would not be seen. The reader at this stage comes to believe that the lodger is hiding out, which seems suspicious. Mrs. Warren, becoming worried about this arrangement, asks Holmes to investigate. He demurs until Mrs. Warren reports that a group of thugs had carried off her husband for an hour but then released him, it being evident that they were trying to capture the lodger. Holmes then becomes involved and with Watson hides in a room opposite the lodger's room to see him when he opens the door to get the meal left for him. All are surprised when the lodger turns out to be a lovely young woman, not a man. This raises the question: How do the man and woman communicate? Holmes, noting that each day the woman receives only one newspaper (the *Daily Gazette*), checks its recent "agony" columns and detects a code and signals that seem relevant. This leads Holmes and Watson to come to the street near where the lodger has a room to watch for signals, which they in fact detect. The messages are in Italian and show a level of desperation. Moreover, they run into Inspector Gregson, who along with a Pinkerton detective is investigating the matter, in hopes of apprehending an internationally known Italian mobster, Giuseppe Gorgiano, who according to the Pinkerton detective is known to be "at the bottom of fifty murders."[14] This is the Gestalt shift point in the story, where what had been seen as a "whimsical problem" takes on a clearly criminal, indeed internationally significant criminal aspect.

Nearly simultaneously, Holmes detects that the signals from the building opposite the room of the lodger have suddenly ceased. This leads the three detectives and Watson to enter the building from which the signals had come. There they find the dead body of a huge man who had been knifed in the throat. After Holmes uses the code to encourage the lodger to come, they learn from her that the dead body is that of Gorgiano. Moreover, she expresses great relief that her husband, Gennaro Lucca, has killed Gorgiano, whose goal was to kill her husband because Gennaro had

[13] Doyle, *Holmes*, II, 1066
[14] Doyle, *Holmes*, II, 1068.

refused to commit a murder assigned him by the Mafia-like group called the Red Circle. In effect, with this the Gestalt shift culminates. Within a short span to time, we come to see the mystery as global (at least international), and the result as being life-saving for Gennaro and Emilia Lucca. Gregson and the Pinkerton detective have finally found Gorgiano and secured clear evidence of his malicious actions. Once again, we are surprised that what appears to be a minor mystery emerges as an internationally significant capture by Holmes, Emilia, Gregson, and the Pinkerton agent. It is important to add that in this delineation of the structure of this case (as in many other instances in this book) numerous clues, subtleties, and details have of necessity been left unmentioned in an effort to highlight the overall dynamic and drama of the story.

"THE ADVENTURE OF THE BRUCE-PARTINGTON PLANS"
(1908)

One feature of the Gestalt approach is that it fits very well with the idea of a Gestalt shift point or Gestalt shift moment. I have become ever more convinced that in many of the stories, one can locate a particular point where Doyle devotes his skills to leading the reader to see that Holmes has attained an insight of singular importance, which convinces Holmes that he is on the right path to solving the mystery and even capturing the evil doer. At this point, Holmes may not yet have a total solution, but he is convinced that among the possible explanations of the events and clues, one particular development is crucial. The "Adventure of the Bruce-Partington Plans" exemplifies this pattern. About one third of the way through the story, Holmes worries that no solution is emerging. It appears that Cadogan West has stolen plans for a revolutionary new submarine, but then has been killed on an Underground carriage and his body thrown near the tracks. At this time, Holmes, Lestrade, and Watson go investigate the area on the Underground line where the body of Cadogan West had been found. Holmes and others are puzzled by the facts that not only are there no witnesses to West's death but also there is very little blood where West's body was found, nor did anyone find blood in any car on the line. At one point, Lestrade asks: "Why, whatever is the matter with Mr. Holmes?" Watson then gives the reader a very clear signal that something is happening.

> My friend was standing with an expression of strained intensity upon his face, staring at the railway metals where they curved out of the tunnel. Aldgate is a junction, and there was a network of points. On these his eager, questioning eyes were fixed, and I saw on his keen, alert face that tightening of the lips, that quiver of the nostrils, and concentration of the heavy, tufted brows which I knew so well.
> "Points," he muttered; "the points."
> "What of it? What do you mean?"
> "I suppose there are no great number of points on a system such as this?"
> "No; they are very few."
> "And a curve, too. Points, and a curve. By Jove! if it were only so."[15]

---

[15] Doyle, *Holmes*, II, 1081–1082.

Shortly thereafter, Holmes and Watson depart, Holmes sends off a telegram to Mycroft, and Watson uses a metaphor to stress again the degree to which this transformed Holmes:

> His eager face still wore that expression of intense and high-strung energy, which showed me that some novel and suggestive circumstance had opened up a stimulating line of thought. See the foxhound with hanging ears and drooping tail as it lolls about the kennels, and compare it with the same hound as, with gleaming eyes and straining muscles, it runs upon a breast-high scent—such was the change in Holmes since the morning. He was a different man from the limp and lounging figure in the mouse-coloured dressing-gown who had prowled so restlessly only a few hours before round the fog-girt room.[16]

Holmes then confides to Watson his assessment of the investigation and also reveals the insight that has so excited him: "The end is dark to me also, but I have hold of one idea which may lead us far. The man met his death elsewhere, and his body was on the *roof* of a carriage."[17] It is important to understand that Holmes's excitement was not solely due to his having attained an explanation of why West's body lay near the tracks and in a particular condition; it was also this recognition that allows Holmes to take his investigation to an entirely new level. Watson gives a hint of this by having Holmes request in the telegram to Mycroft "a complete list of all foreign spies or international agents known to be in England, with full address."[18] Comparing this list with the areas where the Underground had passed allows Holmes to conclude that Oberstein, whose lodgings were adjacent to the track, must be the person who killed West. Further developments occur in the story, but nearly all depend on this key recognition.

In outline, the further developments are that Holmes and Watson burgle Oberstein's lodgings, finding copies of ads in the agony column of a newspaper, which ads Oberstein uses to contact the as yet unknown person who stole the plans. Holmes then places a further communication in Oberstein's style in the newspaper, which brings Colonel Valentine Walter, who admits being the thief but denies committing murder. Holmes then

[16] Doyle, *Holmes*, II, 1082.
[17] Doyle, *Holmes*, II, 1082.
[18] Doyle, *Holmes*, II, 1082.

has Walter contact Oberstein offering further secret materials, which leads to the arrest of Oberstein and the recovery of the original plans.[19]

Watson makes it clear that this was a case of great significance. At his narrative's opening he stresses that it was important enough to bring Mycroft Holmes, who was the "most indispensable man in the country," and at times "*is* the British Government"[20] to seek the assistance of his younger brother. And at story's end, Watson relates that Holmes mentions to him that he had just spent a day at Windsor where an "august [and] gracious lady" had presented him with "a remarkably fine emerald tie-pin."[21]

---

[19] An interesting question that this story suggests is this: In perceiving a Gestalt does one typically see it all at once? The aha experience that usually accompanies a Gestalt shift proceeds very rapidly, but perhaps in various stages. In coming to see the Dalmatian Gestalt, one may first see an ear or a collar or leg, with the dog following on this. In the duck/rabbit Gestalt shift, one first sees the ears of the rabbit turn into the beak of the duck. What is striking in this case is that from recognizing the railway points as significant, one ends up with a major clue to where the murder occurred.

[20] Doyle, *Holmes*, II, 1075–1076.

[21] Doyle, *Holmes*, II, 1096.

"The Adventure of the Dying Detective" (1913)

The structure of this story depends on two Gestalt shifts, one more obvious than the other, but both very important. Holmes, who has taken on many disguises, seeks to convince a criminal, Culverton Smith, that Holmes is dying. To attain this appearance, Holmes takes on various actors' accouterments and also starves himself for five days. To test his success in appearing to be near death, Holmes gets Martha Hudson to contact Watson. She reports: "He's dying, Dr. Watson…. For three days he has been sinking, and I doubt he will last the day." She insists on getting a doctor; Holmes replies: "Let it be Watson."[22] Watson arrives and is deeply saddened to see Holmes's condition and offers medical treatment. Holmes refuses, and in fact will not let Watson near him. When Watson asks Holmes to allow him to get a doctor. Holmes replies:

> "If I am to have a doctor…, let it be one in whom I have confidence," said [Holmes].
> "Then you have none in me?"
> "In your friendship, certainly. But facts are facts, Watson, and, after all, you are only a general practitioner … with mediocre qualifications."
> I was bitterly hurt.[23]

Watson stays with Holmes for a period, during which Holmes seems delirious. Then Holmes instructs Watson to fetch Culverton Smith, a resident of Sumatra then visiting London who is an expert on tropical illnesses, to treat him. Watson does as requested, even forcing his way past Smith's butler, to gain an audience. Smith strongly objects to visiting the sick man until he learns that it is Holmes who requested him and that he is near death. Then he agrees. Holmes had instructed Watson to return before Smith arrives. When Watson does this, he finds Holmes far more coherent but no less sickly in appearance. Holmes then instructs Watson to hide behind the head of Holmes's bed, the reason being that Smith would be more ready to provide a diagnosis if no one else were present. TI₁ ₗₗ₁₁ ₗ₁ ₗₗ₁ W₁₁₁₁₁ "A₁₁₁ ₗₗ₁₁₁'₁ ₗ₁₁₁ₗₗ₁ , ₗₗ₁₁₁ ₁₁ ₁ ₗₗ₁₁₁₁ ₁₁₁"[24]

After Smith arrives, he and Holmes converse, Holmes asking whether he has the same disease that killed Victor Savage, who had told Holmes that

---

[22] Doyle, *Holmes*, II, 1097.
[23] Doyle, *Holmes*, II, 1098.
[24] Doyle, *Holmes*, II, 1104.

Smith had infected him. Smith admits this and also explains to the dying Holmes that Smith had also infected Holmes, using a spring-loaded ivory box. Holmes admits that he had opened the box and was cut in the process. Smith remarks how pleased he is to have outsmarted such an intelligent man and freely discusses his murder method. At one point, Holmes, his voice ever weakening, asks Smith to turn up the lights in the room. As Smith does this, Holmes's voice suddenly sounds better as he asks Smith for a "match and a cigarette."[25] Almost immediately thereafter, Inspector Morton opens the door and soon has Smith in handcuffs. This is the first Gestalt shift and moment: the apparently miraculous cure of the dying Holmes, and the capture with solid evidence of a murderer. Shortly after Smith points out that Holmes had no witness to support any allegations that he might make against Smith, Holmes calls forth Watson from behind the head of the bed! And soon thereafter, the second Gestalt shift occurs. Holmes proceeds to explain to Watson that he was confident that if he could convince Watson and his "astute judgment"[26] that he was near death, Watson would reliably convey this message to Smith. Moreover, Holmes explains that he would not let Watson be near him, because he was convinced that as a skillful physician, Watson would immediately detect that Holmes was not severely ill. As the story ends, Smith is taken to the police station, after which a hungry Holmes and a relieved Watson set off to dine at Simpson's.

[25] Doyle, *Holmes*, II, 1106.
[26] Doyle, *Holmes*, II, 1108.

"The Disappearance of Lady Frances Carfax" (1911)

Arthur Conan Doyle loved contrasts. In fact, he structured this story around four bipolar Gestalt contrasts. And it ends with another Gestalt shift centered on a remarkable murder weapon.

1. Lady Frances Carfax: We encounter her as "a beautiful woman, still in fresh middle age,"[27] "a good and pious lady,"[28] who travels in Europe using funds derived from having inherited precious jewelry. She is also the victim, whose life Holmes desperately tries to save. Holmes sees a contrasting side of her: "One of the most dangerous classes in the world is the drifting and friendless woman. She is the most harmless and often the most useful of mortals, but she is the inevitable inciter of crime in others."[29] An even more fundamental contrast in the story concerns the issue of whether or not Lady Frances has been killed.

2. Philip Green: When we first meet him, Watson suggests to Holmes that Green appears as a "savage." Holmes's response is: "Exactly. ... He is a bulky, bearded, sunburned fellow, who looks as if he would be more at home in a farmers' inn than in a fashionable hotel. A hard, fierce man, I should think, and one whom I should be sorry to offend."[30] Moreover, after encountering Green, Watson describes him as having "a grip of iron, and the fury of a fiend."[31] Readers readily assume he is out to get Lady Frances and her fortune. Soon, however, from a conversation between Holmes and Green, we see that there is another side to him. As Green states:

> I swear to you, Mr. Holmes, that there never was in this world a man who loved a woman with a more wholehearted love than I had for Frances. I was a wild youngster, I know—not worse than others of my class. But her mind was pure as snow. She could not bear a shadow of coarseness. So, when she came to hear of things that I had done, she would have no more to say to me. And yet she loved me—that is the wonder of it!—loved me well enough to remain single all her sainted days just for my sake alone. When the years had passed and I had made my money at Barberton I thought perhaps I could seek her out and soften her. I had heard that she was still unmarried,
> I found her at Lausanne and tried all I knew. She weakened, I think, but her

---

[27] Doyle, *Holmes*, II, 1109.
[28] Doyle, *Holmes*, II, 1109.
[29] Doyle, *Holmes*, II, 1109.
[30] Doyle, *Holmes*, II, 1112.
[31] Doyle, *Holmes*, II, 1113.

will was strong, and when next I called she had left the town. I traced her to Baden, and then after a time heard that her maid was here. ... But for God's sake tell me what has become of the Lady Frances.[32]

3. Dr. Shlessinger: The two sides of Green's rival regarding Lady Frances make an even more stark contrast. The Shlessinger who charms Lady Frances is a cultured clergyman staying in Baden. Watson describes the situation, labeling him

a missionary from South America. Like most lonely ladies, Lady Frances found her comfort and occupation in religion. Dr. Shlessinger's remarkable personality, his whole-hearted devotion, and the fact that he was recovering from a disease contracted in the exercise of his apostolic duties affected her deeply. She had helped Mrs. Shlessinger in the nursing of the convalescent saint.[33]

Holmes, however, manages to see a darker side to Shlessinger. He reports to Watson:

[W]e are dealing with an exceptionally astute and dangerous man. The Rev. Dr. Shlessinger, missionary from South America, is none other than Holy Peters, one of the most unscrupulous rascals that Australia has ever evolved.... His particular specialty is the beguiling of lonely ladies by playing upon their religious feelings, and his so-called wife, an Englishwoman named Fraser, is a worthy helpmate. The nature of his tactics suggested his identity to me, and this physical peculiarity—he was badly bitten in a saloon-fight at Adelaide in '89—confirmed my suspicion. This poor lady is in the hands of a most infernal couple.... That she is already dead is a very likely supposition. If not, she is undoubtedly in some sort of confinement.... All my instincts tell me that she is in London, but as we have at present no possible means of telling where, we can only take the obvious steps....[34]

4. Sherlock Holmes and Dr. John Watson: Holmes and Watson are of course intent upon saving Lady Frances from abduction and murder by Shlessinger. In this, they are clearly champions of the law and working in cooperation with the police. Nonetheless, late in the story, Holmes reaches a point of desperation. He is virtually certain that Shlessinger is holding Lady Frances in his house and intends to kill her in order to secure her

---

[32] Doyle, *Holmes*, II, 1114.
[33] Doyle, *Holmes*, II, 1111.
[34] Doyle, *Holmes*, II, 1115.

jewels. This leads to the following exchange between Holmes and Shlessinger:

> "I *mean* to find her," said Sherlock Holmes. "I'm going through this house till I do find her."
>
> "Where is your warrant?"
>
> Holmes half drew a revolver from his pocket. "This will have to serve till a better one comes."
>
> "Why, you're a common burglar." "So you might describe me," said Holmes cheerfully. "My companion is also a dangerous ruffian. And together we are going through your house."
>
> Our opponent opened the door. "Fetch a policeman, Annie!" said he.[35]

Shlessinger, one must admit, is on the side of the law here, as Holmes admits by leaving the house when the policeman arrives. Ultimately, Holmes triumphs and ends up with the full support of the law.

The Gestalt shift point comes late in the story. Through brilliant detective work and some assistance from Green, Holmes finds himself convinced that Lady Frances is either dead or near death and that the Shlessingers will bury her the next morning. By recalling a chance remark of the coffin maker that the coffin was a special size, Holmes realizes that the Shlessingers plan to use this oversized coffin not just as a way to bury the dead, but also to kill and to dispose of a chloroformed Lady Frances, placed in the coffin atop a very old person who had just died. Holmes rushes to the Shlessinger lodging and manages to open the coffin, after which Watson brings back Lady Frances from the brink, this to the great relief of Philip Green. Thus this is a story of five people, each with two strikingly different sides, and the resolution of the situation in which a criminal had transformed a coffin, typically used to bury the dead, into a murder weapon.

[35] Doyle, *Holmes*, II, 1119.

"THE ADVENTURE OF THE DEVIL'S FOOT" (1910)

Early in this story, Watson, seeking Holmes's input concerning which story to compose next, quotes a telegram from Holmes: "Why not tell them of the Cornish horror—strangest case I have ever handled."[36] The story would also rank high on a gruesomeness scale. Regarding whether the story has a Gestalt component, it is noteworthy that early on, two interpretations of the nature of a solution are advanced: supernatural and natural. Mortimer Tregennis, who prefaces his claim by reporting the death of his sister and the sudden insanity of his two brothers, takes the former view, remarking: "It's devilish, Mr. Holmes, devilish! It is not of this world. Something has come into that room which has dashed the light of reason from their minds. What human contrivance could do that?"[37] Holmes shows his preference for a naturalistic explanation: "I fear that if the matter is beyond humanity it is certainly beyond me."[38] Another champion of a supernaturalist explanation appears the next day when Vicar Roundhay reports: "We are devil-ridden, Mr. Holmes! My poor parish is devil-ridden! Satan himself is loose in it! We are given over into his hands!" Roundhay follows this with startling news: "Mr. Mortimer Tregennis died during the night, and with exactly the same symptoms as the rest of his family."[39]

Holmes's chief response is to search meticulously for details, which eventually indicate that Mortimer Tregennis himself is guilty of causing the terrible fate that befell his siblings, accomplishing this by burning "*Radix pedis diaboli*",[40] the fumes of which destroyed them. Holmes shows that this substance also caused Mortimer's death. In fact, Holmes's investigation of this substance nearly proves fatal for Holmes and Watson. And Holmes also establishes that Dr. Leon Sterndale, an African explorer, had murdered Mortimer by forcing him under gunpoint to inhale the deadly fumes. All of this occurs gradually and at least Sterndale's admission of guilt comes forth gradually, Holmes convincing him that definite evidence points toward his guilt.

What happens suddenly and surprisingly at the end of the narrative is that Holmes agrees not to inform the police of the evidence against Sterndale that Holmes had accumulated and thereby to allow Sterndale to

[36] Doyle, *Holmes*, II, 1124.
[37] Doyle, *Holmes*, II, 1127.
[38] Doyle, *Holmes*, II, 1127.
[39] Doyle, *Holmes*, II, 1127.
[40] Doyle, *Holmes*, II, 1140.

return to Africa, an action that surprises—in some cases outrages—readers. On Holmes's behalf, it should be noted that Sterndale had long loved Brenda Tregennis, whom Mortimer had murdered, but could not marry because English law prohibits this on the grounds that Sterndale is divorced.

Because all this develops gradually, not rapidly, because much of this is local not global, it is difficult to see this story as fitting well with the Gestalt features that appear prominently in so many of the stories. This should not be taken to entail that "The Devil's Foot" is an inferior story, because the thesis of this book is not that a Gestalt pattern is the only way to produce dramatic effects, but is only one particularly effective way.

"His Last Bow" (1917)

This story fits particularly well with the thesis of this book. Like Part II of *The Valley of Fear*, it begins with a mystery: no narrator is named. The first solid clue that we get concerning what is *actually* going on comes when German spy master Von Bork opens the packet of secret documents that his agent Altamont delivers to him, which turns out to contain only a book on bee culture! At this point Holmesians, realizing that they know of someone who has authored a book titled *Practical Handbook of Bee Culture with Some Observations upon the Segregation of the Queen*, begin to understand what is going on. This event is the leading candidate for being the Gestalt shift moment in the story. The reader begins to recognize that this tall, thin, graying Irish-American, so critical of the British and so friendly to the Germans, is none other than Sherlock Holmes, enemy of Germany, benefactor of Britain. Other major changes follow immediately.

For example, Von Bork, who earlier was preparing to celebrate his greatest triumph, has been chloroformed and shackled by Holmes (Fig. 6.1), who then, along with Watson, is sipping Von Bork's Imperial

Fig. 6.1 Holmes chloroforming Von Bork.

Tokay. Soon Martha returns to the scene, transformed from being Von Bork's housekeeper into being another spy allied to England and possibly the Martha Hudson of 221 Baker Street.[41] One reading of the story is that the entrance somewhat earlier of Martha[42] is the first solid clue that Altamont is actually Holmes.

The number and magnitude of the transformations is remarkable. The anti-English Irish-American spying on England and aiding the Germans turns out to be a famous Brit successfully spying on the Germans. Altamont's chauffer, "a heavily built, elderly man with a grey moustache,"[43] turns out to be a former military man (Afghan war) long associated with Holmes. Readers have come to recognize that a number of Von Bork's spies whom Altamont had earlier mentioned as having been apprehended may have been part of the real work that Altamont had been performing. If readers have any doubt as to who Altamont is, the following conversation between Von Bork and Altamont dramatically clarifies the issue:

> "It is really immaterial who I am, but since the matter seems to interest you, Mr. Von Bork, I may say that this is not my first acquaintance with the members of your family. I have done a good deal of business in Germany in the past and my name is probably familiar to you."
>
> "I would wish to know it," said the Prussian grimly.
>
> "It was I who brought about the separation between Irene Adler and the late King of Bohemia when your cousin Heinrich was the Imperial Envoy. It was I also who saved from murder, by the Nihilist Klopman, Count Von und Zu Grafenstein, who was your mother's elder brother. It was I—" Von Bork sat up in amazement. "There is only one man," he cried.
>
> "Exactly," said Holmes.
>
> "And most of that information came through you," he cried. "What is it worth? What have I done? It is my ruin forever!"[44]

Von Bork not only chastises Holmes and Watson for the illegality of what they are doing but also, as they pass through small towns on the way to London, threatens to yell out that he is being kidnapped. In response, Holmes approves this idea, cautioning Von Bork that such an action might

---

[41] Doyle, *Holmes*, II, 1157.

[42] Doyle, *Holmes*, II, 1147. My reading of the story is that the first appearance of Martha may be an important clue that she is Martha Hudson of Baker Street. Others disagree. For a well-regarded analysis taking the opposite view, see Catherine Cooke, "Mrs. Hudson: A Legend in Her Own Lodging-House," which is available on the internet. See http://www.bakerstreet-journal.com/images/Catherine_Cooke_Mrs_Hudson.pdf. Viewed January 10, 2015.

[43] Doyle, *Holmes*, II, 1147.

[44] Doyle, *Holmes*, II, 1153.

enlarge the "limited titles of our village inns by giving us 'The Dangling Prussian' as a signpost."[45] Moving from the persons involved to the international level, we see that the direction in which military secrets had been moving is not West to East but East to West. Moreover, to move to a meta-level, we see Arthur Conan Doyle emerge in this story not only as a skillful author writing fiction, but also as a patriot and commentator crafting a story in support of the War effort.[46]

In short, a number of rapid, unexpected, distinctive, and global changes are at the core of this story. As the story develops, all the characters and nearly all their relations are seen very differently from what they at first seemed to be. Although none of the words from the first eighty percent of the story have changed, many have altered, indeed sometimes totally reversed, their meaning. These changes can be described as Gestalt shifts.

BIBLIOGRAPHY

PRINTED SOURCES

Dakin, D. Martin. *A Sherlock Holmes Commentary* (Newton Abbot: David & Charles, 1976).
Doyle, Arthur Conan. *The Complete Sherlock Holmes,* 2 vols. (New York: Doubleday, 1953).

INTERNET SOURCES

Cooke, Catherine, "Mrs. Hudson: A Legend in Her Own Lodging-House," which is available on the internet at http://www.bakerstreetjournal.com/images/Catherine_Cooke_Mrs_Hudson.pdf. Viewed 10 January 2015.
http://dickens.stanford.edu/sherlockholmes/2007/notes12_1.html. Viewed 10 January 2015.
Klinger, Leslie S. "The Textual Problem of the Resident Patient" at http://www.sherlockian.net/canon/klinger.html. Viewed 31 December 2014, and http://en.wikipedia.org/wiki/The_Adventure_of_the_Cardboard_Box. Viewed 31 December 2014.

---

[45] Doyle, *Holmes,* II, 1154.

[46] It is interesting to ask how Doyle came to write "His Last Bow." One source reports that Doyle wrote it in the following context: "It was … meant to answer a question that blindsided the author while he was reviewing troops at the French front in 1916. Taken by surprise when asked if Holmes was serving in the English army, he answered, 'He is too old to serve.' Apparently, Conan Doyle rethought that answer, and this story is the result." See http://dickens.stanford.edu/sherlockholmes/2007/notes12_1.html. Viewed January 10, 2015.

CHAPTER 7

The Case-Book of Sherlock Holmes (1927)

"THE ADVENTURE OF THE ILLUSTRIOUS CLIENT" (1924)

In a Gestalt shift, an entity can be seen two or more different ways. This story features many entities that fit this characterization and hence many Gestalts. Consider Baron Adelbert Gruner: Violet de Merville sees him as an excellent person whose marriage proposal she welcomes even though some malign him. Among Gruner's detractors are General de Merville (i.e., Violet's father), Kitty Winter, whom Gruner had courted and abused, as well as Sir James Damer, who contacts Holmes at the request of an unidentified "Illustrious Client," who sees Gruner as a murderer and also a most undesirable mate for Miss de Merville. Holmes, whose assignment is to persuade Violet to break off her engagement to Gruner or, to put it differently, to experience a Gestalt shift in her image of him, also has his Gestalt(s). After Gruner sends two thugs to beat up Holmes, the public perceives him as severely (according to some accounts, nearly fatally) wounded. These reports combined with Watson's deceptions put Gruner off his game. Readers and the English public see Holmes as also an upholder of the law, an image that for readers may alter as they witness Holmes, his head "girt in bloody bandages,"[1] successfully burgle Gruner's home, where with help from Kitty he secures Gruner's diary of his abuse of an array of women. Watson, under Holmes's direction, tries (only partially successfully) to appear as a specialist in classic Chinese pottery, but

[1] Doyle, *Holmes*, II, 1176.

© The Author(s) 2018
M. J. Crowe, *The Gestalt Shift in Conan Doyle's Sherlock Holmes Stories*, https://doi.org/10.1007/978-3-319-98291-5_7

Gruner fairly soon sees through this ruse. Gruner, a handsome fellow, goes through a major change in his appearance after Kitty Winter disfigures him by tossing vitriol in his face. Violet eventually sees Gruner's catalog of his conquests, his "lust diary,"[2] which Holmes, with help from Watson and from Kitty, had stolen from Gruner. These records enable Violet to see how disfigured a person her fiancé actually is.

Ultimately, readers must confront the dilemma of witnessing a champion of the law committing burglary for the good purpose of saving Violet from marriage to one of the most repulsive characters in the Conan Doyle canon. These tensions as well as the concern for the future of Kitty Winter are relieved by the fact that Holmes's "Illustrious Client" used his influence to spare Holmes from charges in the police courts and also to secure a mild sentence for Kitty Winter. As Watson puts it, a newspaper reported on "the first police-court hearing of the proceedings against Miss Kitty Winter on the grave charge of vitriol-throwing. Such extenuating circumstances came out in the trial that the sentence … was the lowest that was possible for such an offence. Sherlock Holmes was threatened with a prosecution for burglary, but when an object is good and a client is sufficiently illustrious, even the rigid British law becomes human and elastic."[3] Nonetheless, Watson never quite unmasks the "Illustrious Client," but offers a clue (a sighting of the armorial bearings on his carriage), which clue Sherlockian scholars have succeeded in reading as indicating England's King Edward VII.[4] Does this case qualify as one of Holmes's most important cases? Watson sees it as "in some ways, the supreme moment of my friend's career."[5]

One final comment before leaving this story, which in effect deals with the changing Gestalts associated with each of the main characters. While revising this analysis, I stumbled onto what may be a significant discovery. I have had the worry for some time that another author may "scoop" me on taking a Gestalt approach to the Holmes stories. To check this, I periodically use Google's search functions to see whether this is the case. My current effort has been to search "Holmes Gestalt," which seemed likely

---

[2] Doyle, *Holmes*, II, 1177.

[3] Doyle, *Holmes*, II, 1178–1179.

[4] D. Martin Dakin, *A Sherlock Holmes Commentary* (Newton Abbott: Dayton and Charles, 1974), 259. See also Arthur Conan Doyle. *The New Annotated Sherlock Holmes*, annotated. by Leslie S. Klinger, vol. II (New York: W. W. Norton, 2005), 1481.

[5] Doyle, *Holmes*, II, 1160.

to turn up writings that associated Holmes with the idea of a Gestalt, if such exist. In other words, I wanted Google to find only publications where both words appeared, even if separated by many sentences. This is not what Google did; rather it looked only for cases where these two words appeared next to each other; in other words, it sought for cases where authors were saying that there is a particular Gestalt associated with Holmes. It found 219 cases of either "Holmes Gestalt" or "Holmes-Gestalt." It thus appears that authors are regularly characterizing Holmes as exhibiting some particular Gestalt. Thus they are finding the word Gestalt to be very useful in specifying the particular characteristics that distinguish Holmes. Searching for "Sherlock Gestalt" was similarly productive. Moreover, the search for these two pairs showed that this practice is becoming worldwide. This was evident from the fact that both words in each pair are thoroughly international. French or German authors wanting to refer to Holmes use the word Holmes; similarly, the German word Gestalt is now a common term in English and one assumes in other major languages. Reference to home in English can be house; in German one would use "Haus." All this suggests that noting the usefulness of the idea of Gestalt in discussing Holmes is already a common practice; what seems to be rare is to give the idea the centrality proposed in the present publication.

"The Adventure of the Blanched Soldier" (1926)

This story is one of only two stories in the Holmes canon written by Holmes himself. It centers on two soldiers who were comrades in the Boer War, Godfrey Emsworth and James Dodd, the former of whom had been wounded. Dodd desires to reconnect with his mate, but encounters resistance from Godfrey's father, Colonel Emsworth, who claims that his son cannot be contacted because he is spending a year traveling around the world. Dodd visits the father, but is distressed at the father's resistance to giving any information about his son. On the night of his first visit to the family estate, Dodd hears the butler speak of his friend in the past tense, but later he sees his friend pressing his face against a window, his face seeming very white and also deformed. Godfrey then flees. The next day Dodd notices a cabin on the property with its windows shuttered and staffed by a person who appears to have medical training. The father, distressed by this, orders Dodd to leave. Dodd then turns to Holmes with whom he returns to the house to demand an explanation. Holmes by this time has developed three hypothetical explanations of what has been happening: (1) Godfrey is "in hiding for a crime"; (2) Godfrey is "mad and that they wanted to avoid an asylum"; and (3) Godfrey has "some disease which caused his segregation."[6] Holmes applies the rule of logic that "when you have eliminated all which is impossible, then whatever remains, however improbable, must be the truth."[7] Holmes, applying this rule to what he observes when visiting Colonel Emsworth's estates, concludes for the disease option; in particular, he believes that Godfrey suffers from leprosy. Having already become convinced that this is the most likely explanation, Holmes arranges for a prominent dermatologist to accompany them. This physician offers the consoling diagnosis that Godfrey suffers not from leprosy but from ichthyosis, which was known to be treatable.

With this, the scene greatly changes. The father is not only relieved, but comes to be seen as a loving though gruff parent very concerned for his son. The son is viewed as a person who need not be an outcast, but as a person able to return to society. And the family now perceives Dodd not as a busybody who may do more harm than good, but rather as a person whose persistence has greatly helped his friend.

---

[6] Doyle, *Holmes*, II, 1192.

[7] Doyle, *Holmes*, II, 1192. One wonders whether other plausible hypotheses would be that Godfrey was hiding from an enemy, feared being charged with a paternity suit, or was writing a book.

"THE ADVENTURE OF THE MAZARIN STONE" (1921)

Gestalt shifts repeatedly occur in this story. It is almost like popcorn is going off, or possibly a magician who is performing rapid-fire tricks. It is very possible that the reason for this is that Doyle first wrote this story as a drama, "The Crown Diamond," and then converted it to a short story.[8] This explains why all the events recounted occur in Holmes's rooms. Some examples of shifts: Early on, Holmes using various disguises follows Count Sylvius. The Count, who is no dolt, picks up on this, thinking that Holmes's henchmen (or perhaps the word should be henchpeople) are following him. Sylvius, for example, notices that an older lady is following him and even helps her by picking up her parasol. Later in the story, Sylvius expresses amazement when he learns that the lady was in fact Holmes, who in proof produces the parasol![9] Also, Holmes has a model of himself in his flat. Sylvius at one point advances on it with the idea of striking Holmes dead. Just before he is about to strike with his walking stick Holmes emerges and gets Sylvius to back off. Sylvius is amazed at the quality of the likeness.[10] Holmes gets Sylvius (and the stolen Mazarin Stone as well) by another trick. He leaves the room, goes into his bed-room, and begins playing his violin. This gives Sylvius a chance to talk to his bruiser, Merton, in privacy to see whether they want to surrender the stone. They are certain that Holmes cannot overhear them because he is playing his violin. But in fact he is not: it is a recording. This and a second door from his bedroom allow Holmes to replace the dummy by himself and thus overhear the conversation. Moreover, when Sylvius gets out the Mazarin stone, Holmes (the dummy has turned into the real Holmes) snatches the stone away.[11] Moreover, Holmes now has proof that Sylvius and Merton are criminals. And yet another example: Holmes works his magic on Lord Cantlemere, who has been skeptical of Holmes's powers. He slips the stone into Cantlemere's coat and asks him whether the person who is in possession of the stone is guilty. After Cantlemere agrees to this, Holmes has Cantlemere reach into his own pocket. Cantlemere goes from first doubting Holmes, then being angry with him for having fooled him, but then recovers and ends up praising Holmes.[12]

---

[8] http://en.wikipedia.org/wiki/The_Adventure_of_the_Mazarin_Stone. Viewed January 20, 2015.

[9] Doyle, *Holmes*, II, 1198.

[10] Doyle, *Holmes*, II, 1197.

[11] Doyle, *Holmes*, II, 1203.

[12] Doyle, *Holmes*, II, 1206.

"The Adventure of the Three Gables" (1926)

Holmes's client in this story is Mrs. Maberley, a widow, who comes to him with a strange problem: someone wants to purchase her home for significantly more than it is worth, but has specified that she must include all the contents of her house as part of the sale. To understand the structure of this story, one must pause to realize that this must be an extraordinarily rare event in the history of hiring detectives, including fictional detectives. One goes to detective fiction expecting to encounter such serious problems as beatings, blackmail, robbery, or murder. Indeed, Doyle built his reputation on skillfully portraying such activities. The Gestalt shift in this story is related to the fact that this elderly lady's request becomes a launching pad for dealing with traditional services by detectives.

The process begins when the lady remarks that the potential purchaser of her house made the non-standard requirement that she would not remove anything from the house. This surprises the lady because she believes that there is nothing in the house that has substantial value. Holmes comes to see the house, learning in the process that she is the mother of Douglas Maberley, a gifted young man, "a magnificent creature," "debonair and splendid," who while serving as "attaché at Rome" had recently become a "moody, morose, brooding creature," who died about a month earlier.[13] His death was related to a romance he had had with Isadora Klein, "the richest as well as the most lovely widow upon earth."[14] Klein broke off the relationship with Maberley when a far better prospect, the Duke of Lombard, took an interest in marrying her. Moreover, she expressed her disdain for Maberley by hiring a bruiser to thrash him outside her house.

Holmes eventually learns that in the last days of Douglas's life, he had written a novel, which in effect chronicled his romance with Klein and her final treatment of him, and that his mother had acquired this manuscript when she received his possessions after his death. Recognizing Klein's conviction that the information in this manuscript would lead the Duke to break off their engagement, makes it clear to Holmes that it is Klein who wants to purchase the house and its contents to enable her to destroy Douglas's novel. Holmes therefore urges Mrs. Maberley to arrange for someone to stay with her overnight, which she neglects to do. Persons

[13] Doyle, *Holmes*, II, 1208.
[14] Doyle, *Holmes*, II, 1215.

hired by Klein then burgle the house, carrying off the manuscript but leaving behind its last page. From this page, Holmes infers what had been happening and with this page in hand he goes to Klein who by then had burned the manuscript. Watson comments about the meeting that "of all Holmes's criminals this was the one whom he would find hardest to face."[15] Holmes makes clear to Klein that he had enough information to expose Klein and ruin her chance of marrying the Duke. Holmes proposes, moreover, that Klein give Mrs. Maberley £5000 to allow her to travel around the world, which Holmes admits would have him "compound a felony as usual."[16]

Put differently, Holmes's achievement when confronted with the information Mrs. Maberley provided him was to discern a pattern that helped her both to understand the state of affairs and also to benefit from them. This summary leaves out mention of Holmes's extensive contacts not only with various criminals such as bruiser Steve Dixie and criminal agent Barney Stockdale and also tabloid gossip columnist Langdale Pike, who add color to the narrative but are not central to its structure, which centers on the Gestalt shift that involves understanding the special value of what Mrs. Maberley owned.[17]

---

[15] Doyle, *Holmes*, II, 1217.

[16] Doyle, *Holmes*, II, 1218.

[17] This analysis may go some way toward redeeming this story from the indictment of it by D. Martin Dakin in his generally excellent *Sherlock Holmes Commentary* (Newton Abbot: David & Charles, 1974), 265. Dakin describes it as "[m]uch the poorest story" in the sixty stories that make up the Holmes canon.

"THE ADVENTURE OF THE SUSSEX VAMPIRE" (1924)

It is clear that a Gestalt shift occurs in this story. At the beginning Holmes's client, Robert Ferguson, seeks help because he believes that his second wife, a Peruvian woman, not only has abused his fifteen-year-old crippled son from his former marriage but also has twice bitten their own baby on the throat. Holmes agrees to take the case, which leads to Holmes and Watson going to Lamberly to meet the persons involved. By this point, the wife is confined to their bedroom and refuses to see her husband who has made such hurtful accusations against her. Holmes meets Jacky, Ferguson's crippled son, and the wife's maid; he also sees the family dog (which is crippled) and the baby with a mark on her throat, and talks with Ferguson's wife, who is clearly suffering. Pressed by Ferguson for a solution to this delicate and complex problem, Holmes makes what seems an astonishing statement that marks the Gestalt shift moment in this story:

> It is certainly delicate ... but I have not been struck up to now with its complexity. It has been a case for intellectual deduction, but when this original intellectual deduction is confirmed point by point by quite a number of independent incidents, then the subjective becomes objective and we can say confidently that we have reached our goal. I had, in fact, reached it before we left Baker Street, and the rest has merely been observation and confirmation.[18]

Holmes then, in the presence of the wife and son, explains to Ferguson that his wife "is a very good, very loving, and very ill-used woman."[19] The source of the problems has been Ferguson's son, Jacky, who has taken poison from various Peruvian artifacts in the house, tested it on the family dog, and then at least twice attempted to poison the baby. The wife, recognizing what Jacky had done, had sought to save the baby by sucking out the poison, but concealed this action because she was unsure that her husband would believe her because of his great love for his son. Robert Ferguson realizes that this is a correct account of what has been happening. Holmes suggests and Ferguson accepts Holmes's suggestion that "a year at sea would be my prescription for master Jacky."[20]

---

[18] Doyle, *Holmes*, II, 1228.
[19] Doyle, *Holmes*, II, 1228.
[20] Doyle, *Holmes*, II, 1230.

It is rare indeed that one can find a comment made directly by Doyle on one of the Holmes stories. But in regard to this story such a statement is available.

> People have often asked me whether I knew the end of a Holmes story before I started it. Of course I did. One could not possibly steer a course if one did not know one's destination. The first thing is to get your idea. We will suppose that this idea is that a woman … is suspected of biting a wound in her child, when she was really sucking that wound for fear of poison injected by someone else. Having got that key idea, one's next task is to conceal it and lay emphasis upon everything which can make for a different explanation. Holmes, however, can see all the fallacies of the alternatives, and arrives more or less dramatically at the true solution by steps which he can describe and justify.[21]

These are the words of an author deeply attached to creating contrasts and to providing readers with dramatic resolutions of them. And who also recognizes the value of using even the story's title to mislead the reader into expecting another outcome.

[21] Arthur Conan Doyle, *Memories and Adventures and Western Wanderings* (Newcastle on Tyne: Cambridge Scholars Publishing, 2009), 75.

"THE ADVENTURE OF THE THREE GARRIDEBS" (1924)

In this story, as in a number of other narratives, Holmes's first task in serving a client is not to solve a crime, but to determine whether a crime is contemplated. Such is the substance in this instance, although Nathan Garrideb does not realize this. He believes that Holmes needs only to find a third Garrideb, which will entitle Nathan to a third of about fifteen million dollars left by an American Garrideb to three surviving male Garridebs, provided that three exist and can be found. Moreover, the good news is that John Garrideb, an American lawyer residing in England, has notified Nathan of this bequest, meaning that only one more Garrideb must be located. Holmes is visited not by the reclusive Nathan but by the fast-talking John, who hails from Kansas and happens to know Holmes's long-time friend from Topeka, Kansas, Dr. Lysander Stark. Because Holmes in fact knows no such person, he is immediately suspicious of John. That suspicion grows all the greater when John claims to have located a third Garrideb living in Birmingham, England, and displays a newspaper advertisement showing that Howard Garrideb sells various items including hand plows and artesian wells. Holmes, recognizing that the British do not use plows (they prefer ploughs) and have little taste for artesian wells, is skeptical of John's honesty and Howard's existence. After John informs the reclusive Nathan that he will have to leave his lodgings to go to Birmingham, Holmes recognizes that John has launched this elaborate scam in order to gain access to Nathan's lodging, which he has scarcely ever left in the five years since he had moved there. Holmes investigates who lived there before Nathan, finding that it was an American forger named Rodger Prescott, now deceased. In fact, Scotland Yard was able to inform Holmes that the person who killed Prescott was a notorious American known as Killer Evans, whose appearance turns out to be very similar to John Garrideb! All this points to Evans, aka John Garrideb, planning to burgle Nathan's lodgings while Nathan was bringing the good news to the non-existent Howard Garrideb in Birmingham, which Holmes understands as creating the opportunity for Evans to recover the plates used by Prescott in his counterfeiting career. This marks the Gestalt moment in the story. Watson records that immediately after Garrideb/Evans had made these arrangements with Nathan, Watson "noticed that my friend's face cleared when the American left the room, and the look of thoughtful perplexity had vanished."[22]

---

[22] Doyle, *Holmes*, II, 1237.

What happens is that Evans arrives at the lodging, locates the plates in a compartment under the floor, and then finds that Holmes and Watson had preceded him to the premises. They succeed in capturing him, but not without Watson being wounded, though not seriously. This leads to an exchange that may not be central to the story although it is central to the canon. In fact, Watson describes it as producing a "revelation," which may justify us in labeling it as global.

> "You're not hurt, Watson? For God's sake, say that you are not hurt!"
>
> It was worth a wound—it was worth many wounds—to know the depth of loyalty and love which lay behind that cold mask. The clear, hard eyes were dimmed for a moment, and the firm lips were shaking. For the one and only time I caught a glimpse of a great heart as well as of a great brain. All my years of humble but single-minded service culminated in that moment of revelation.[23]

---

[23] Doyle, *Holmes*, II, 1241.

"The Problem of Thor Bridge" (1922)

This story certainly centers on a bipolar Gestalt shift. Convincing evidence throughout much of the story points to the conclusion that Grace Dunbar (the beautiful governess in the Gibson household) murdered Maria Gibson (the aging South American wife of fabulously wealthy Neil Gibson, who had become infatuated by Grace). Maria had been found dead on a bridge near the Gibson estate, shot in the head by a pistol found in Dunbar's wardrobe. Also Maria clutched in her hand a note from Dunbar agreeing to meet Grace on the bridge. The presumed motive was that Neil loved Grace, but could not marry her because he was already married to Maria. Neil Gibson hires Holmes, pleading with him to prove Grace's innocence. Holmes informs Grace of the seriousness of her situation:

> "My dear young lady," cried Holmes earnestly, "I beg you to have no illusions upon the point. Mr. Cummings [her barrister] here would assure you that all the cards are at present against us, and that we must do everything that is possible if we are to win clear. It would be a cruel deception to pretend that you are not in very great danger. Give me all the help you can, then, to get at the truth."[24]

It is true that there is another suspect. Sergeant Coventry asks Holmes: "Don't you think there might be a case against Mr. Neil Gibson himself?"[25] Holmes agrees that this is worth consideration.

Holmes comes to believe in Grace's innocence, this chiefly because of two considerations. The first involves flipping the strongest evidence against Dunbar: the fact that a gun with one shell missing was found in her wardrobe. To Watson, this was "the most damning incident of all."[26] Holmes, however, becomes convinced that if Grace were the murderer, this is just the reverse of what she would do. The decisive reason, however, was a clue that others saw as no clue at all: Both Holmes and the police had noticed that there was a chip in the stonework on the bridge near where Maria had been shot. Coventry and Watson saw it as irrelevant, until Holmes presented the possibility that the "murdered" Mrs. Gibson might have tied a gun to a cord attached to a rock, arranging it so

[24] Doyle, *Holmes*, II, 1256.
[25] Doyle, *Holmes*, II, 1252.
[26] Doyle, *Holmes*, II, 1254.

that she could shoot herself and then have the pistol fly into the stream and disappear. In fact, the person whom everyone believed had murdered Gibson had devised a plot to have the state murder Dunbar, although the plan cost Gibson her life. At this point, Holmes assures Dunbar by saying: "I will give you a case which will make England ring."[27] Borrowing Watson's gun, Holmes tests this hypothesis, finds it plausible, and then searches the stream and successfully finds the murder gun.

Major changes come with this discovery. The reader sees that the murdered Mrs. Gibson was in fact a suicide, who was employing suicide as a method for murdering Dunbar. The gun in the wardrobe was not the murder gun; rather, the gun that killed Mrs. Gibson was near her body, but invisibly lying in the stream. Neil Gibson, despite his many bad actions to his wife and others, was correct in his assessment of the goodness of Grace Dunbar, who so clearly seems to be the murderer of his wife.

This story nicely illustrates the problematic nature of one mandate viewed as central to detective work: the detective must carefully examine every clue. This claim assumes that clues are the starting point for detection. The problem is that there are typically hundreds, if not thousands, of potential clues at a crime scene. Some (e.g., blood splatter) are evident as clues. Others (e.g., a chip on a nearby stone surface) may seem entirely irrelevant, until a brilliant detective perceives their possible importance. Yet others may be planted clues (the gun in the wardrobe), which are meant to mislead. This is significantly similar to the process by which we see a previously invisible image in a Gestalt; for example, seeing that what we have been seeing as a rabbit's ears can also be seen as a duck's bill.

[27] Doyle, *Holmes*, II, 1258.

"THE ADVENTURE OF THE CREEPING MAN" (1923)

As in a number of other Holmes stories, a dog plays an important role in this story. In fact, early in this story Holmes remarks to Watson: "I have serious thoughts of writing a small monograph upon the uses of dogs in the work of the detective."[28] This story has another feature that also regularly reappears. Holmes is initially contacted not because a crime has occurred, but rather from fear that some serious and unwelcome action will take place. The central character in this story is Professor Presbury, a distinguished sixty-one-year-old physiologist, whose assistant, Jack Bennett, correctly categorizes the problem that led him to seek Holmes's assistance: "It is not a case in which we can consult the police, and yet we are utterly at our wit's end as to what to do, and we feel in some strange way that we are drifting towards disaster."[29] In particular, the professor has been exhibiting strange behaviors. These started not long after he became engaged to a much younger woman and after he made an unexplained trip to Prague. One such behavior is showing sharpness of temper; another is acting strangely toward his dog and his dog toward him. Holmes notes that the period between the erratic behaviors is nine days, which period coincides with mailings Presbury receives from London. Another surprising behavior is Presbury's tendency to climb the ivy and trees around the house. Holmes, aided by Bennett and by Presbury's daughter, studies this behavior without hitting on an explanation until (and this brings on the Gestalt shift point) Holmes notices Presbury's knuckles. He points out to Watson that these had become "[t]hick and horny." And he adds: "Oh … what a fool I have been! It seems incredible, and yet it must be true. All points in one direction. How could I miss seeing the connection of ideas? Those knuckles—how could I have passed those knuckles? And the dog! And the ivy! It's surely time that I disappeared into that little farm of my dreams."[30]

What Holmes had concluded, and soon successfully proves, is that Presbury while in Prague had consulted a specialist, H. Lowenstein, who was experimenting with treating humans seeking to rejuvenate themselves with serum from the langur, "the great black-faced monkey of the Himalayan slopes, biggest and most human of the climbing monkeys."[31] This serum

[28] Doyle, *Holmes*, II, 1262.
[29] Doyle, *Holmes*, II, 1266.
[30] Doyle, *Holmes*, II, 1273.
[31] Doyle, *Holmes*, II, 1275–1276.

was sent to Presbury through London every nine days, which fits exactly with Presbury's periods of aberrant behavior. Presbury was in effect experiencing Gestalt shifts between being a distinguished if aging university professor and exhibiting behaviors characteristic of a langur monkey. By detecting and recognizing that shift, Holmes succeeds in saving Presbury's life and reputation. We are not told how Professor Presbury reacted to Holmes's analysis, but the fact that almost exactly at the time that Holmes had reached this conclusion, Presbury's dog had attacked its master, nearly costing the professor his life, makes it seem probable that he agreed with Holmes about the dangers of this therapy.

Holmes's comments on Presbury's actions no doubt reflect Dr. Doyle's sentiments: "The real source lies, of course, in that untimely love affair which gave our impetuous professor the idea that he could only gain his wish by turning himself into a younger man. When one tries to rise above Nature one is liable to fall below it. The highest type of man may revert to the animal if he leaves the straight road of destiny."[32]

---

[32] Doyle, *Holmes*, II, 1276.

"THE ADVENTURE OF THE LION'S MANE" (1926)

To say the least, this is an unusual Holmes tale. It is the next to last story in Holmes's life, "His Last Bow" being the final one. Because Holmes is retired in Sussex, Watson plays no part either as character or narrator. No crime is involved, although a man and a dog are killed and another man is nearly killed. Moreover, there is no client in this case.

One morning as Holmes and a neighbor, Harold Stackhurst, head of a local academy, are walking near the ocean, Fitzroy McPherson, science master at the academy, coming up from the shore where he has been swimming in a tidal pool, confronts them and immediately dies, muttering the words "the Lion's Mane" as he expires. The cause was obvious: "His back was covered with dark red lines as though he had been terribly flogged by a thin wire scourge."[33] Along comes Ian Murdoch, math coach at the academy, who it turns out had earlier had an incident with his fellow teacher McPherson and, moreover, both had sought the attentions of the lovely Maud Bellamy. Holmes sends Murdoch for the local police while he investigates this case, "as strange a case as had ever confronted me."[34] He visits the Bellamys, learning that in fact McPherson was secretly engaged to their daughter Maud. Already by this time, Murdoch emerges as a suspect. A few days later, McPherson's dog is found dead in the same area of the beach where his master had been attacked. Then Holmes tells his readers that he has hit upon an idea that may prove promising, this idea arising not directly from his observations, which were extensive, but from his memory. He explains: "My mind is like a crowded box-room with packets of all sorts stowed away therein—so many that I may well have but a vague perception of what was there,"[35] but he does not as yet tell us what he has recovered. If this is not quite the Gestalt moment, it is the beginning of it.[36]

Matters take a turn shortly thereafter when Murdoch, the leading suspect, returns from the same swimming area where McPherson had been attacked with the same sort of wounds, except that they were not fatal, partly because brandy brought him back. At this point, Stackhurst and the inspector ask Holmes: "Can you do nothing for us?" Holmes then leads them to the tidal pool area of the beach where swimming had been ideal

---

[33] Doyle, *Holmes*, II, 1278.
[34] Doyle, *Holmes*, II, 1279.
[35] Doyle, *Holmes*, II, 1285.
[36] Doyle, *Holmes*, II, 1287.

before the death of McPherson. Holmes bursts "into a shout of triumph." What he proceeds to say is: "Cyanea! Behold the Lion's Mane." At this moment, he points to a creature barely visible in the water looking "like a tangled mass torn from the mane of a lion. It lay upon a rocky shelf some three feet under the water."[37] It was this strange aquatic creature that had killed McPherson, later his dog, and eventually attacked Murdoch. Holmes uses a large rock to kill this giant jellyfish sometimes known as the Lion's Mane. It was this that Holmes remembered, which enabled him to determine that there was no crime or murder, though there had been a killer jellyfish. Murdoch was especially pleased by this result, because it proved his innocence. Moreover, Holmes's solution enabled him to take actions that prevented any further killings by *Cyanea*. Such broadly significant results support the case that Holmes had once again managed a Gestalt shift. Part of this achievement was that his solution was such that it involved a category shift, or to put it differently, he avoided making what was earlier described as a category error.

[37] Doyle, *Holmes*, II, 1288.

"The Adventure of the Veiled Lodger" (1927)

Let us begin by noting various Gestalts that appear in this story. First, there is Eugenia Ronder, with veil and without veil. Eugenia with veil is a lovely woman. Eugenia without veil is a woman whom most would hesitate to behold. Then there is Eugenia as portrayed in the public story: a woman who was tragically attacked by a lion whom she was trying to feed. Eugenia's true story is very different; she and her lover Leonardo were engaged in murdering her husband, but their plans misfired because the smell of the blood of her husband, whom Leonardo with her help had killed, incited the lion to pounce on her. And also there is the Eugenia, seven years after the tragedy and nearing her death, who wishes to reveal the true story. And finally there is the Eugenia, who after informing Holmes of the true story plans to take another life, her own, but who heeds Holmes's message: "Your life is not your own. Keep your hands off it." She heroically sends him her bottle of prussic acid.[38] For Eugenia's husband, there are only two images: a "human wild boar," and "[r]uffian, bully and beast,"[39] and the dead man who was killed not as the public thinks by the lion but murdered by Leonardo in collusion with Eugenia. Leonardo is "a professional acrobat … of magnificent physique"[40] and loving man, who successfully murders Ronder, but loses his nerve when he needs to rescue the woman whom he loves, leading Eugenia to scream "Coward! Coward!"[41] And then there is Leonardo who apparently abandoned Eugenia not only at the scene of the crime but also afterwards, and now there is Leonardo dead. One person who in a sense does not change is Holmes himself: he makes no startling deductions; he listens, learns, consoles, and advises.

In this narrative, a major Gestalt shift does occur: We see that the public story of the killing of Ronder by lion Sahara King was actually the murder of Ronder by Leonardo in collusion with Eugenia and that the mighty Leonardo was both killer and coward. But Holmes does not bring about the shift that we see, although he does record it. He does rather more, however, for his client; he offers her understanding and wise counsel. These seem to be characteristics that Doyle in his final Holmes stories wishes to emphasize.

---

[38] Doyle, *Holmes*, II, 1297–1298.
[39] Doyle, *Holmes*, II, 1295.
[40] Doyle, *Holmes*, II, 1295.
[41] Doyle, *Holmes*, II, 1294.

"THE ADVENTURE OF SHOSCOMBE OLD PLACE" (1927)

The challenge of this story is not finding Gestalts, but deciding which is most central. Among the lesser Gestalts is the fact that Holmes and Watson enter the scene disguised as fishermen. Eventually fisherman Holmes will appear on the scene as a detective. Another lesser Gestalt is the fake and the real Shoscombe Prince, whom Sir Robert Norburton hides from the public by having the horse's half-brother practice in public before the big race, thereby trying to get betters to wager on another horse in the race, thus raising his profits if Shoscombe Prince wins. More central to the story is Sir Robert, whom John Mason, head trainer at the Norburton stables, hints is behaving rather oddly. Mason informs Holmes that Sir Robert does not own the house or stables. These are properties that Norburton's elderly widowed ailing sister, Lady Beatrice Falder, owns; in fact, if she dies, he will receive nothing, the estate going to the brother of Lady Beatrice's deceased husband. Moreover, Mason notes that recently Lady Beatrice has been behaving strangely. For example, for the past week she has remained in her room, except for her daily carriage ride, and even then, her dog barks furiously when she goes out, leading Norburton to give the dog to an innkeeper. Norburton, known as irascible, has been seen visiting a very old crypt on the property; in fact, Mason has found bones present in it, which he believes were not previously there. In short, it appears possible that Norburton may be up to no good, possibly even having murdered his sister, but as yet no direct evidence is available. It is my suggestion that the central Gestalt issue in the story concerns the real identity of Norburton.

Holmes's first line of investigation is to borrow from the innkeeper the sister's dog and to release it near her carriage as she travels about. The dog runs to the carriage, but then begins barking furiously. Holmes's comments that the dog "thought it was his mistress, and he found it was a stranger. Dogs don't make mistakes."[42] That night, Holmes and Watson go to the crypt, where they find that the bones mentioned by Mason have been removed. Holmes then begins to examine some of the coffins, finding a coffin containing the body of Norburton's sister, a result that indicates to readers that Mason's worries were not without reason. At this point Norburton arrives and when confronted by this fact and other inferences that Holmes has attained reveals the actual situation. He states that about a week earlier, his sister had died a natural death. Had this become known, he would have

[42] Doyle, *Holmes*, II, 1307.

lost his house, stables, and horse. His only chance of avoiding all this was to hide the fact of his sister's death until after the race, which race he believed would make him financially secure. Holmes's response to Norburton was that "this matter must, of course, be referred to the police. It was my duty to bring the facts to light, and there I must leave it. As to the morality or decency of your conduct, it is not for me to express an opinion."[43] It turned out that Shoscombe Prince won the Derby, Norburton cleared eighty thousand pounds, and the police and coroner issued only a mild rebuke. The real Norburton has emerged, and all the other Gestalts fall in line.

Holmes's achievement was to learn enough of what actually had happened to make Norburton realize that a full account of his actions provided the best chance for him to save his livelihood and reputation. The Gestalt shift point can be identified as Holmes's showing Norburton that he had found his sister's corpse. One is, however, tempted to attribute a special significance to the dog and its infallibility, and to Holmes's letter that led Norburton to the crypt.

[43] Doyle, *Holmes*, II, 1311.

"The Adventure of the Retired Colourman" (1926)

The structure of this story involves a Gestalt shift. In its opening lines, Watson describes Josiah Amberley, Holmes's new client, as "an old fellow," in fact a "pathetic, futile, broken creature," and Holmes fully agrees.[44] Holmes explains that at age sixty-one, Amberley had retired with a house and nest egg to Lewisham, where he soon married a woman twenty years younger than he. Within two years, he was a broken man, the cause according to Holmes was a "treacherous friend and a fickle wife," the "faithless spouse [having] carried off the old man's deed-box with ... a good part of his life's savings within."[45] Holmes, busy with another case, sends Watson to Lewisham to assess the situation. Watson visits Amberley's home, listens to his tale, and learns some details; for example, that Amberley had purchased theater tickets for a performance the previous night, but his wife at the last minute felt sickly and stayed home. When he returned from the theater, he found his financial assets gone and also his wife and a male family friend had disappeared. Strangely, Amberley was attempting to cope by painting parts of his house. Holmes, using the telephone, confirms that Amberley had a reputation for being "a miser as well as a harsh and exacting husband."[46] Soon Holmes sends Watson and Amberley to visit a vicar in a remote area, which is actually a ruse to get Amberley away from his home.

The next day Holmes summons Amberley to Baker Street, where he opens the conversation with a question that marks the beginning of the Gestalt shift point in the story: "What did you do with the bodies?"[47] Amberley's response:

> The man sprang to his feet with a hoarse scream. He clawed into the air with his bony hands. His mouth was open, and for the instant he looked like some horrible bird of prey. In a flash we got a glimpse of the real Josiah Amberley, a misshapen demon with a soul as distorted as his body. As he fell back into his chair he clapped his hand to his lips as if to stifle a cough. Holmes sprang at his throat like a tiger and twisted his face towards the ground. A white pellet fell from between his gasping lips.
>
> "No short cuts, Josiah Amberley. Things must be done decently and in order."[48]

[44] Doyle, *Holmes*, II, 1312.
[45] Doyle, *Holmes*, II, 1313.
[46] Doyle, *Holmes*, II, 1316.
[47] Doyle, *Holmes*, II, 1319.
[48] Doyle, *Holmes*, II, 1319.

Amberley is then led off to police headquarters, where understandably they ask: "We don't seem to have got any real facts yet, Mr. Holmes. You say that the prisoner, in the presence of three witnesses, practically confessed by trying to commit suicide, that he had murdered his wife and her lover. What other facts have you?"[49] Holmes then explains that his "first clue [was] the smell of paint." That along with the fact that Amberley had constructed an hermetically sealed room led him to get Amberley out of town by a ruse, while Holmes came to Lewisham, checked with the theater and found that *no one* had occupied either of the theater seats reserved for the Amberleys. Then Holmes proceeds "to burgle the house,"[50] where he finds gas lines running into the hermetically sealed room, along with markings on the wall, indicating that Amberley had locked the couple in the room and flooded it with gas, the odor of which he sought to mask by the new painting. Holmes also suggests that the bodies might be found in an abandoned well on the property, a suggestion that proves correct. Holmes's assessment of Amberley was that his future "destination is more likely to be Broadmoor than the scaffold."[51] Overall, this is a grim story that involves a rapid and global change. We see that even the word "retired" in the title is just the reverse of the truth.

---

[49] Doyle, *Holmes*, II, 1320.
[50] Doyle, *Holmes*, II, 1321.
[51] Doyle, *Holmes*, II, 1320.

BIBLIOGRAPHY

PRINTED SOURCES

Dakin, D. Martin. *A Sherlock Holmes Commentary* (Newton Abbot: David & Charles, 1976).

Doyle, Arthur Conan. *The Complete Sherlock Holmes,* 2 vols. (New York: Doubleday, 1953).

Doyle, Arthur Conan. *Memories and Adventures and Western Wanderings* (Newcastle on Tyne: Cambridge Scholars Publishing, 2009).

Doyle, Arthur Conan. *The New Annotated Sherlock Holmes,* annotated. by Leslie S. Klinger, vol. II (New York: W. W. Norton, 2005).

INTERNET SOURCE

http://en.wikipedia.org/wiki/The_Adventure_of_the_Mazarin_Stone. Viewed 20 January 2015.

CHAPTER 8

Conclusion: The Sixty Holmes Stories

It is now time to ask: Do the analyses of the sixty Conan Doyle Sherlock Holmes stories presented in this book support the thesis of this book? In particular, is there a Gestalt structure in a substantial majority of the Holmes stories?

Before presenting my conclusions on this matter, some qualifications. I have no direct evidence that Conan Doyle expressed enthusiasm for writings from the point of view that is now called Gestalt psychology. On the other hand, it appears that early Gestalt psychology did not discuss what are now called Gestalt figures. I have searched through numerous sources on Doyle looking for the word Gestalt and have come away without a single hit. I would be surprised if someone did locate such a reference, but the key issue is whether Doyle was consciously aware of the idea of a Gestalt shift. Because Doyle was a trained ophthalmologist and as such very interested in issues of perception, he might have found some early figures such as the duck-rabbit figure interesting (they were not then called Gestalt figures). I have cited in this volume numerous cases where he shows an interest in perception. The most striking of these appears in *The Hound of the Baskervilles*, where he describes in almost clinical detail the revelation that Holmes had while staring into a family portrait in Baskerville Hall.[1] Also, periodically in his stories Doyle explicitly refers to the idea, originated by Aristotle in his *Poetics*, of a *dénouement*, which has

---

[1] Doyle, *Holmes*, II, 879. See also Chap. 1 of this book.

© The Author(s) 2018
M. J. Crowe, *The Gestalt Shift in Conan Doyle's Sherlock Holmes Stories*, https://doi.org/10.1007/978-3-319-98291-5_8

some affinities with the idea of a Gestalt shift. It is clear that his writings show a penchant not only for the dramatic but also for the visibly dramatic. The various costumes worn by Holmes are examples of this. It is also true and relevant that Doyle was passionate about creating contrasts. His Holmes stories are filled with extraordinarily diverse characters, which is also a feature of Gestalt images. What is so striking about the young lady/older lady Gestalt shift is that one collection of lines can be seen as showing either a young damsel or an elderly lady. Also, Doyle took delight in having Holmes perform what can be called magic.

Another qualification relates to a difficulty I sometimes experienced in discerning the key Gestalt(s) in a story. I have been reading the Holmes stories for decades. Their content, however, is so rich and diverse that I need to reread them periodically. I had a good chance to do this seven years ago when I began teaching a course on the Holmes stories. I've now taught seven such Holmes courses. It was while presenting Holmes that I began to see the merits of a Gestalt approach. An attorney Denis Burke, who co-taught most of the classes, especially contributed to my thought about the Holmes stories. I cannot tell exactly how much I owe to him. But I know that I learned a great deal from interactions with him. In any case, I gradually saw a book emerging, which would entail carefully rereading and analyzing all sixty stories.

My first task in analyzing the stories was to reread them and listen to them as brilliantly recorded by David Timson.[2] Then I would write a paragraph or so about the structure of the story, which gave me thirty or so pages of notes. This experience reinforced my conviction that the project would be productive. Then I began afresh, typically first reading the Hoy summary of a story[3] and the analysis of it from the McMurdo camp.[4] This proved useful in recalling the names and situations. It was, however, of surprisingly little help in delineating the Gestalts. I am convinced that the

---

[2] *Sir Arthur Conan Doyle. The Complete Sherlock Holmes*, read by David Timson. Naxos Audiobooks.

[3] James Hoy has produced summaries of all sixty stories. These are available on the internet at http://www.diogenes-club.com/hoyadventures.htm. Viewed February 4, 2015.

[4] By going to the Sherlockian.Net at http://www.sherlockian.net/ and locating the section called "The Original Sherlock Holmes Stories," one can access summaries of all sixty stories. These typically have names such as "Story Summary from McMurdo's Camp." The summary for *A Study in Scarlet* is located at https://mcmurdoscamp.wordpress.com/story-summaries/stud/. Viewed February 4, 2015. McMurdo's Camp is a Sherlockian society in Michigan. See https://mcmurdoscamp.wordpress.com/. Viewed February 4, 2015.

stories as told in such summaries are very different in structure from the stories as crafted by Doyle. An example may make this plausible. Typically such a summary, say of Doyle's "His Last Bow," begins by revealing that Altamont is Sherlock Holmes, which is a revelation that Doyle hid throughout most of the story. Then I would read the written story and listen to the Timson reading. Although these are identical in words, the impact of each was sometimes significantly different. Then I would let what I had read/heard marinate for some hours in my brain as I tried to figure out what to write. Perhaps in the subsequent twenty-four hours, I would have a feeling that I was prepared to do a topical or opening sentence. Two hours later, I would have my mini-essay drafted. Sometimes I would look into the books of various commentators. Martin Dakin's commentary[5] has long been a favorite source. I also frequently turned to the wonderful annotated editions done by William S. Baring-Gould[6] and by Leslie Klinger,[7] because they supplied relevant information and insightful commentary. I also found that internet rich in information on the Holmes stories.

Let us now turn to the question: Is there a correlation between the dramatic quality of the story and whether it fits with a Gestalt shift analysis? A key part of my approach was to discern Gestalts or structures that were central to the dramatic impact to the narrative. Sometimes this took a good deal of searching. Sometimes the contrasts central to the Gestalts were between people or even within a person. Sometimes they were about the nature of the story: Is this primarily a detective story, a sports story, or a love story (think of "The Missing Three-Quarter")? From early in the process, I was fully aware that what I wanted to locate was a Gestalt shift. What I gradually learned was that linked to this in most cases was a Gestalt shift point, a specific place in the story that corresponds to what happens when we are looking at the duck/rabbit Gestalt, seeing only the duck when suddenly a rabbit appears and the duck disappears. Typically in the stories, this shift first occurs in Holmes, then in those around him (e.g., Watson, the official detective, the reader, etc.). This suggests that Doyle

---

[5] D. Martin Dakin. *A Sherlock Holmes Commentary* (Newton Abbot: David & Charles, 1974).

[6] Arthur Conan Doyle. *Annotated Sherlock Holmes: The Four Novels and the Fifty-Six Short Stories* Complete, annotated by William S. Baring-Gould, 2nd ed., 2 vols. (New York: C. N. Potter, 1975).

[7] Arthur Conan Doyle. *New Annotated Sherlock Holmes*, annotated by Leslie Klinger, 3 volumes (New York: Norton, 2005).

faced a major challenge: he needed to structure the story in such a way that at the Gestalt shift point the reader would not have suspected the Gestalt that would then be revealed, but Doyle would also need to structure his narrative in such a way that the reader would relatively quickly see the correctness of Holmes's solution. Doyle, I am suggesting, wanted the reader to respond with an "AHA" or an "how could I have missed this?" He or she might say "Of course, the trainer was killed by Silver Blaze" or "How did I miss that Jack McMurdo was actually Birdy Edwards?" Put differently, Doyle wanted to produce the Gestalt shift effect, even if that effect had not yet been named or carefully studied.

Enough background. These efforts allowed me to divide the sixty stories into three groups. In Group One, I placed stories in which I see a clear-cut Gestalt shift or a set of Gestalt shifts. I have listed forty-two stories in this group. As readers of this book will realize, Doyle's *The Valley of Fear* strikes me as a particularly splendid example.

Group One

1. "Black Peter"
2. "The Blanched Soldier"
3. "The Bruce-Partington Plans"
4. "A Case of Identity"
5. "Charles Augustus Milverton"
6. "The Crooked Man"
7. "The Dancing Men"
8. "The Dying Detective"
9. "The Empty House"
10. "The Engineer's Thumb"
11. "The Final Problem"
12. "The Golden Pince-Nez"
13. "His Last Bow"
14. "The Illustrious Client"
15. "The Disappearance of Lady Frances Carfax"
16. "The Lion's Mane"
17. "The Mazarin Stone"
18. "The Missing Three-Quarter"
19. "The Musgrave Ritual"
20. "The Naval Treaty"
21. "The Norwood Builder"

22. "The Priory School"
23. "The Red-Headed League"
24. "The Resident Patient"
25. "The Retired Colourman"
26. "A Scandal in Bohemia"
27. "The Second Stain"
28. "Shoscombe Old Place"
29. *The Sign of the Four*
30. "Silver Blaze"
31. "The Six Napoleons"
32. "The Solitary Cyclist"
33. "The Speckled Band"
34. "The Stock-Broker's Clerk"
35. *A Study in Scarlet*
36. "The Sussex Vampire"
37. "Thor Bridge"
38. "The Three Students"
39. "The Twisted Lip"
40. *The Valley of Fear*
41. "The Veiled Lodger"
42. "The Yellow Face"

Group Two contains fifteen cases where although I believe that Gestalt shifts occur, the shifts are less clear or less dramatic than in the first group. I see them as supporting my thesis, but to a lesser degree.

Group Two

1. "The Abbey Grange"
2. "The Beryl Coronet"
3. "The Blue Carbuncle"
4. "The Boscombe Valley Mystery"
5. "The Cardboard Box"
6. "The Copper Beeches"
7. "The Creeping Man"
8. "The Five Orange Pips"
9. "The *Gloria Scott*"
10. *The Hound of the Baskervilles*
11. "The Noble Bachelor"

12. "The Red Circle"
13. "The Three Gables"
14. "The Three Garridebs"
15. "Wisteria Lodge"

A third group, with three members, lists stories in which I struggled to see a Gestalt shift. This does not necessarily indicate that they are weak stories or stories with less drama. It may simply mean that I failed to see or appreciate the structure of the story.

Group Three

1. "The Devil's Foot"
2. "The Greek Interpreter"
3. "The Reigate Puzzle"

Dramatic Quality

It is interesting to ask whether the use of a Gestalt approach in a Holmes story correlates with the dramatic quality of the story. I had earlier commented that the Gestalt shift might add to the drama of the narrative. One approach to this is to compare the ranking of the stories based on a survey conducted by the *Baker Street Journal*.[8]

The Baker Street Journal Ranking

1. "The Speckled Band"
2. "The Red-Headed League"
3. "A Scandal in Bohemia"
4. "Silver Blaze"
5. "The Blue Carbuncle"
6. "The Musgrave Ritual"
7. "The Final Problem"
8. "The Empty House"
9. "The Dancing Men"

[8]For more information, see http://www.bestofsherlock.com/story/storyhm.htm and http://bookclubs.barnesandnoble.com/t5/Mystery/Conan-Doyle-s-Favorite-Sherlock-Holmes-Stories/td-p/191527.

10. "The Six Napoleons"
11. "The Bruce-Partington Plans"
12. "The Man with the Twisted Lip"

It seems significant that of these twelve stories, eleven are in the first group; one appears in the second group and none appears in the third group, which contains the three stories that resist a Gestalt interpretation.

Another ranking of the stories came from Conan Doyle himself. His list of his nineteen favorite short stories does not include "The Blue Carbuncle." Moreover, the only story that appears in Doyle's list that is not from my Group One is "The Five Orange Pips."[9]

Overall, it appears that there is impressive agreement between my categorization and these two lists of favorite stories. Looked at more broadly, the fact that many readers recognize Doyle as the most gifted author of detective stories can in part be explained by my thesis that he was a master at writing stories with a Gestalt shift structure.

DOYLE AS DRAMATIST

What does this Gestalt shift analysis suggest regarding Doyle's approach in writing his sixty Holmes stories? As noted before, I have found no direct evidence that Doyle was consciously aware of the idea of a Gestalt shift. On the other hand, I believe that the research presented in this book supports making some suggestions about various ideas/practices central to Doyle's writing style. For example, it is clear that Doyle was especially attracted to featuring contrasts in his stories. He designed Watson as a contrast to Holmes and also delighted in contrasting Holmes with various official detectives. Mycroft contrasts with Holmes almost as much at Holmes contrasts with Moriarty (despite their similarities). Doyle at times sent forth Holmes disguised as an old lady with a parasol ("The Mazarin Stone"), an elderly bibliophile ("The Empty House"), or an up-and-coming plumber ("Charles Augustus Milverton"). Doyle also contrasts Holmes on his deathbed with Holmes rejuvenated by Culverton Smith's revelations ("The Dying Detective")! In "The Crooked Man," he contrasts Colonel James Barclay with all his distinctions with the broken-down nearly penniless Henry Wood, and then shows how differ-

[9] http://www.trivia-library.com/b/sir-arthur-conan-doyle-favorite-sherlock-holmes-stories.htm.

ently each eventually appears to Nancy Barclay, when at the end of the story it becomes clear who the real "Crooked Man" is. The entities in these pairings are certainly *distinct*. And the transformations they undergo are *unexpected*.

Doyle also took great delight is serving up *rapid* plot twists or transformations in his stories. In seconds, Holmes in *The Valley of Fear* raised Jack Douglas from the dead and later he transformed the nefarious Jack McMurdo into the heroic Birdy Edwards, whom we realize is actually Jack Douglas. With a little soap and water and a few moments, we see the beggar with the twisted lip become the upstanding Neville St. Clair. The same substances turn an undistinguished horse into Silver Blaze and also into a killer. When Von Bork opens the packet of stolen British military secrets and finds only a book on bee culture, savvy readers immediately recognize that a great detective has returned from retirement and emerged as a war hero. Not only do these pairings change rapidly, the pairs are clearly distinct from each other and correspondingly the shifts are *unexpected*. The point is that these and many other cases, because they have all four marks of a Gestalt shift, can be characterized as Gestalt shifts. Moreover, Doyle in numerous cases identifies what we have called the Gestalt shift point or moment; Holmes, seemingly out of the blue, announces regarding a case: "I have solved it," or, after stating that he has determined who the criminal is, opens the door and in a few minutes turns the cabman into Jefferson Hope, who was central to the death of Drebber and Stangerson (*A Study in Scarlet*).

We have direct testimony from Doyle on the importance in writing a story of hiding the key idea that the author has formulated: "Having got that key idea, one's next task is to conceal it and lay emphasis upon everything which can make for a different explanation."[10] This is exactly what the creator of a Gestalt must do. In his wonderful essay titled "How to Write a Detective Story," which Gilbert Keith Chesterton published in 1921, he stressed a relevant point and illustrated it by discussing Doyle's "Silver Blaze." He wrote: "the fact or figure explaining everything should be a familiar fact or figure. The criminal should be in the foreground, not in the capacity of criminal, but in some other capacity which nevertheless gives him a natural right to be in the foreground." And he adds, regarding "Silver Blaze":

---

[10] Arthur Conan Doyle, *Memories and Adventures and Western Wanderings* (Newcastle on Tyne: Cambridge Scholars Publishing, 2009), 75.

[T]he point is that the horse is very obvious. The story is named after the horse; it is all about the horse; the horse is in the foreground all the time, but always in another capacity. As a thing of great value he remains for the reader the Favourite; it is only as a criminal that he is a dark horse. It is a story of theft in which the horse plays the part of the jewel until we forget that the jewel can also play the part of the weapon. That is one of the first rules I would suggest, if I had to make rules for this form of composition. Generally speaking, the agent should be a familiar figure in an unfamiliar function. The thing that we realize must be a thing that we recognize; that is it must be something previously known, and it ought to be something prominently displayed.[11]

CAN A GESTALT SHIFT STRUCTURE BE DETECTED IN OTHER DETECTIVE STORIES?

I have no good direct evidence to give me confidence that this is the case. Nonetheless, I feel somewhat more confident that this is the case than when I began to explore this thesis. Recently, I happened on a test of the possibility of the correctness of this idea. Totally independently of the writing of this book but late in the process, I began to read some stories about a detective of roughly the same time period as Holmes by an author who was known to be very fond of Holmes. Overall, this British author attained a literary reputation that rivals and may surpass that of Doyle, and he designed his detective to be comparably clever but in almost every other way different from Holmes. The author: Gilbert Keith Chesterton. His detective: Father Brown. This led me to test my technique on the first Father Brown story, which was published in 1910: "The Blue Cross." My analysis of this story appears as an appendix to this book. I was delighted by how well it seemed to fit the thesis of this volume. Moreover, a less careful reading led me to the belief that at least some of the other stories in *The Innocence of Father Brown* (1911), the first Father Brown anthology, exhibit a structure that fits the Gestalt shift pattern. This probably will not surprise persons who know Chesterton's nickname: The Prince of Paradox.

---

[11] G. K. Chesterton, "How to Write a Detective Story," which essay is available on the internet at http://www.chesterton.org/how-to-write-detective/ and was viewed on September 19, 2015.

BIBLIOGRAPHY

PRINTED SOURCES

Dakin, D. Martin. *A Sherlock Holmes Commentary* (Newton Abbot: David & Charles, 1974).

Doyle, Arthur Conan. *Annotated Sherlock Holmes: The Four Novels and the Fifty-Six Short Stories* Complete, annotated by William S. Baring-Gould, 2nd ed., 2 vols. (New York: C. N. Potter, 1975).

Doyle, Arthur Conan. *Memories and Adventures and Western Wanderings* (Newcastle on Tyne: Cambridge Scholars Publishing, 2009).

Doyle, Arthur Conan. *New Annotated Sherlock Holmes.* annotated by Leslie Klinger, 3 volumes (New York: Norton, 2005).

INTERNET SOURCES

"Story Summary from McMurdo's Camp" at https://mcmurdoscamp.wordpress.com/story-summaries/stud/. Viewed 4 February 2015.

Chesterton, G. K., "How to Write a Detective Story," which essay is available on the internet at http://www.chesterton.org/how-to-write-detective/ and was viewed 19 September 2015.

Hoy aummaries of the Sherlock Holmes stories; http://www.diogenes-club.com/hoyadventures.htm. Viewed 4 February 2015.

http://bookclubs.barnesandnoble.com/t5/Mystery/Conan-Doyle-s-Favorite-Sherlock-Holmes-Stories/td-p/191527.

http://www.bestofsherlock.com/story/storyhm.htm.

http://www.trivia-library.com/b/sir-arthur-conan-doyle-favorite-sherlock-holmes-stories.htm.

Sherlockian.Net at http://www.sherlockian.net/.

AUDIO SOURCE

Sir Arthur Conan Doyle. The Complete Sherlock Holmes, read by David Timson. Naxos Audiobooks.

Appendix A: G. K. Chesterton's "The Blue Cross" (1910)

In assessing whether this story has a Gestalt shift structure, it is imperative to keep in mind that with it Gilbert Keith Chesterton (1874–1936) sought to launch a new detective. During the first decade of the twentieth century, various authors, influenced by the extraordinary success of Doyle's Sherlock Holmes stories, explored writing detective fiction. As a fan of detective stories and a prolific author, Chesterton was among those aware of this opportunity. In fact, in 1904 he had already made an attempt to enter this market, the chief result of which was a book he published that year titled *The Club of Queer Trades*.[1] In 1910, Chesterton decided to try this market again. His goal was to create a detective who could compete with Holmes's remarkable array of talents and long list of successes, despite being a very different type of person using quite different techniques. This presented no small challenge. But more than this, Chesterton's great concern throughout his life was to champion various religious, philosophical, and political causes. Doyle also favored various causes, but refrained from burdening Holmes with these issues; for example, Holmes never championed spiritualism, whereas Doyle spent much of the last decade of his life writing and lecturing on spiritualist claims. Chesterton probably realized

---

[1] John Peterson, "Introduction," *Collected Works of G. K. Chesterton*, XII (San Francisco: Ignatius Press, 2005), 15–18.

© The Author(s) 2018
M. J. Crowe, *The Gestalt Shift in Conan Doyle's Sherlock Holmes Stories*, https://doi.org/10.1007/978-3-319-98291-5

he needed not only a Holmes substitute but also a Watson, a Moriarty, and a Lestrade for his stories. And, not least important, he desired a detective able to succeed using at least some techniques comparable in power but quite different from those employed by Holmes.

Chesterton opened his "The Blue Cross" by introducing Valentin, the "most famous investigator of the world."[2] It would be natural for readers of this first story to assume that Valentin would be the hero of the story. Chesterton devoted his second and third paragraphs to introducing that "colossus of crime," Hercule Flambeau, on whom Chesterton remarks that on "his best days (I mean, of course, his worst) Flambeau was a figure as statuesque and international as the Kaiser."[3] As is well known, Flambeau ends up doing double duty: after serving as Father Brown's Moriarty, he emerges in later stories as Brown's Watson.

This sets the stage for Chesterton to introduce (seemingly as an aside) a "little priest" named Father Brown; as Chesterton states, "he had a face as round and dull as a Norfolk dumpling; he had eyes as empty as the North Sea."[4] Brown's mission is to bring a precious crucifix to a Eucharistic Congress, a fact that Valentin specifically advises Brown not to mention, whereas Brown with "moon-calf simplicity" does exactly the opposite. The reader naturally expects that this rather hopeless bungler will be the victim.

Father Brown then links up with another priest (who turns out not to be a priest, but rather to be the infamous Flambeau, who is disguised as a priest) attending the conference. He accompanies Brown as they travel through the London area, chatting about various matters and stopping periodically for snacks. In the course of their rambles, they encounter such strange events as salt in a sugar dish at one restaurant, apples knocked out of their basket at a grocery, signs shifted in a store window, a splash on the wall of another eatery, a broken window, and so on. The bungler priest seems to be the source of these problems. None of this makes any sense to anyone except to the astute Valentin, who is desperately looking for clues yet finds nothing but these anomalies. The two priests then reach Hampstead Heath, where they engage in a discussion of the question of intelligent life in outer space. Suddenly the taller priest interrupts this discussion by telling the little priest to hand over the cross. The tall priest,

[2] G. K. Chesterton, "The Blue Cross" in Chesterton's *The Innocence of Father Brown* (New York: Penguin Books, 1975), 7.

[3] Chesterton, *Innocence*, 8.

[4] Chesterton, *Innocence*, 28.

we recognize, is Flambeau in disguise; the short priest responds simply "No," and explains that he has already sent the cross to its destination. Moreover, this "celibate simpleton," as Flambeau describes him, turns out to have substantial knowledge of crime and criminals, which he attributes partly to his many hours in the confessional. We then gradually learn in the final paragraphs that this apparent bungler has known all along that his fellow priest is not a priest and that Valentin accompanied by then by two police has been following them, attracted by the bizarre trail that Brown has been leaving (e.g., misplaced sugar and a broken window). They eventually emerge and capture the master criminal. The final lines of the story are these:

> And even as [Flambeau] turned away to collect his property, the three policemen came out from under the twilight trees. Flambeau was an artist and a sportsman. He stepped back and swept Valentin a great bow.
> "Do not bow to me, *mon ami*," said Valentin with silver clearness. "Let us both bow to our master."
> And they both stood an instant uncovered while the little Essex priest blinked about for his umbrella.[5]

In these few minutes, a Gestalt shift has occurred. The "most famous investigator of the world" and the "colossus of crime" have recognized this bungling clergyman, Fr. Brown, as a master detective working, it seems, on new principles forged in such sources as a confessional. Valentin is deposed as the *ne plus ultra* detective. Flambeau for the first time has met more than his match; in fact, after years he has now been identified and is under arrest. The Cross is saved. The reader finally recognizes that Chesterton has created a new detective who has emerged suddenly and only at the very end of this story. Probably even Chesterton was unaware that this unique detective would over the next twenty-five years succeed in attaining solutions in fifty-one more stories and an international reputation.

What I am suggesting is that although Chesterton's Fr. Brown was drastically different from Doyle's Holmes in appearance and methods from the great detective that Doyle had so successfully created, Chesterton seems to have carried over from Doyle a dramatic technique present in the Holmes stories: structuring his stories in accordance with a form of change that would decades later be described as a Gestalt shift. Moreover, Chesterton

[5] Chesterton, *Innocence*, 29.

in 1925 in his "How to Write a Detective Story," suggested: "The first and fundamental principle is that the aim of a mystery story, as of every other story and every other mystery, is not darkness but light. The story is written for the moment when the reader does understand, not merely for the many preliminary moments when he does not understand. The misunderstanding is only meant as a dark outline of cloud to bring out the brightness of that instant of intelligibility."[6]

[6] G. K. Chesterton, "How to Write a Detective Story," available on the internet at http://www3.dbu.edu/mitchell/chesterton_on_detective_fiction.htm.

Appendix B: Some Questions and Some Answers

Of the Recent Characters Modeled on Sherlock Holmes Character, Which Is Most Authentic?

In the last two decades, characters modeled on Doyle's Sherlock Holmes have appeared in numerous films and television shows, leading critics to discuss which production is most faithful to the original stories. Among such dramatizations are *Elementary* with Johnny Lee Miller, British television's *Sherlock* with Benedict Cumberbatch, and the films featuring Robert Downey as Holmes. A few years ago a friend suggested another candidate for the distinction of having come closest to the spirit of the original stories. This seemed at first a most unlikely candidate because the central figure is not named Holmes and rather than being a detective is a physician. Nonetheless, I followed up on her lead and have come to accept its plausibility. To offer a definitive answer to this question would take a person with far more knowledge of the candidates than I can claim, but my investigation has led to a suggestion.

The candidate is named *House, M.D.*, a television show featuring Hugh Laurie as physician Gregory House. The show's 177 episodes ran from 2004 to 2012; in fact, it was the most watched series in the world in 2008. The evidence that David Shore, who created House, used Doyle's stories as models is compelling. For example, Shore explicitly stated that he drew upon Doyle's stories in creating House (whose name is a variant of

© The Author(s) 2018
M. J. Crowe, *The Gestalt Shift in Conan Doyle's Sherlock Holmes Stories*, https://doi.org/10.1007/978-3-319-98291-5

Holmes) and whose first name, Gregory, comes from Inspector Gregson. House, like Holmes, has an addiction (vicodin), a closest friend, Dr. James Wilson (think Dr. John Watson), and a brusque manner. More significantly, although a rather irascible figure, House has a genius for diagnosing diseases, typically rare diseases. Many more shared traits could be and are cited by authors who discuss the nature of the House stories.[7]

Examined from my perspective, most discussions of the similarities of the *House* stories miss the most crucial point: the structure (but of course not the content) of the *House* stories is nearly identical to the **structure** of the Holmes stories. Both fit the pattern of featuring a Gestalt shift. It is clear that the structure of each *House* episode is that House and his team of physicians engage a puzzle: how to diagnose and cure a patient. As in the Holmes stories, the author offers the reader various promising solutions to this problem. Then as the story comes to an end, House discerns a solution that typically reconciles all the complexities and usually saves the patient's life. House's theory rapidly draws together all the diverse information that has been gathered and convinces other experts that he has solved the case.[8] Three of the fourteen writers of the *House* stories were brought together for an interview in which they discussed how they write the stories. At one point they state: "We need to find a really cool disease that a genius diagnostician can't figures out immediately ... but we can,

---

[7] See, for example, Barbara Barnett, *Chasing Zebras: The Unofficial Guide to House, M.D.* (Toronto: ECW Press, 2010), esp. pp. 17–19; Jerold Abrams, "The Logic of Guesswork in Sherlock Holmes," in Henry Jacoby (ed.), *House and Philosophy: Everybody Lies* (Hoboken, N.J.: John Wiley & Sons, c. 2009), 55–70; Susan Rowland, "House and Ho(l)mes," in Luke Hockley and Leslie Gardner, *House: The Wounded Healer on Television* (New York: Routledge: 2011), 133–151; Leah Wilson (ed.), *House Unauthorized: Vasculitis, Clinic Duty, and Bad Bedside Manner* (Dallas Texas: BenBella Books, 2007); and Donna Andrews, "Sex, Lies, and MRIs" in Leah Wilson, *House Unauthorized*, 221–234.

[8] This information is available in many sources, the most conveniently accessible being the article "House (TV Series)" available on the internet on Wikipedia; see file:///Volumes/SilverPassport/Desk%20Top/HolmesSherlock%20Stuff/House%20TVSeries/House%20 (TV%20series)%20and%20Holmes.webarchive, viewed August 4, 2016. See also file:/// Volumes/SilverPassport/Holmes%20House%20Connection.webarchive and file:/// Volumes/SilverPassport/HolmesHouseConnection.webarchive, also viewed on August 4, 2016. For textual material, see Jerold Abrams, "The Logic of Guesswork in Sherlock Holmes," in Henry Jacoby (ed.), *House and Philosophy: Everybody Lies* (Hoboken, N.J.: John Wiley & Sons, c. 2009), 55–70.

even though we don't know anything about medicine." They add that they face "the challenge of how to hide the disease" and also seek to find diseases that are "plausible but wrong."[9]

In reading the literature on *House*, I have been especially impressed by Barbara Barnett's highly regarded *Chasing Zebras: The Unofficial Guide to House, M.D.* In this context, it is noteworthy that in summarizing every story in the first six seasons, Barnett delineates various characteristics that appear in nearly every story. The most important of these is what she calls the "epiphany," which she describes as "House's (usually) 'lightbulb moment.' The final piece of the diagnostic puzzle falls into place."[10] The transformations to which she is referring are what I call a Gestalt shift. I recognize that the word epiphany expresses that the section contains the key revelation in the story and also conveys the idea that it was previously invisible. I prefer the term Gestalt shift because it is free of religious connotations and because it gives prominence to the pervasive nature of the idea. Moreover, an epiphany is typically injected into a story, whereas for a Gestalt shift, the pattern is present in the story but remains invisible until the hero, by an effort of intellect, finally sees and reveals it.

Is a Gestalt Shift a Necessary Feature of Good Fiction or Does It Provide a Criterion by Which One Can Rank the Quality of Fictional Works?

I do not claim that the presence of a Gestalt switch is a necessary or a sufficient condition for judging the quality of a work of literature. I do suggest that the presence of a Gestalt shift may enhance the dramatic effect of some stories by increasing, for example, the level of engagement or delight that readers experience. Moreover, I believe that the idea of Gestalt shift can help explain the dramatic quality found in a large number of Holmes stories. In addition, some classic works of fiction written before 1900 have as a central feature a sort of Gestalt shift. I think, for

[9] These quotations are taken from a filmed recording titled "Meet the Writers," which is included as a special on the published version of a collection of the Fourth series of *House* shows.

[10] Barnett, *Zebras*, 163.

example, of Sophocles's King Oedipus going through a Gestalt shift when he realizes who it was that killed his predecessor as king. Or consider the transformation that Jane Austen's Elizabeth Bennett experiences in *Pride and Prejudice* as she begins to see Fitzwilliam Darcy in an entirely different way from how she first saw him. Also it seems plausible to suggest that the skillful use of a Gestalt shift can be one factor that is especially helpful in describing the effect of a fictional work on a reader. Think of the section of Doyle's *The Valley of Fear* that centers on the lines: "Birdy Edwards is here. I am Birdy Edwards."[11] I also believe that asking whether a Gestalt shift occurs in a work of fiction can frequently be productive. It leads to a more careful reading of the text and to a sensitive analysis of the reader's reaction to developments in the story. Moreover, it has the advantage that it does not impose categories, which at times may distort the reading of a text.

Another form in which we can consider this question is to ask whether it applies primarily to detective fiction. It is certainly possible that investigating whether a work of fiction features a Gestalt shift is appropriate for detective stories, but not for other genres of literature. Perhaps it would be appropriate for romances, but not for historical fiction. An interesting case is the fiction of William Sydney Porter (1862–1910), who wrote under the pen name O. Henry. The two most famous of his short stories, "The Gift of the Magi," and "The Ransom of Redchief," feature a surprise ending, which has the form of a Gestalt shift. In the former story, a wife in a poor family cuts and sells her luxuriant hair to buy her husband a watch chain, whereas he secretly sells his valuable watch to purchase expensive combs for his wife! O. Henry's fame may in good part have been due to his skill in devising such engaging climaxes. On the other hand, making a surprise ending a necessary condition for judging a work of fiction as superior would seem to run into trouble by leading one to deny the greatness of Flaubert's *Madame Bovary* or Tolstoy's *Anna Karenina*, both of which strike me as stories of unrelenting decline.

Another very prominent near contemporary of Conan Doyle who made use of a structural form that may be comparable to Doyle's Gestalt shifts was James Joyce (1882–1941). In 1914, Joyce published a collection of short stories titled *Dubliners*, which stories portray life in Ireland in the early years of the twentieth century. In many of the stories, the main

---

[11] Doyle, *Holmes*, II, 1014.

character undergoes what Joyce called an Epiphany, in which the main character experiences at the very end of the story a life-changing illumination or insight into his life. Joyce at one point referred to it as a "showing forth." One example is the story "Araby," in which a young man recounts his efforts to form a relationship with a young woman. To this end, he sets off to purchase a gift for her at a bazaar in Dublin called Araby, but ultimately fails at this. The story ends with a few lines in which the youth recognizes the actual state of his life:

> I lingered before her stall, though I knew my stay was useless, to make my interest in her wares seem the more real. Then I turned away slowly and walked down the middle of the bazaar. I allowed the two pennies to fall against the sixpence in my pocket. I heard a voice call from one end of the gallery that the light was out. The upper part of the hall was now completely dark.
>
> Gazing up into the darkness I saw myself as a creature driven and derided by vanity; and my eyes burned with anguish and anger.[12]

These final lines transform the rest of the story. In fact, it is sometimes suggested that Joyce was actually writing about Ireland, which he viewed as failing to establish itself as a modern nation. Joyce also employed epiphanies in some of his other writings, famously so in for example his *Portrait of the Artist as a Young Man* and also in his most famous work, *Ulysses*. Of course, the content of Doyle's Gestalt shifts was very different from those of Joyce's epiphanies, but their structures and functions seem comparable.

HAVE SHERLOCKIANS PREVIOUSLY SUGGESTED THAT THERE IS A GESTALT SHIFT PATTERN IN THE HOLMES STORIES?

Although I have repeatedly searched for studies of this form, I have not located any. Nor have I encountered critics of literature in general who take this approach. This admittedly is somewhat worrying! On the other hand, my failure to find examples of such an approach encourages me to think that I may be onto something. My investigation would have ended long ago had I found either that an earlier investigator had built a case for my thesis that has been favorably received, or if the reaction had been

---

[12] James Joyce, *Dubliners* (New York: Modern Library, 1916), 41.

rejection. The single somewhat relevant instance that I located was especially meaningful to me. I discovered this author's views totally by chance when reading an article titled "Father Brown, Sherlock Holmes, and the Mystery of Man," by a now deceased University of Notre Dame colleague, Frederick J. Crosson, who was a teacher, mentor, and friend to me for many decades. At one point in his essay, he comments that in a good detective story, what distinguishes it is that

> the real meaning of the events is partly revealed and partly concealed—or rather, is almost wholly revealed, but so camouflaged by non-pertinent data that we do not perceive until the detective discloses it to us. It is possible to have the elements of a gestalt before us, and still to miss the pattern; and that is what makes a successful detective story, in large part. As gestalt psychology has taught us, in such a pattern it is the whole which gives meaning to the parts....[13]

I take this as evidence that Fred Crosson might have agreed with my analysis.

How Did I Come to the View that It Is Productive to Analyze the Holmes Stories in Terms of Gestalt Shifts?

I am not a literary scholar, but rather a professor in a Great Books program whose specialty is the history of science. This is relevant because various historians and philosophers of science have suggested that at least some scientific theories function as wholes; for example, we can most effectively view the Copernican and ancient Ptolemaic systems as competing wholes, rather than as directly testable scientific theories. In other words, in deciding between them, scientists have typically considered not only observations, but also such factors as the methodological features associated with each, its philosophical and religious implications, the elegance of the theories, and much else. As Thomas Kuhn stressed in his *Structure of Scientific Revolutions*, scientists typically choose not between theories but between more capacious entities he called paradigms. This influenced my thought

---

[13] Frederick J. Crosson, "Father Brown, Sherlock Holmes, and the Mystery of Man" in *A Chesterton Celebration*, ed. Rufus William Rauch (Notre Dame, IN: University of Notre Dame Press, 1983), 21–33.

when I began to wonder how Doyle could be so successful in making his stories very dramatic. It occurred to me that this characteristic might productively be analyzed as comparable to a Gestalt shift. Kuhn in his *Structures* drew on the idea of a Gestalt shift.[14] This is particularly evident in the cover of the third edition of his book, which features a version of the Necker Cube. Moreover, as noted earlier, Kuhn in formulating his position drew on Wittgenstein's analysis of the duck/rabbit Gestalt shift, pointing out that what is seen in this image depends not only on what lines are in the drawing but also on what is in the head of the person who sometimes sees the figure as a rabbit, and other times as a duck.

This connection is significant in that it sheds light on an important feature of Doyle's overall philosophy of science. Periodically, Doyle sends a message of this form: A case can be solved decisively if one carefully seeks all the relevant facts and views them without bias. Most present-day philosophers of science have backed away from this position, noting that in some cases a given set of facts and observations can be explained in terms of two or more different theories. Gestalt psychology provides numerous examples of cases where an extensive collection of information can be interpreted in two or more ways. This is a central claim in a highly respected study of Holmes's methodology, which asserts that Holmes's method is actually a version of what Charles Peirce called Abduction.[15] In other words, I came to the Holmes stories with years of experience analyzing developments in the history of science that in many cases show a pattern corresponding to a Gestalt shift.

---

[14] Thomas S. Kuhn, *The Structure of Scientific Revolutions*, 2nd. ed. (Chicago: University of Chicago Press, 1970), 111–114.

[15] [illegible] *in Semiotics*) (Bloomington: Indiana University Press, c. 1983). This volume contains essays by, among others, Thomas A. Sebeok, Marcello Truzzi, Carlo Ginzberg, Gian Paolo Carettini, and Jaakko Hintikka. The key essay in the volume seems to be: Thomas Sebeok and Jean Umiker Sebeok, "You know My Method: A Juxtaposition of Charles S. Peirce and Sherlock Holmes," 11–54. Numerous Sherlockian scholars have accepted this analysis. See, for example, Douglas Kerr, *Conan Doyle: Writing, Profession, and Practice* (Oxford University Press, 2012), 128–129.

IT IS SOMETIMES CLAIMED THAT THERE ARE TWO TYPES OF HOLMESIAN LITERARY STUDIES. WHICH TYPE APPEARS IN THIS BOOK?

There is a curious feature evident in the abundant serious writings about the Sherlock Holmes stories. By serious writings, I mean writings based on substantial, typically referenced research written in a somber tone. Such writings in the great majority of cases fall into two *very* different categories, which usually dictate where and how they are published.[16] **First category**: these writings look very much like other serious writing about literature; their authors typically publish them in journals or as books printed by publishers who serve readers interested in serious scholarship. In fact, in every way they are comparable to typical writing about good literature. **Second category**: these publications, sometimes called Sherlockian Studies, although in format nearly identical to the first group, are radically different. Studies in this form have their origin in a paper, now somewhat forgotten, published in 1912 by a young man known as gifted not only with unusual seriousness and brilliance of thought but also with extraordinary wit. This was Ronald Knox, who in 1912 while studying at Oxford to become an Anglican priest published a paper critical of what theologians call the "Higher Criticism." He titled his paper "Studies in the Literature of Sherlock Holmes."[17] In this essay, Knox treated the Holmes stories not as literature but as history, as tales recorded by John Watson, a retired physician, whose literary agent was Arthur Conan Doyle. Just as the "Higher Critics" were intent on pointing out inconsistencies in the scriptures, Knox noted that Watson has two first names in the Holmes stories. Similarly, whereas the Higher Critics were intent upon arguing that the Old Testament *Isaiah* was written not by one person but by a proto-Isaiah and a deutero-Isaiah, Knox argued that some of the Holmes stories were written by a proto-Watson and others by a deutero-Watson, bodily the same but the latter having succumbed to alcohol. Gradually, this sort of approach caught on among some persons who not only read the Holmes stories but also wrote about them. Dorothy L. Sayers famously described the spirit in which such authors write:

---

[16] For a helpful discussion of this distinction, see Christopher Redmond, *Sherlock Holmes Handbook*, 2nd ed. (Toronto: Dundurn Press, 2009), 310–315.

[17] Michael J. Crowe (ed.), *Ronald Knox and Sherlock Holmes: The Origin of Sherlockian Studies* (Indianapolis: Gasogene Imprint of Wessex Press, 2011). For Knox's famous essay, see 33–57.

The game of applying the methods of the "Higher Criticism" to the Sherlock Holmes canon was begun, many years ago, by Monsignor Ronald Knox, with the aim of showing that, by those methods, one could disintegrate a modern classic as speciously as a certain school of critics have endeavoured to disintegrate the Bible. Since then, the thing has become a hobby among a select set of jesters here and in America. The rule of the game is that it must be played as solemnly as a county cricket match at Lord's: the slightest touch of extravagance or burlesque ruins the atmosphere.[18]

A well-known expert on the Holmes stories, Steven Doyle, estimated to me that the number of such writings must exceed ten thousand. It is important to stress that, in format, these publications are typically identical to Category One publications.

Two tests distinguish between these types. The first test is easily applied but not infallible. It consists of checking for the appearance of one word; it appears in the first type, but almost never in the second type: the word is Doyle (i.e., Watson's literary agent). The other test is to examine the face of the author when writing, asking: Is the author's tongue in his/her cheek? Because this test is hard to apply, a variant is to read an essay suspected of being Category Two type to a sane person. If the person either begins serious laughing or alternatively looks at you with an expression that seems to indicate that the person doubts your sanity, then you are reading a study of the second type.

This raises the question: Into which category does the present study fall? It is possible that different readers of this book will see it rather differently. My own view is that although recognizing the attractions of writings in Category Two and the brilliance of many of its practitioners, I nonetheless find that having practiced academic (Category One type) research and writing throughout my career, I revert to the Category One approach, but with significant enthusiasm for Category Two type Holmesian studies. Part of the explanation of this may be that I admire Knox's thought and approach and believe that although he created the Category Two approach, he did it for Category One reasons.

---

[18] Dorothy L. Sayers, *Unpopular Opinions: Twenty-One Essays* (New York: Harcourt Brace, 1947), v vi.

Appendix C: Table of the Types of the Sixty Sherlock Holmes Stories in Terms of Their Gestalt Shifts

A Study in Scarlet (novel, 1887)	B (2 bipolar shifts: transformation of Holmes from pompous airhead into an extraordinary detective; and transformation of Hope from ruthless killer into a person with whom we can sympathize)
The Sign of the Four (novel, 1890)	B (2 bipolar shifts: in one case, a great treasure is lost; in the other case, a great treasure is gained)
The Adventures of Sherlock Holmes, 1892	
A Scandal in Bohemia, 1891	B (3 bipolar shifts: King, Adler, Holmes)
The Red-Headed League, 1891	B (2 bipolar shifts: the case and Clay)
A Case of Identity, 1891	B (2 bipolar shifts: Hosmer and the case)
The Boscombe Valley Mystery, 1891	B (3 bipolar shifts: the case, McCarthy, and Turner)
The Five Orange Pips, 1891	B (1 bipolar shift: nature of the case changes)
The Man with the Twisted Lip, 1891	B (2 bipolar shifts: the case and St. Clair)
The Blue Carbuncle, 1892	B (1 bipolar shift: the case; maybe the hat; maybe Turner)
The Speckled Band, 1892	B (2 bipolar shifts: the case and Dr. Roylott)
The Engineer's Thumb, 1892	B (1 bipolar shift: how to guess how far they traveled)

(continued)

© The Author(s) 2018
M. J. Crowe, *The Gestalt Shift in Conan Doyle's Sherlock Holmes Stories*, https://doi.org/10.1007/978-3-319-98291-5

(continued)

The Noble Bachelor, 1892	D (1 Dalmatian shift: Lady St. Simon does not exist)
The Beryl Coronet, 1892	B (3 bipolar shifts: Arthur, Mary, and Burnwell are transformed)
The Copper Beeches, 1892	B (1 bipolar shift: country house seems ideal but is actually dangerous)
The Memoirs of Sherlock Holmes, 1894	
Silver Blaze, 1892	D and B (D for the horse as absent; B for the horse as killer)
The Yellow Face, 1893	B (3 bipolar shifts: surprise to Munro and Holmes; Munro then surprises Effie; and Holmes learns some humility)
The Stock-Broker's Clerk, 1893	B (1 bipolar shift: crash of the Franco-Midland Hardware Co.)
The *Gloria Scott*, 1893	D (2 Dalmatian shifts: the first in Trevor's father, the second in Holmes)
The Musgrave Ritual, 1893	D (1 Dalmatian shift, with at least three parts)
The Reigate Puzzle, 1893	B and D (B being Holmes's recovery of health; D being his detection of the nature of the crime)
The Crooked Man, 1893	D and B (D being the discovery of what really happened; B being the reversal of the images of Barclay and Wood)
The Resident Patient, 1893	B (1 bipolar shift: discovering who the criminals are)
The Greek Interpreter, 1893	B (numerous small bipolar shifts)
The Naval Treaty, 1893	B (1 major Dalmatian shift, seen first by Holmes, who then reveals it to Watson, Phelps, and the Foreign Office)
The Final Problem, 1893	B (numerous bipolar shifts)
The Hound of the Baskervilles (novel, 1901–1902)	B (2 bipolar shifts: seventeenth-century Hugo Baskerville versus Stapleton; Stapleton versus his wife as the killer.) D and B (1 Dalmatian and one bipolar shift, the first being Holmes's seeing Stapleton in the Baskerville painting; the second being Holmes's solution to the case versus Bayard's solution)
The Return of Sherlock Holmes, 1905	
The Empty House, 1903	B (3 bipolar shifts that occur in Holmes, Moran, and Lestrade)
The Norwood Builder, 1903	B (1 bipolar shift, occurring when Oldacre suddenly appears)
The Dancing Men, 1903	B (2 bipolar shifts: deciphering the code and capturing he criminal)
The Solitary Cyclist, 1903	B (1 bipolar shift: the cyclist revealed as friend, not enemy)
The Priory School, 1904	B (1 bipolar shift, which leads us to see that the kidnapper of Lord Holdernesse's son was the Lord's illegitimate son, and in a sense the Lord himself)

(*continued*)

(continued)

Black Peter, 1904	B (1 bipolar shift: from Hopkins's analysis to Holmes's)
Charles Augustus Milverton, 1904	B (2 bipolar shifts: Holmes and Watson commit criminal actions; Milverton is executed)
The Six Napoleons, 1904	B (1 bipolar shift, which contrasts the methods of Lestrade with those of Holmes)
The Three Students, 1904	B (1 bipolar shift, which suggests that the most successful method of solving a crime involves approaching it in an oblique rather than a direct manner)
The Golden Pince-Nez, 1904	D (1 Dalmatian shift with Holmes making the figure appear)
The Missing Three-Quarter, 1904	B (1 Dalmatian shift: we see that Staunton, rather than being missing, was exactly where he should have been)
The Abbey Grange, 1904	B (1 bipolar shift, between two accounts of the murder)
The Second Stain, 1904	B (1 bipolar or possibly multipolar shift regarding the letter)
The Valley of Fear (novel, 1914–1915)	B (3 bipolar shifts: Douglas dead, Douglas alive; McMurdo arch criminal, McMurdo arch detective; Douglas is Edwards.)
His Last Bow, 1917	
Wisteria Lodge, 1908	B (3 bipolar shifts, centering on Baynes, Henderson, and England versus South America)
The Cardboard Box, 1893	B (1 bipolar shift, with Holmes's view supplanting Lestrade's)
The Red Circle, 1911	B (1 bipolar shift, centering on the death of Georgiano)
The Bruce-Partington Plans, 1908	B (1 bipolar shift, centering on Holmes's view of what happened in this case)
The Dying Detective, 1913	B (2 bipolar shifts, one involving Holmes's health, the other regarding Holmes's views of Watson's medical abilities)
Lady Frances Carfax, 1911	B (5 bipolar shifts, centered on Carfax, Green, Shlessinger, Holmes, and a coffin)
The Devil's Foot, 1910	B (Possibly 1 bipolar shift between the demonic and the naturalistic)
His Last Bow, 1917	B (1 giant bipolar shift, which entails a number of smaller shifts)
The Case-Book of Sherlock Holmes, 1927	
The Illustrious Client, 1924	B (1 giant bipolar shift, which entails a number of smaller shifts)
The Blanched Soldier, 1926	B (1 giant bipolar shift, entailing smaller shifts)
The Mazarin Stone, 1921	B (1 giant bipolar shift, tying together various small shifts)

(*continued*)

(continued)

The Three Gables, 1926	B (1 bipolar shift regarding the value of a house)
The Sussex Vampire, 1924	B (1 bipolar shift, showing that the mother's actions were not those of a vampire but of a responsible mother)
The Three Garridebs, 1924	B (1 large bipolar shift, which Holmes shows is a scam)
Thor Bridge, 1922	B (1 bipolar shift, which drastically changes how Dunbar and both Gibsons are viewed)
The Creeping Man, 1923	B (1 bipolar shift in the actions of Presbury, which Holmes shows is linked to Presbury taking a serum from langur monkeys)
The Lion's Mane, 1926	D (1 Dalmatian shift, detected by Holmes by using his memory)
The Veiled Lodger, 1927	B (2 or more bipolar shifts, corresponding to Rondo and Eugenia; Eugenia even undergoes one further change of mind)
Shoscombe Old Place, 1927	B (1 bipolar shift when Holmes's discovery that Norburton's sister had died a natural death saves Norburton from ruin)
The Retired Colourman, 1926	B (1 bipolar shift, when Holmes shows that a supposedly retired and abused man is actually the murderer of two persons)

BIBLIOGRAPHY APPENDICES

PRINTED SOURCES

Abrams, Jerold. "The Logic of Guesswork in Sherlock Holmes," in Henry Jacoby (ed.), *House and Philosophy: Everybody Lies* (Hoboken, N.J.: John Wiley & Sons, c. 2009), 55–70.

Andrews, Donna. "Sex, Lies, and MRIs" in Leah Wilson, *House Unauthorized: Vasculitis, Clinic Duty, and Bad Bedside Manner* (Dallas Texas: BenBella Books, 2007), 221–234.

Barnett, Barbara. *Chasing Zebras: The Unofficial Guide to House, M.D.* (Toronto: ECW Press, 2010).

Chesterton, G. K. "The Blue Cross" in Chesterton's *The Innocence of Father Brown* (New York: Penguin Books, 1975), 7–29.

Crosson, Frederick J. "Father Brown, Sherlock Holmes, and the Mystery of Man" in *A Chesterton Celebration*, ed. Rufus William Rauch (Notre Dame, IN: University of Notre Dame Press, 1983), 21–33.

Crowe, Michael J. *Ronald Knox and Sherlock Holmes: The Origin of Sherlockian Studies* (Indianapolis: Gasogene Imprint of Wessex Press, 2011).

Doyle, Arthur Conan. *Annotated Sherlock Holmes: The Four Novels and the Fifty-Six Short Stories* Complete, annotated by William S. Baring-Gould, 2nd ed., 2 vols. (New York: C. N. Potter, 1975).

Eco, Umberto, and Thomas A. Sebeok. *The Sign of Three: Dupin, Holmes, Peirce (Advances in Semiotics)* (Bloomington: Indiana University Press, c. 1983).

Joyce, James. *Dubliners* (New York: Modern Library, 1916).

Kuhn, Thomas S. *The Structure of Scientific Revolutions*, 2nd ed. (Chicago: University of Chicago Press, 1970).

© The Author(s) 2018
M. J. Crowe, *The Gestalt Shift in Conan Doyle's Sherlock Holmes Stories*, https://doi.org/10.1007/978-3-319-98291-5

Peterson, John. "Introduction," *Collected Works of G. K. Chesterton*, XII (San Francisco: Ignatius Press, 2005), 15–18.

Rowland, Susan. "House and Ho(l)mes," in Luke Hockley and Leslie Gardner, *House: The Wounded Healer on Television* (New York: Routledge: 2011), 133–151.

Sayers, Dorothy L. *Unpopular Opinions: Twenty-One Essays* (New York: Harcourt Brace, 1947).

Wilson, Leah (ed.). *House Unauthorized: Vasculitis, Clinic Duty, and Bad Bedside Manner* (Dallas Texas: BenBella Books, 2007).

INTERNET SOURCES

"House (TV Series)" available on the internet on Wikipedia; see file:///Volumes/SilverPassport/Desk%20Top/HolmesSherlock%20Stuff/House%20TVSeries/House%20(TV%20series)%20and%20Holmes.webarchive, viewed 4 August 2016.

"House (TV Series)" on Wikipedia: see file:///Volumes/SilverPassport/Desk%20Top/HolmesSherlock%20Stuff/House%20TVSeries/House%20(TV%20series)%20and%20Holmes.webarchive, viewed 4 August 2016, and file:///Volumes/SilverPassport/HolmesHouseConnection.webarchive, also viewed on 4 August 2016.

Chesterton, G. K. "How to Write a Detective Story," available on the internet at http://www3.dbu.edu/mitchell/chesterton_on_detective_fiction.htm.

file:///Volumes/SilverPassport/Holmes%20House%20Connection.webarchive and file:///Volumes/SilverPassport/HolmesHouseConnection.webarchive, also viewed 4 August 2016.

BIBLIOGRAPHY

PRINT PUBLICATIONS AND RECORDINGS REGARDING HOLMES

Accardo, Pasquale J. *Diagnosis and Detection: The Medical Iconography of Sherlock Holmes* (Rutherford: Fairleigh Dickinson University Press; London: Associated University Presses, 1987).

Baggett, David. "Sherlock Holmes as Epistemologist." In Philip Tallon and David Baggett (eds.) *The Philosophy of Sherlock Holmes* (University Press of Kentucky, 2012), 7–21.

Bayard, Pierre. *Sherlock Holmes Was Wrong: Reopening the Case of The Hound of the Baskervilles* (New York: Bloomsbury, 2008).

Bird, Alexander. "Abductive Knowledge and Holmesian Inference". In Tamar Szabo Gendler and John Hawthorne. *Oxford Studies in Epistemology*, vol. 1 (Oxford: Oxford University Press, 2005), 1–31.

Bird, Alexander. *Thomas Kuhn* (Princeton, N.J.: Princeton University Press, 2000).

Boring, Edwin. *A History of Experimental Psychology*, 2nd ed. (New York: Appleton-Century-Crofts, 1950).

Boring, Edwin. "A New Ambiguous Figure," *American Journal of Psychology, 42:3* (July, 1930), 444–445.

Boring, Edwin. *Sensation and Perception in the History of Experimental Psychology* (New York, London, D. Appleton-Century Co., 1942).

Brugger, Peter. "One Hundred Years of an Ambiguous Figure: Happy Birthday, Duck/Rabbit!" *Perceptual and Motor Skills, 89* (1999), 973–977.

Brugger, Peter, and Susan Brugger. "The Easter Bunny in October: Is It Disguised as a Duck?" *Perceptual and Motor Skills, 76* (1993), 577–578.

Carr, John Dickson. *The Life of Sir Arthur Conan Doyle: The Man Who Was Sherlock Holmes* (New York: Vintage, 1975).

Cat, Jordi. "Switching Gestalts on Gestalt Psychology: On the Relation between Science and Philosophy," *Perspectives on Science, 15: 2* (Summer 2007), 131–177.

Covey, Stephen R. *The Seven Habits of Highly Effective People* (New York: Simon and Schuster, 1989).

Chesterton, G. K. "The Blue Cross" in Chesterton's *The Innocence of Father Brown* (New York: Penguin Books, 1975).

Crosson, Frederick J. "Father Brown, Sherlock Holmes, and the Mystery of Man" in *A Chesterton Celebration*, ed. Rufus William Rauch (Notre Dame, IN: University of Notre Dame Press, 1983), 21–33.

Crowe, Michael J., "A New Interpretation of Conan Doyle's Sherlock Holmes Stories," in Mary Ann Bradley, Louise Haskett, and Melanie Hoffman (eds.), *70 Years of Gas Lamp: The Illustrious Clients' Sixth Casebook* (Indianapolis: Gasogene Imprint of Wessex Press, 2018), 100–137.

Crowe, Michael J. (ed.). *Ronald Knox and Sherlock Holmes: The Origin of Sherlockian Studies* (Indianapolis: Gasogene Imprint of Wessex Press, 2011).

Dakin, D. Martin. *A Sherlock Holmes Commentary* (Newton Abbot: David & Charles, 1974).

DesAutels, Peggy. "Gestalt Shifts in Moral Perception," in Larry May, Marilyn Friedman, and Andy Clark, eds., *Mind and Morals* (Bradford/MIT Press, 1996), 129–143.

Doyle, Arthur Conan. *Annotated Sherlock Holmes: The Four Novels and the Fifty-Six Short Stories Complete*, annotated by William S. Baring-Gould, 2nd ed., 2 vols. (New York: C. N. Potter, 1975).

Doyle, Arthur Conan. *Complete Sherlock Holmes*, 2 vols. (New York: Doubleday, 1953).

Doyle, Arthur Conan. *Complete Sherlock Holmes*, read by David Timson. Naxos Audiobooks.

Doyle, Arthur Conan. *Memories and Adventures and Western Wanderings* (Newcastle on Tyne: Cambridge Scholars Publishing, 2009).

Doyle, Arthur Conan. *The New Annotated Sherlock Holmes*, annotated by Leslie Klinger, 3 vols. (New York: W. W. Norton, 2005).

Doyle, Steven, and David A. Crowder. *Sherlock Holmes for Dummies* (Hoboken, NJ: Wiley, 2010).

Eco, Umberto, and Thomas A. Sebeok (eds.). *The Sign of Three: Dupin, Holmes, Peirce (Advances in Semiotics)* (Bloomington: Indiana University Press, c. 1983).

Frank, Lawrence. "Reading the Gravel Page: Lyell, Darwin, and Conan Doyle," *Nineteenth Century Literature, 44:3* (Dec., 1989), 364–387.

Frank, Lawrence. *Victorian Detective Fiction and the Nature of Evidence* (New York: Palgrave Macmillan, 2003).

Ginzburg, Carlo, "Clues: Roots of an Evidential Paradigm," in *Clues, Myths, and the Historical Method*, trans. by John and Anne C. Tedeschi (Baltimore: Johns Hopkins University Press, 1989), 96–125

Ginzburg, Carlo. "Morelli, Freud, and Sherlock Holmes: Clues and Scientific Method," *History Workshop, 9* (Spring, 1980), 5–36.

Gladwell, Malcolm. *The Tipping Point: How Little Things Can Make a Big Difference* (New York: Little Brown, 2000).

Gutting, Gary (ed.). *Paradigms and Revolutions: Appraisals and Applications of Thomas Kuhn's Philosophy of Science* (Notre Dame, IN: University of Notre Dame Press, 1980). Contains various essays and an extensive bibliography listing essays in which authors have applied Kuhn's ideas of conceptual change to various intellectual disciplines.

Hafner, E M. "The New Reality in Art and Science," *Comparative Studies in Society and History, 11* (1969), 385–397.

Hanson, Norwood Russell. *Patterns of Discovery: An Inquiry into the Conceptual Foundations of Science* (Cambridge University Press, 1958).

Henle, Mary, Julian Jaynes, and John J. Sullivan (eds.). *Historical Conceptions of Modern Psychology* (New York: Springer, 1976).

Hunt, Morton. *The Story of Psychology* (New York: Doubleday, 1993).

Jastrow, Joseph. *Fact and Fable in Psychology* (Boston: Houghton-Mifflin, 1900).

Jastrow, Joseph. "The Mind's Eye," *Popular Science Monthly, 54* (1899), 299–312.

Joyce, James. *Dubliners* (New York: Modern Library, 1916).

Kerr, Douglas. *Conan Doyle: Writing, Profession, and Practice* (Oxford University Press, 2012).

Kornmeier, J. and M. Bach. "The Necker Cube—An Ambiguous Figure Disambiguated in Early Visual Processing. *Vision Research, 45*(8) (2005), 955–960.

Kuhn, Thomas. "Historical Structure of Scientific Discovery," *Historical Conceptions of Psychology*, ed. Mary Henle, Julian Jaynes, and John J. Sullivan (New York: Springer, 1973), 1–12.

Kuhn, Thomas. "Reflections on the Relations of Science and Art" in Kuhn's *The Essential Tension: Selected Studies in Scientific Tradition and Change* (Chicago: University of Chicago Press, 1977), 340–352.

Kuhn, Thomas. *The Essential Tension: Selected Studies in Scientific Tradition and Change* (Chicago: University of Chicago Press, 1977).

Kuhn, Thomas. *The Structure of Scientific Revolutions*, 2rd ed. (Chicago: University of Chicago Press, 1970).

Lycett, Andrew. *The Man Who Created Sherlock Holmes: The Life and Times of Sir Arthur Conan Doyle* (New York: Free Press, 2007).

MacPherson, Fiona. "Ambiguous Figures and the Content of Experience," *Nous, 40:1* (Mar., 2006), 82–117.

McQueen, Ian. *Sherlock Holmes Detected* (New York: Drake, 1974).

Miller, Russell. *Adventures of Arthur Conan Doyle: A Biography* (New York: Thomas Dunne Books: St. Martin's Press, 2008).

Murphy, Gardner, and Joseph Kovach. *Historical Introduction to Modern Psychology*, 3rd ed. (New York: Harcourt Brace Jovanovich, 1972).

Naughton, John. "Thomas Kuhn: The Man Who Changed the Way the World Looked at Science," *Manchester Guardian*, August 19, 2012. Accessed on May 13, 2015 at http://www.rawstory.com/2012/08/thomas-kuhn-the-man-who-changed-the-way-the-world-looked-at-science/.

Necker, Louis Albert. "Observations on Some Remarkable Optical Phaenomena Seen in Switzerland; and on an Optical Phaenomenon Which Occurs on Viewing a Figure of a Crystal or Geometrical Solid," *London and Edinburgh Philosophical Magazine and Journal of Science, 1* (5) (1832), 329–337.

Peterson, John (ed.). *G. K. Chesterton on Detective Fiction* (Sauk City, Wisconsin: The Battered Silicon Dispatch Box: 2010).

Peterson, John. "Introduction," *Collected Works of G. K. Chesterton*, XII (San Francisco: Ignatius Press, 2005), 15–18.

Pigliucci, Massimo. "Sherlock's Reasoning Toolbox" in Philip Tallon and David Baggett (eds.) *The Philosophy of Sherlock Holmes* (University Press of Kentucky, 2012), 49–60.

Polanyi, Michael. *Personal Knowledge: Towards a Post-Critical Philosophy* (New York: Harper and Row, 1964).

Postelwait, Thomas. "Historical Evidence: Induction, Deduction, Abduction, and Serendipity," *Journal of Dramatic Theory and Criticism, 31:2* (2017), 9–31.

Redmond, Christopher (ed.). *About Sixty: Why Every Sherlock Holmes Story Is the Best* (Wildside Press, 2016).

Redmond, Christopher. *Sherlock Holmes Handbook*, 2nd ed. (Toronto: Dundurn Press, 2009).

Richards, Robert, and Lorraine Daston (eds.). *Kuhn's Structure of Scientific Revolutions at Fifty: Reflections on a Scientific Classic* (Chicago: University of Chicago Press, 2016).

Sayers, Dorothy L. *Unpopular Opinions: Twenty-One Essays* (New York: Harcourt Brace, 1947).

Schaefer, Bradley E. "Sherlock Holmes and Some Astronomical Connections," *Journal of the British Astronomical Association, 103* (1993), 30–34.

Sebeok, Thomas, and Jean Umiker Sebeok. "You know My Method: A Juxtaposition of Charles S. Peirce and Sherlock Holmes" in Umberto Eco and Thomas A. Sebeok. *The Sign of Three: Dupin, Holmes, Peirce (Advances in Semiotics)* (Bloomington: Indiana University Press, c. 1983), 11–54.

Snyder, Laura J. "Sherlock Holmes: Scientific Detective," *Endeavour: Review of the Progress of Science, 28* (Sept., 2006), 104–108.

Stashower, Daniel. *Teller of Tales: The Life of Arthur Conan Doyle* (New York: Henry Holt, 1999).

Steiff, Josef (ed.). *Sherlock Holmes and Philosophy: The Footprints of a Giant Mind* (Chicago: Open Court, 2011).

Sullivan, John J. (eds.). *Historical Conceptions of Modern Psychology* (New York: Springer, 1976).

Thagard, Paul. *Conceptual Revolutions* (Princeton: Princeton University Press, 1992).

Timson, David. *Sir Arthur Conan Doyle. The Complete Sherlock Holmes, read by David Timson*. Naxos Audiobooks.

Tondre, Michael. *Vision, Science and Literature, 1870–1920: Ocular Horizons* (London and Brookfield, Vermont: Pickering and Chatto, 2011).

Truss, Lynne. *Eats, Shoots & Leaves: The Zero Tolerance Approach to Punctuation* (New York: Gotham Books, 2006).

Wade, Nicholas. *Art and Illusionists* (New York: Springer, 2016).

Wagner, E. J. *The Science of Sherlock Holmes: From Baskerville Hall to the Valley of Fear, the Real Forensics Behind the Great Detective's Greatest Cases* (Hoboken, NY: John Wiley & Sons, 2006).

Willis, Martin. *Literature and Science* (Basingstoke: Palgrave Macmillan, 2015).
Willis, Martin, *Vision, Science and Literature, 1870–1920: Ocular Horizons* (London and Brookfield, VT: Pickering & Chatto, 2011).
Wittgenstein, Ludwig. *Philosophical Investigations*, trans. by G. E. M. Anscombe, 2nd ed. (New York: Macmillan, 1958).

INTERNET RESOURCES

"Adventure of the Mazarin Stone," See http://en.wikipedia.org/wiki/The_Adventure_of_the_Mazarin_Stone. Viewed 20 January 2015.
Bird, Alexander. "Thomas Kuhn," *The Stanford Encyclopedia of Philosophy* (Fall 2013 Edition), Edward N. Zalta (ed.), URL: http://plato.stanford.edu/archives/fall2013/entries/thomas-kuhn/. Viewed 23 February 2015.
"Category Mistake." See http://en.wikipedia.org/wiki/Category_mistake. Viewed 25 January 2015.
Chesterton, G. K. "How to Write a Detective Story," which essay is available on the internet at http://www.chesterton.org/how-to-write-detective/. Viewed 19 September 2015.
Cooke, Catherine. "Mrs. Hudson: A Legend in Her Own Lodging-House." See http://www.bakerstreetjournal.com/images/Catherine_Cooke_Mrs_Hudson.pdf. Viewed 10 January 2015.
Doyle: see http://dickens.stanford.edu/sherlockholmes/2007/notes12_1.html. Viewed 10 January 2015.
"Duck-Rabbit Illusion." See http://en.wikipedia.org/wiki/Rabbit–duck_illusion. Viewed 22 February 2015.
"His Last Bow," origin of this Holmes story; see http://dickens.stanford.edu/sherlockholmes/2007/notes12_1.html. Viewed 10 January 2015.
Hoy, James. James Hoy has produced summaries of all sixty stories. These are available on the internet at http://www.diogenes-club.com/hoyadventures.htm. Viewed 4 February 2015.
Kihlstrom, John F. "Joseph Jastrow and His Duck – Or Is It a Rabbit?" See http://ist-socrates.berkeley.edu/~kihlstrm/JastrowDuck.htm.   Viewed   3 March 2015.
Klinger, Leslie S. See "Adventure of the Cardboard Box." At http://en.wikipedia.org/wiki/The_Adventure_of_the_Cardboard_Box. Viewed   31   December 2014.
Klinger, Leslie S. See "The Textual Problem of the Resident Patient" at http://www.sherlockian.net/canon/klinger.html. Viewed 31 December 2014.
McMurdo Summaries of the Holmes stories: http://www.sherlockian.net/.
"My Wife and My Mother-in-Law" image. See https://en.wikipedia.org/wiki/My_Wife_and_My_Mother-in-Law. Viewed 17 September 2015.

Painting by Eugène Burand named "The Disciples Peter and John Running to the Sepulcher on the Morning of the Resurrection." Viewed on the internet at https://en-gb.facebook.com/hsmresources/posts/285076478236418. Viewed 10 October 2014.

Rankings of Holmes stories: see http://www.bestofsherlock.com/story/storyhm. htm and http://bookclubs.barnesandnoble.com/t5/Mystery/Conan-Doyle-s-Favorite-Sherlock-Holmes-Stories/td-p/191527.

"Rubin did not discover the Rubin Vase," http://figuresambigues.free.fr/ArticlesImage/rubin1.html#axzz41DIKsvFm.

Speed Painter website: http://www.liveleak.com/view?i=829_1360099797. Viewed 23 September 2015.

HOUSE BIBLIOGRAPHY

Abrams, Jerold. "The Logic of Guesswork in Sherlock Holmes," in Henry Jacoby (ed.), *House and Philosophy: Everybody Lies* (Hoboken, N.J.: John Wiley & Sons, c. 2009), 55–70.

Andrews, Donna. "Sex, Lies, and MRIs" in Leah Wilson, *House Unauthorized: Vasculitis, Clinic Duty, and Bad Bedside Manner* (Dallas: BenBella Books, 2007), 221–234.

Barnett, Barbara. *Chasing Zebras: The Unofficial Guide to House, M.D.* (Toronto: ECW Press, 2010).

DuBose, Mike S. "Morality, Complexity, Experts, and Systems of Authority in House, M. D., or 'My Big Brain is My Superpower,'" *Television and News Media*, 11:12 (2010), 20–36.

Hockley, Luke and Leslie Gardner (eds.). *House: The Wounded Healer on Television* (New York: Routledge: 2011).

Holtz, Andrew. *The Medical Science of House, M.D.* (Berkley Boulevard Books, 2006).

"House (TV Series)," which is a 32 pp. study available at https://en.wikipedia. org/wiki/House_(TVseries). Viewed July 2016.

Jackman, Ian. *House, M.D.: The Official Guide to the Hit Medical Drama* (It Books, 2010).

Jacoby, Henry (ed.). *House and Philosophy: Everybody Lies* (Hoboken, N.J.: John Wiley & Sons, 2009).

Rowland, Susan. "House and Ho(l)mes," in Luke Hockley and Leslie Gardner, *House: The Wounded Healer on Television* (New York: Routledge: 2011), 133–151.

Wilson, Leah (ed.). *House Unauthorized: Vasculitis, Clinic Duty, and Bad Bedside Manner* (Dallas Texas: BenBella Books, 2007).

Index[1]

---

[1] Note: Page numbers followed by 'n' refer to notes.

© The Author(s) 2018
M. J. Crowe, *The Gestalt Shift in Conan Doyle's Sherlock Holmes
Stories*, https://doi.org/10.1007/978-3-319-98291-5